Dom Moraes (1938–2004), poet, novelist, and columnist, is seen as a foundational figure in Indian English Literature. In 1958, at the age of twenty, he won the prestigious Hawthornden Prize for his first volume of verse, *A Beginning*, going on to publish more than thirty books of prose and poetry. He was awarded the Sahitya Akademi Award for English in 1994. He has won awards for journalism and poetry in England, America, and India. He also wrote a large number of film scripts for BBC and ITV, covering various countries such as India, Israel, Cuba, and Africa.

Also by Dom Moraes

Green Is the Grass: Essays on Cricket (1951)

A Beginning: Poems (1957)

Poems (1960)

Gone Away: An Indian Journey (1960)

John Nobody: Poems (1965)

Mrs Gandhi: A Biography (1980)

Absences: Poems (1983)

Collected Poems: 1957–1987 (1987)

Serendip (1990)

Never at Home: A Memoir (1992)

Out of God's Oven: Travels in a Fractured Land, co-authored with Sarayu Srivatsa (2002)

The Long Strider: How Thomas Coryate Walked from England to India in the Year 1613, co-authored with Sarayu Srivatsa (2003)

A Variety of Absences: The Collected Memoirs of Dom Moraes (2003)

Selected Poems, Ed. Ranjit Hoskote (2012)

MY SON'S FATHER
An Autobiography

DOM MORAES

SPEAKING
TIGER

SPEAKING TIGER BOOKS LLP
12 5 A, Ground Floor Shahpur Jat, Near Asiad Village
New Delhi 110049

First published in the UK by Secker and Warburg 1968
This edition published in India by Speaking Tiger in paperback 2020

ISBN: 978-81-944729-7-1
eISBN: 978-81-944729-8-8

10 9 8 7 6 5 4 3 2

Typeset in Adobe Garamond Pro by Jojy Philip, New Delhi Printed
at Chaman Enterprises, New Delhi

Contents

A Piece of Childhood

Poor meagre life is mine, meagre and poor:
Only a piece of childhood thrown away.

—David Gray

1

Almost I can recall where I was born,
The hot verandahs where the chauffeurs drowse,
Backyard dominion of the ragged thorn
And nameless servants in my father's house…
—'A Letter' from *Poems* (1960)

Missing my father is my first real memory of him. The summer before he went to war he had been a loved, distant figure, sitting at evening on the verandah of our flat with a sequence of young English officers on their way to the Burma front (the poet Alun Lewis, who died there, was one of them), all inhaling the rich flesh of cigars, sipping beer, talking: not my world that summer. My world was in the oval park outside our flat in Bombay, a park eyelashed with palm trees, above which, like a school of enormous airborne white whales, barrage balloons floated. Above these the glaring sun pulsed like an eye: vultures soared up towards it on tremendous, idle wings. Down on my knees in the rough scurfy park grass, a vigilant nanny nearby, I stared at the texture of the earth, the texture of a stone, the texture of a fallen leaf, all eroded to red dust by the sun. A spy, I hovered above ants busy in the red dust; grasshoppers stilting up into the air; briefly settled, hairy flies. Vivid colours stained my eye. Behind our flat was the Arabian Sea, an ache and blur of blue at noon, purpling to shadow towards nightfall: then the sun spun down through a clash of colours like a thrown orange, and was sucked into it: sank, and the sea was black shot silk, stippled and lisping, and it was time for bed.

At morning the sea was a very pale, indolent colour, ridged with wavy lines like Greek statuary. When I woke, I went into my parents' room. They lay in twin teak beds: above them, on a wooden stand, loomed a three-foot plaster Christ, fingers clapped to where a raw heart swelled from its chest, for my mother was religious. Sometimes on Sundays she took me to church, though my father never came. He was not religious, my mother explained mysteriously to me, because he had been educated in England.

Anyway, there they lay, my gods, tranquil and powerful, in charge of the day ahead, my father reading the newspapers, my mother varnishing her nails. I ran to my mother first, since except in moments of stress I was gruff and shy with my father. Even so early in the day, she smelt of flowers. I buried my head between her small breasts, and was happy. Over us that summer Christ cocked an apparently benevolent eye.

The day unfolded like a year: breakfast, served silently by the bearer: scraping up cornflakes as I listened to my parents talk: shopping in the car with my mother (waiting, impatient, for her to emerge from the Army & Navy Stores, while the chauffeur strove to amuse me with funny faces): then the park with my nanny: the weeks, months, years, of one burning afternoon, breathing the turning world, vigilant: nightfall, my father on the verandah, the English officers drinking beer: bedtime, when I thought the chirping of crickets was the noise the stars made. It seemed to go on forever, before my father went to war.

After he went, the first monsoon I remember broke: the sky went coppery, and was filled always with a dirty fleece of cloud, infested by winged creatures, aimless and concentric. Thunder rumbled on the horizon, where the grey, maned sea neighed and reared. Lightning leapt, and a brown wall of rain shut off the park. The gutters croaked with overflow: everything was damp, chairs, books, my bed: the vultures hunched wetly on the neighbouring rooftops, slowly raising and lowering their dingy enormous wings. The barrage balloons turned brownish, and quavered in their tethers. Letters came from Burma: my father drew sketches for me in the margin, one of himself, standing in a jungle, slashed at by the slanting rain. When I saw this sketch, I felt my heart make the exact stilted upward movement of a grasshopper in the park.

'Where is my daddy?' I asked my mother.

'He's in Burma, darling. In the war.'

When I asked her what war was, she replied, in the cloudy way that was becoming common in her, 'Bangs and flashes, lots of fire, and lots of noise.'

Towards the end of that monsoon, my nanny took me for an afternoon walk. We didn't go to the park, but along the seafront, where the beggars, armless, legless, eyeless, lolled on the seawall: for me a part of the scenery, like grass or earth or grasshoppers: I had never imagined they were people. We moved slowly down the seafront past this sad, withered regiment, hands raised in salute for alms: then came a sudden tremendous thump underfoot, bucketing me off my feet, and a moment later the long wash of an explosion. Then the dull, cluttered sky filled with trails of flame: the pavement shook, and each time the sky flashed came the crump of another explosion. The beggars lay quietly looking up at the sky, almost with interest: I suddenly realized that they were people after all.

Meanwhile my nanny had knelt down (she was a good Catholic), and was telling her beads. 'Let's go home,' I said. 'What is the use, baba,' she answered, 'when it is the end of the world?' She began to cry. The beggars did not cry: they watched the flaming sky, they suffered the crump and sway of the explosions: I felt they had the right attitude. My nanny implored me to kneel too, and pray: I must save my soul. But I wouldn't. Eventually, amidst the explosions, a car drew up: ours: my mother came out of it, smelling of flowers. She put the nanny and me into the car. The nanny said, 'Madam, it is the end of the world.'

My mother said, 'Don't be more silly than you can help, Natal. An oil tanker has blown up in the harbour.'

We reached home. My mother put my nanny to bed and stood with me on the balcony, looking at the sky. Across the grey clouds the spurts and rushes of flame multiplied, and the thuds of the explosions deepened, as the orgasm of the burning tanker neared its climax.

I said, 'This is like what it's like with Daddy in Burma.'

My mother said, 'What do you mean?'

'Lots of fire, and lots of noise.'

My mother did not reply, and when I looked at her I was amazed to discover that she was crying. I could see the tears, but she made no sound whatever, so I was puzzled, until she said, 'I've got something in my eye,' and I didn't believe her, and was confirmed in my belief that she was crying.

'Never mind,' I said. 'Daddy'll be back soon.'

She still didn't reply, and when I looked at her I saw that she was still crying. The flat still shook with the explosions, regular as heartbeats: the flames in the sky were turning into fascinating colours: blue, gold, orange, green, crimson. Then the thick seasonal rain began to fall, the flames faded, the explosions receded, and then suddenly hundreds of mad vultures were blundering drunkenly round the sky.

As a child I knew my mother was very beautiful. Her face was a pearly heart, in which her large candlelit eyes were luminous under moth-soft lashes. I identified her with the Christ above her bed.

She was about thirty when my father went to war, a poised women, known for her dry and acid wit. My father and she adored each other: they had met when she was sixteen and he twenty-one. Then he went to England, and for eight years was at Oxford and Lincoln's Inn. During this time they wrote constantly to each other. When my father came back, he was a qualified barrister, but not a very prosperous one. However, he was a literary sort of person, and in due course was offered the post of Literary Editor on the *Times of India.* He took it, and got married. There was immediate opposition from the respective families. My mother's parents were both doctors (her mother, in fact, was the first Indian woman doctor, and there is a hospital endowed in her name in Bombay) and Roman Catholics. My paternal grandfather was an engineer, and a Roman Catholic too, but the Hindu caste system of their forefathers had worked on Indian Catholics over the years, splitting them into communities: and my parents' families came from different Catholic communities. A great deal of fuss ensued, but in 1937 my parents married, and on 19 July 1938, I was born.

By the time my father was accredited as the first Indian war correspondent, and sent to the Burma front, my parents were one of the bright young couples of Bombay. They gave and attended expensive cocktail parties: my father had a weekly radio programme, to which, in the nursery, my nanny and I listened with bewilderment and pride. My parents both drank and smoked, and, unusual in Indian Christians, held nationalist views. They supported Gandhi and Nehru: the flat was always full of unshaven and furtive young nationalists who had either just emerged from prison or were hiding from the police.

In the tradition of her family, my mother was a doctor, a pathologist: she worked in a large hospital half the week, and in a research laboratory the other half. After my father went to war, she sometimes took me with her to the hospital, with its disinfectant smell and its rows of sad cow-eyed patients in white shrouds overflowing the cramped wards, corpses before they were dead. In my mother's office there were puckered purple foetuses pickled in bottles of alcohol. The eyes of the foetuses were dilated and whitish: they hung in their bottles, discoloured shadows, but their eyes followed and accused me. My mother, moved by some educative impulse, once lifted a bottle off the shelf and held it in front of me. As the alcohol in the bottle swirled, the purple dwarf in the shallows turned slowly, malevolently, displaying its huge white-eyed head, then its hunched back and pinched buttocks. It was the first time I had ever felt pity, but I also felt extreme disgust: I had hysterics and was sent home.

The foetuses apart, I liked to watch my mother at work. Her small caressive fingers were delicate with microscopes and slides, her large eyes absorbed and secretive. She was a very good pathologist, and in 1944 when Gandhi was on a hunger strike, was sent to look after him. He was at this time encamped at Juhu, a beach near Bombay, and once my mother took me there with her.

The encampment was a dishevelled squad of tents, pinned down like washing on the yellow line of the beach. Numbers of policemen surrounded it, and through the tents drifted a long sequence of people dressed in white, men, women, and children. It was a monsoon day, with a low-crowded sky overhead. Beside the camp the grey sea lay like a cat.

Among Gandhi's followers in the camp was Mrs Sarojini Naidu, who in her youth had lived in England and written quantities of appalling verse which was praised by Yeats and Gosse. By the time I met her she was about sixty, a large, grey-haired, talkative lady, who had long since abandoned verse to become a heroine of the revolution. In her, as in the whole camp, I felt a lively, striving quality of desire and pursuit, of which somehow even the watchful policemen were part, for they saluted Mrs Naidu, not their English officers.

My mother entrusted me to Mrs Naidu, who promptly, as a token of friendship, handed me an orange. Then she led me to the central tent to see Gandhi.

He was sitting on a charpoy, legs crossed, an old shrunken man, naked except for a loincloth. He wore enormous spectacles, and when he smiled I saw he had no teeth. He frequently smiled: he was surrounded by people: from time to time a disciple fished an awed child out of the crowd and brought him up to be blessed. Now, when I look back on that scene, I think of encampments in Galilee: then, unliterary, I only felt a sort of happiness that I was there.

Mrs Naidu was no respecter of persons. She bulldozed a way through the crowd, and, arriving beside the charpoy, inquired in thunderous affectionate tones, 'How's my Mickey Mouse today?' She was an unlikely Mary Magdalene, but Gandhi laughed. He then addressed me in Hindi. Unluckily my family, like many Christian families in India, had only spoken English for the previous two generations. The only Hindi I knew was the pidgin Hindi in which I spoke to the servants. I confessed this fact to Gandhi.

He clicked his tongue, but switched to English, and asked Mrs Naidu whose son I was. 'Beryl's,' Mrs Naidu said. Gandhi said, 'I must tell Beryl to teach him. All our children should speak Hindi.' I was by this time rather crushed, but he turned back to me, laughing, pulled my ears (at this time somewhat protuberant) and said, 'You have ears like mine, beta.' This cheered me up, and with a sudden, inexplicable impulse of love, I offered him Mrs Naidu's orange, still clutched damply in my hand.

He said, 'You have a good heart, beta, but keep the orange. I don't eat much these days, so you will need it more than I will.' As Mrs Naidu prepared to ferry me back through the crowd, he asked abruptly, 'Is your father still in Burma?' I nodded. He said, 'Then you must look after your mother, beta. Take care of her. Till he comes back, she is your responsibility.'

In the days that followed, I became aware of what he meant. Before my father went away I remembered my mother, at bedtime, coming in to kiss me on her way to a party, radiant, a rustle of scent and silk. Now she didn't go to parties: after my nanny had put me to bed she would come in and sit for hours by my bed, talking in a wan vague way. She talked mainly about her own childhood, in a house on a hill above the sea, where my uncle now lived, and about her own parents, recently dead. Sometimes she brought the gramophone in and played it. Like a wilted flower, petalled by her sari, she sat by my bed, head bent, listening. One night, soon after my visit to Juhu, she played various negro spirituals. One of these had a chorus which went, 'Don't cry, ladies, don't cry, sweet ladies.' As the voice on the disc moaned on, my mother actually did start to cry, the same soundless tears I had seen before. The pity I felt for the pickled foetuses, for the ravaged Christ above my mother's bed, came back to me: I couldn't bear it, I sat up and said, 'Don't cry, Mummy. Why are you crying, Mummy? You're always crying now.'

Then, to my utter astonishment, my mother slapped me. It was not a very hard slap, but she had never done it before, and I couldn't understand it. I never understood it, till years later, with slow strokes on a bed, I first nailed a woman to her cross.

My father came back from the war. He was resplendent in a correspondent's uniform: he brought with him a Gurkha kukri to hang like a moon on his study wall, a dented American Army helmet, and hundreds of presents. He had flown the Hump, and walked with Stilwell on the long retreat from Burma. He was unscratched, intact: my mother became hysterically gay, and for days the flat was a roar of parties. During these parties my father would enter my bedroom every fifteen or twenty minutes, and, since the noise always kept me awake, would talk to me, stroke my hair, or read me a story. In this way he spent as much time with me as he did at the party. When he left me he would hold me hard against his shark-skin dinner jacket for a moment. My elbows bumped against the buttons, but I inhaled the delicious smell of cigars, whisky, aftershave with deep pleasure. Once I demanded, 'Why do you come in so often, Daddy? Mummy only comes in at bedtime.' He said humbly, 'I haven't seen you for a long while, son, and I just want to make sure you're all right.' In a curious, patronizing way, I felt touched.

At this time we had five servants. Besides my nanny, there was a chauffeur, a cook, a bearer, and a hamal. The bearer, Ram, had been with my parents since their marriage. He was a dark young man from Cannanore, with frizzy hair and lips that were normally purple with betel. He and I got on very well; on my sixth birthday he presented me, for some reason, with a scholarly history of Napoleon's campaigns. He sometimes took me for walks when my nanny didn't feel like it. I was forbidden more than a certain number of sweets, but Ram occasionally smuggled extra ones to me in bed. I was very fond of him.

One day, soon after my father's return, there was an uproar. My mother's jewellery, which she kept in a box on her dressing table, had vanished. The police arrived, and searched the flat. They discovered a bracelet, tucked away under the pillow of the hamal, a shy boy from the country who had only recently been employed. The hamal was dragged, weeping, into my father's study. My father was terrible, thunderous, in his wrath. So thunderous, he became unfamiliar, and I clutched his leg for reassurance, staring at the smug khaki policemen, and the weeping boy on the floor. The hamal was shaking with terror: he crawled to my father's feet and attempted to lay his head on them in supplication. My father hastily withdrew them, and stood looking down at him with a mixture of pity and the disgust I had already learnt goes with it.

'Sahib,' wept the hamal, 'you are my father and my mother, don't let the police take me away, I swear I have stolen nothing. Don't let them take me away.'

One of the policemen suggested gently, 'If we take him now, sir, be sure that we will extract a full confession. He may tell us where the jewellery is also. Won't you, raper of your sister?' he roared suddenly, and stepped hard on the hamal's bare foot.

This apparently decided my father. 'You can go,' he told the hamal, 'but get out at once, and don't come back, or I'll call the police.'

The hamal, sobbing still, fled: the policemen looked disappointed: my father offered the inspector a drink. I returned to my own room, where I met Ram. 'Burra sahib is too kind,' he said, gravely wagging his head. 'He let that devil go free with memsahib's jewellery. Anyone who steals from his employer should be punished. Still, baba, that is not our concern, so let us go for a walk. There is a stall in the park today selling sugarcane.'

A few weeks later, my mother discovered that my nanny, who wasn't married, was pregnant. She also discovered that Ram was the father, and, further, that Ram and my nanny between them had stolen the jewellery, in order to have enough money to marry on. The flat shook with my father's fury. Eventually, Ram brought back what he had stolen: he hadn't yet sold it: and my nanny and he were sacked. I shut myself in my room, away from the angry voices, the repentant voices, the world. Presently there was a knock. I opened the door. Ram stood there, red-eyed, beside a pathetically small tin trunk which contained all his possessions.

'I am going now, baba,' he said, 'but I came to say goodbye. Perhaps when you are grown up I may see you, and we shall talk of when you were a little boy.'

A sudden savage impulse seized me, and I said, 'I don't want to see you ever any more.'

His face twitched, and before I could unsay it, he picked up his little trunk and went away.

In my bed, in the depths of darkness, I asked myself for pardon. I had experienced a kind of vicarious satisfaction in the downfall of the hamal, because he was wicked and I wasn't: and now it turned out the hamal wasn't wicked at all. But I couldn't believe that Ram was wicked really. I must be wicked instead, because I had thought wickedly about the hamal, and spoken wickedly to Ram. Who is ever guilty, who is ever innocent? In the dark familiar nursery I asked the question for the first time, but the twirled world spun in a galaxy of chirping stars, and did not answer.

I had started to read a lot. The war was over, my father was at the office all day every day, except at the weekend. On Saturday he would take me to the Royal Asiatic Library. We climbed a long spiral of ringing marble stairs, with pallid marble busts of donors and founders in every alcove, to an immense room with racked books everywhere: it reeked of books, of old yellowing paper and type, and the dust books make as they disintegrate. In the alleyways of the shelves I wandered about for hours, carefully burrowing out the works of Edgar Rice Burroughs, Jeffrey Farnol, and Conan Doyle.

After that we went to Cuffe Parade, on the seafront, where a bearded Muslim owned a small bookstall selling American comic books. These were in great demand by the servicemen then infesting India. I delved amidst the glossy, coloured covers for *Superman*, *Batman*, *Plastic Man,* and *Wonder Woman*. The comic books smelt quite different from the library books: they smelt shiny: with an armful of them I returned from the stall to the car, and we drove on to a restaurant called the Parisian Dairy, where I drank a chocolate milkshake and ate two chicken sandwiches with quantities of mustard. My father meanwhile sipped a desultory cup of coffee and thoughtfully eyed the bar across the street. The boredom of his morning was perhaps increased by the fact that I never spoke, being deep in a book as I ate. This habit has persisted.

One weekday at home, I was lying on the floor of my father's study, reading, when my mother came in. I did not really see as much of her now as I used to. After the first euphoria that followed my father's return, she had become pale, withdrawn, and unfriendly. She passed much of her day by herself, saying the rosary, and her appearance had changed. She had always been very spruce and quick: now her movements were slow, her glossy hair had become dull and untidy, and she seldom made up. I loved my mother, but a child's wariness kept me away from this altered woman, and she made no approaches to me.

My mother sat down and began to talk to me. She told me a long rambling story about a party she and my father had been to the previous night. There they had been introduced to an American woman on a visit to Bombay. Though my father had pretended it was the first time he had met this woman, my mother said she had proof that he had known her for years. Indeed, she said, while my father had pretended to be in Burma, be had been with this woman in America.

Even to a child with a vivid imagination, this sounded highly unlikely. Moreover, I now had a nervous feeling about my mother: for the first time, I had ceased to trust her. I shied like a green pony from the proposition she now put to me: that I should accompany her to the American woman's hotel, and plead with her to leave my father alone. 'I don't want to,' I said, and immediately a leap of fury came to my mother's voice. I needn't think, she said, that my father and I could plot against her. Whether I liked it or not, I was to come with her.

She herself had not made up, and her eyes and hair were alarming: but she now washed and dressed and brushed me with jerky care. She polished me like an object: when I gleamed, she ordered the car, and we drove in silence to the Taj Hotel, by the seafront. I have never entered this hotel since, without feeling once more the pressure of apprehension that I felt then.

We went up to the American woman's room. She opened the door, a tough handsome woman in her forties, smart in slacks. A swell of shame swamped me, and I attempted a retreat, but my mother's hand was firm on my arm.

'I want to speak to you,' she said in a high trembly voice, 'about my husband.'

The American woman looked very puzzled. However, she held the door open. 'Do come in,' she said. 'We met yesterday, didn't we? Is this your little boy?'

My mother did not answer, but in the same high, trembly voice launched into an interminable speech about my father's misdeeds, while I tried not to hear. The American woman stared at her in amazement. When my mother paused for breath, she said very kindly, 'Look, honey, you're not well. Come sit down a moment, and have a cool drink. You wait here, sonny,' she said to me. 'There's some picture books in that shelf there. Don't worry, your Mommy's fine.'

She led my mother into the verandah. I stood in the middle of acres of carpet, my fists clenched, listening to the indecipherable trembly tones of my mother and the kind voice of the American. It seemed hours before the verandah door opened and they returned. To my horror, my mother was crying. She didn't say goodbye, but seized my hand, pushed me through the door, and so downstairs, through a crowded lobby that paused and stared, to the car.

On the way home she dried her eyes, and, inexplicably, became her old self.

'What a silly ass your Mummy is,' she said. 'Isn't she?'

'Yes,' I said coldly.

'Shall we stop for some ice cream on the way?'

'No, thank you.'

When we got home my mother went into her bedroom. I returned to my father's study, lay down on the floor, and went on reading *Batman.*

My imagination, naturally vivid, was fired and flowered by anything I read. I found that what was actually in a book was not enough for me. I wanted to extend the myth of the book into my own mind, to create new situations for the characters of the book. I told myself stories, therefore, based on the characters I had just read about: Tarzan, Black Bartlemy, Sherlock Holmes, Allan Quartermain, among others. At first I simply told myself these stories in bed: then I began to do it walking up and down my bedroom. Finally I wandered through the flat, murmuring to myself, and gesturing fiercely with my hands as the tension of the plot mounted. My father and his friends, sitting on the verandah, often watched astounded, as I slowly paced the drawing room, mouthing and flapping my hands. My father was already worried about my mother's mental health: he now began to worry about mine.

'You ought to be with more boys of your own age,' he said tersely one day, and sent me to school.

It was a Catholic prep. school, called Campion School, sited on the far side of the park. Though I was eight years old, and it was scarcely half a mile off, I was carefully driven there by the chauffeur every morning, and driven back every evening. At lunchtime, moreover, he delivered my lunch, and when I had finished, wrapped it all up and took it home. Few of the other boys received such excessive attentions, and I was, not unnaturally, very unpopular.

This did not greatly worry me, since contrary to the expectations of my father I had not the slightest desire to have friends of my own age. A beastly little boy, I sat apart from the others at break, reading. This did not endear me to my classmates, but did to the Jesuits who ran the place. They cited me, in class, as an example to the others. So did our teacher, Miss James, a young Scotswoman, very pretty as I remember, with red hair and freckles. This pleased me more than secular praise, and I became much attached to her. She smelt of flowers, as my mother used to do, but affected me in a different way from my mother: Miss James's sturdy Scottish brogues trod on my dreams and in the stories I told myself she and I were now the main characters. I constantly rescued her from fire, flood, and murderers. She rewarded me, chastely, with kisses on the cheek.

My affection must have showed: Miss James started to lend me books, and once, to my joy, took me shopping with her. Then, one day, rather to my annoyance, the small son of a family friend joined the class. He was occasionally brought to our flat by his parents, and then I became an unwilling host: so also in school. I was supposed to introduce him to the other boys: since I knew none of them, this was difficult, but Ashok was himself a friendly, gregarious person, and, to my even greater annoyance, made friends with them all, and then introduced them to me. Gradually, I began to like some of them, and eventually I became a fairly accepted member of the class.

After Ashok had been in school a few weeks, he took me aside one break and whispered mysteriously, 'I found something out yesterday.'

'What?'

'Do you remember I dropped my rubber and went to pick it up? It fell just in front of Miss's desk. When I bent to pick it up I saw right up her skirt.'

I assumed my disdainful look, but felt curiously interested.

'I've told all the others in the front row,' whispered Ashok, 'so they're all going to do it. You do it too.'

'Why should I?'

I knew, however, that I wanted to. Ashok's giggle at my query only confirmed my knowledge. 'All right,' I said, with an air of boredom, 'I will if you like.'

From that day on a rain of rubbers fell at the foot of Miss James's desk. There was scarcely a moment when some small boy wasn't rooting about on the floor at her feet, while the rest giggled ostentatiously. Miss James was obviously puzzled: she wrinkled her pretty brow. One day she asked me why we were all so frequently convulsed with mirth.

I wouldn't tell her. Indeed, I now avoided all contact with her outside class hours, and fled if she approached me during break. I don't think she understood the change in me at all. I am not sure if I entirely understood it myself.

Being now at school all day, I didn't see as much of my mother as before, and was, therefore, surprised afresh each time I saw her. She had become ravaged and dishevelled, with the indefinable terrifying look of madness. She locked herself away in her bedroom for hours, but would suddenly erupt from it in causeless fury, shrieking words I had not known she knew. Doctors began to appear in the flat, sepulchral and whispery. One recommended a change of scene.

'How would you like to go to Ceylon?' my father asked me.

'The *Times of Ceylon* want me to be Editor. We'd have to live in Colombo.'

'I don't mind,' I said.

'I'll have to tell your mother,' said my father a little wearily. Apparently, that evening, he did. The first I knew about it was an explosive crash which brought me flying into the drawing room. My mother had just smashed a decanter on the wall. She emitted a curious batlike shriek and rushed past me into the hall, where she smashed a picture. My father and I followed her into the bedroom in time to see her reach up to the tall plaster Christ in his niche on the wall. He had not moved from there within my memory, but now my mother lifted him down and with a careful and deliberate sweep of the arm smashed him against the wall. I was dumbstruck. At this moment the phone went. My mother rushed to it. My father obviously thought she was about to break that as well, and went after her, but she picked it up quite decorously and said calmly into it, 'Hullo. Oh, it's Gladys.' (Her sister.) 'Darling, how are you. I've got a wonderful bit of news. Frank's just told me we're going to live in Ceylon.'

On the floor of the bedroom Christ lay broken. I had always known he was plaster, and could break, but not that his intestines were straw, and bits of old newspaper. They spilled out through his breached belly, as his brain, a hard roll of paper, dropped from his fractured skull. I stared in wonder, as though at a real crucifixion. In some mysterious way, this was the end of one part of my life.

2

That was an innocent country,
Warlock and dwarf, the hairy forest, dragons
Somewhere there, they said…
—'That Was' from *A Beginning* (1957)

The weeks before we left for Colombo were a confusion of parties. At the office party, my father was presented with a silver salver: I touched its smooth surface, bemused by the unfamiliar. So much was unfamiliar: daily my home melted away where I stood. Chairs, tables, cupboards, that had stood in their places, gentle and solid, since I had been born, were lifted from around me by strangers, and bedded in straw in huge plywood cases. Lids came down on the cases, in a thunder of hammers, a strange wood smell filled the flat. On the fitted carpets where our furniture had stood, there were paler patches rimmed with dust: and eventually the carpets rose like spectres, revealing stone floors I had never known were there, floors with the odour of absence.

We left one evening, the servants bowing and weeping on the pavement as we climbed into the car and were driven to the station. None of them had wanted to come with us to Ceylon, so my father had employed two men who did: a bearer, Vincent, and a driver, Kutthalingam. They were with us in the car, Kutthalingam driving. I had not met them before, and their presence underlined the strangeness of departure that I felt. The night smelt as always, of talcum powder and the sea.

In the station there was a noise and smell of people, and of trains. The trains shrieked wildly and rushed into darkness: a spatter of sparks, receding like an alley of stars. Numbers of people had come to see us off: they all shook hands with me, the women in sudden downpours of scent stooped to kiss me: they talked incessantly; hours seemed to pass like this. Then we climbed into a small compartment filled with the sullen buzz of air conditioners, like climbing into a cold bath from the moist heat of the platform. The train snorted, shook, plunged forward, shaking off the station and the cloudy waving hands and smiling faces, and the night started to pass the window. Soon we clattered over a bridge, a glycerine sea gleaming below us. My father said, 'We're leaving Bombay.'

After this I settled back in my seat and started to read my comic books. My parents sat opposite, talking in low voices. Presently the steward came in with dinner, shepherded by Vincent. Vincent was a skinny smiling young man with black hair that smelt of brilliantine, and a small moustache. 'The arrangements in this train aren't very good,' he told my father. 'They only had mutton curry in the restaurant car. It was bad curry, sir, so I myself with my own hands made three omelettes in the kitchen.' I decided I didn't like him, but the omelettes were delicious and runny.

Later Vincent came in once more, and made the bunks up. I slept up on top, the sway of the train rolling me gently from one side to another, like being suspended in a cloud. The lights blinked off, and in the smell and sway of the train I eventually fell asleep.

Vincent awoke me with a tray. He placed it neatly across my knees, and said, 'Nice breakfast, baba. Rissoles, I made them myself, with my own hands.' I did not reply. When I had finished the rissoles, which were excellent, I climbed down to find my father reading the papers and my mother varnishing her nails.

Except that this was in a train, not in their bedroom in Bombay, and that the plaster Christ I knew was irretrievably broken, it was like earlier days. I looked out of the window at a curious new world.

To get to Ceylon from Bombay by train, at least then, one had to travel down to Dhanushkodi, at the extreme southern tip of India, before crossing the short sea. The landscape grew progressively drier: it stretched vastly out as the train rippled by, but that first morning the earth was black, with patches of lustrous bushes and trees, and fields where peasants worked, clad in bright colours: and by evening the earth was red, with an occasional stunted tree; black, loinclothed men, skimpy as ants, pecked at it with sad scythes. As the train roared south, too, the heat increased: to step from our compartment into the corridor was scalding, incendiary. Windows notwithstanding, all day first black dust, then red, covered the seats of the compartment, making my fingers and eyes gritty and uncomfortable. From time to time curious faces were pressed to our window, as the train rumbled and hammered dustily south. My parents appeared to ignore them, and I had a feeling that I was dreaming these brown, inquisitive faces, covered in black and red dust like the faces of clowns. Only when I climbed out to stretch my legs with my father at some wayside halt did I discover that the entire external length of the train, like a dead snake infested by ants, was swarmed over by people who stood on the foot-boards as it moved, clinging to any appreciable protuberance, or to each other. At the halts occasional railway officials would brush a few of them off: but they only climbed on again further down the train. 'They can't afford to buy tickets,' my father said.

The wayside halts were usually small, dusty stations lonely in a waste of fields, or adjacent to some decrepit village: the third-class travellers and those who clung antlike to the train-skin would rush across the platform to the solitary water tap: dirty trickles coiled through the dust. One palm tree standing, dishevelled, with open wings, against a dying red sky: and like the harsh voices of birds, the voices of the passengers calling.

In the large stations, there was always turmoil: great masses of people ran aimlessly first one way, then another, carrying bundles and tin trunks: they cried out constantly, as though in pain, and the faces of the women clutching children showed an imbecile terror. At these stations Vincent and Kutthalingam stood guard at the compartment door, preventing anyone from entering. On all sides whiteclad, hysterical people pressed against them, shrieking their need for space: but 'This is a reserved compartment,' said Vincent in the black earth area of the north, in Hindi, and Kutthalingam in the red earth area of the south in Tamil. At one point I asked my father why we couldn't let some of these people in: he replied, with one of his stern looks, 'Don't be silly.'

Vincent was always there: with meals, with iced water, with fruit, with beer for my father. He was wearing a suit of some sort: 'Excuse me, sir and madam,' he would say at every entry, 'that I am not in my proper uniform.' Kutthalingam, less decorous, had donned the costume of the south, his own territory, a vest and sarong, and instead of perching in one of the wicker chairs that Vincent had set up in the servant's alcove by the compartment, sat phlegmatically and comfortably, cross-legged in a heap of his bedding.

Dust, and bottles of iced water, and as the train pounded further and further south, bottles of warm water: Vincent in his suit fetching meals, Kutthalingam fat and happy in his accustomed clothes, the little spaniel puppy I had recently acquired whining and nosing my hand: then at last the sea, vividly blue, under the bullnose of a ship, and gulls racing like scraps of blown paper over green palm-spiked headlands and white beaches spread out like drying washing. It was the end of the first of my journeys. We had come to Colombo.

Slowly, the rain slipped down the hotel window, and my mother clasped her head in her hands as though it were someone else's, and filtered tears through her fingers.

Her head in fact did look like someone else's: her sleek black hair wisped out untidily, a peculiar dead colour, on every side: her face had become shrunken and waxy. She scarcely ever spoke. Cooped up with her in the hotel suite while my father was at his new office, I wandered around her as round some obelisk in the desert, or sat moodily trying to read. I did not know what to do.

My father was trying to find a house: meanwhile we were staying in an expensive and ugly red brick hotel by the sea. A long sweep of polished turf ran down from the hotel to the ugly House of Parliament, also in red brick, opposite. On this flourish of turf, on morning walks, we usually encountered the prime minister, Mr Senanayake, thudding along on a huge, sweaty horse. The prime minister had a walrus moustache, and was rather stout: he greeted us always with a beam and a bow, and I thought of him as the White Knight in *Alice in Wonderland.* Some years later he was shot dead by a Buddhist monk.

Things were splendid when we first arrived. Green Colombo was spread out for our inspection, under a hot and clammy blue sky: the sea beat its drums beside the hotel, brilliant birds spired out of violently coloured trees. My spaniel, Kumar, had to be boarded out with friends, and the servants were living in a hostel nearby. These were minor sorrows, for a week.

During this time my mother was gay, witty, her old self: swathed in peacock saris of shot silk, she departed with my father to parties in the evening: in the morning she put on slacks, and we all walked by the sea. One day, however, as we started on our walk, one of the hotel servants came up and advised us to take an umbrella. 'Monsoon he break very sudden in Colombo, master,' he said. 'He break today, I can smell him.' My father looked up at the sky, and laughed.

But by the time we had reached the far end of the green, quite a considerable distance, little rags of wind were shipping up from the sea: large grey waves raised hostile heads over the seawall, and dark clouds obscured the sky. 'Let's turn back,' said my father. As he spoke, a gun of thunder thumped dully overhead, and the rain swept in from the sea, a loud barbarous rain, so thick in its fall as to obscure vision. We stumbled through it towards the hotel. Somewhere on the way my mother lost a sandal. When we got back all three of us were like waterfalls walking. My father and I laughed when we looked at ourselves in the mirror.

Then we discovered my mother was in tears, and nothing we could do could stop these tears. They rippled on like the rain. Finally, through them, she said dully to us, 'You've humiliated me in a strange country.' Then she went on crying. From time to time, in the same leaden, uninterested way, she would repeat her remark.

Since then she had been like that nearly all the time. My father as yet knew nobody in Ceylon who could stay with her, and did not want to leave her alone. Equally, he did not want me to be with her all day, but there was no alternative. 'She'll be better when we get a house,' said my father hopefully.

Meanwhile, slowly the rain slipped down the hotel window, and my mother clasped her head in her hands as though it were someone else's.

We found a house. It was a whitewashed modern house in a fairly fashionable part of town: in the garden the grass was as fat as butter, and sunbursts of flowers made the air heavy. Ceylon is almost on the equator, and the garden soil was so rich, so blackly fertile, that if one dropped a seed, a shoot would rise within hours. Rather inappropriately in these green ferocious environs, the house was called 'Salcombe'.

Here the huge plywood cases that had followed us from India found their last home: they were split open, and books, furniture, crockery lifted out, only distantly familiar now, and found new positions. The servants were installed, Kumar was reclaimed, and we moved in.

My mother took no interest in the house, or indeed in anything else. She stayed in her room and cried impossible reservoirs of tears. Streams of doctors appeared once more. They recommended that my mother return to India. This seemed rather foolish: my father summoned some of her relatives, and they strove without success to penetrate her veils of tears and silence. To me she was now an utter stranger: I breakfasted and dined with my father, but while he was at the office lunched alone, ministered to by Vincent. To him and Kutthalingam I turned increasingly in the time when my father was at work.

Kutthalingam sometimes, when his duties permitted, took me for drives around Colombo. He was a plump, kindly man, very black, with a pug face and a little grey moustache, and had seven children of his own in India. He told me about them. 'The eldest be damn rascals, baba. But the young-young ones, they be good. When you be old, be good to your Daddy and Mummy. Very bad otherwise.' He was proud of his knowledge of Colombo, he had driven for a planter in Ceylon for twenty years before the war. He took me to the parks and the zoo, and showed me the big shops. Once he drove me to Negombo, a beach outside Colombo, and watched with pleasure as I lunched off what I still think were the best crabs I have ever eaten. He himself wouldn't have any. 'Master not liking if I eat at same-same table as baba,' he said undemocratically. 'Also,' he added, 'I not liking crabs.'

He was puzzled by my mother, and worried by her. 'Why she no take some air?' he demanded of me. 'No good for health, if you taking no air.' One day, to my dismay, as we were about to drive off on an excursion to Mount Lavinia, another nearby beach, he switched the engine off and said with determination, 'I going ask your Mummy to come.' I tried to dissuade him, but he marched upstairs and tapped my mother's door. Very gently, he began to wheedle her out. 'It be fine place, memsahib,' he said. 'Lovely beach there, hotel, everything...you come take one look, if you not liking I bringing you straight home.'

To my amazement, my mother consented. Pallid, dishevelled, her eyes red with weeping, her hair straggling and lank, she came stiffly downstairs and got in the car. We drove off. All the way to Mount Lavinia Kutthalingam pointed out places of interest, and my mother listened, and even asked questions.

The beach at Mount Lavinia twined like a white ribbon through explosively vivid trees: a dazzling blue sea shone and lifted beside it. My mother and I walked rather desultorily down the beach, Kutthalingam following at a respectful distance, then we went back to the smart tourist hotel on the headland for a lemonade. The lounge of the hotel was full of Americans who looked as if they had just climbed off Rockefeller's yacht. My mother wisped through them like a ghost, and reluctantly I followed her. I knew I was ashamed to be seen with her, and did not want to be ashamed. However, at eight years old, my mother's pallid unkemptness seemed to me a deliberate attempt to embarrass my father and me, which I hated and did not understand. To make matters worse, it transpired that she had not brought out any money, so Kutthalingam had to pay for us. But he was obviously delighted by the fact that my mother had come with us, and 'taken some air'. He beamed as he opened the car door for us, but his smile faded as my mother, having got in, began to weep.

We belted back on the open road to Colombo. Kutthalingam still made attempts to point out beauty spots, but my mother wept on in silence. Then, suddenly, as we swept round a curve above the sea, she lurched forward, grabbed the door handle, and wrenched it open. A great fist of wind reached into the car, and seemed to draw her with it. She made to jump out.

Kutthalingam, while I sat paralysed, slammed the brakes on. With his right hand he reached over and pulled my mother back, with his left he dragged the car out of a swirling spin that took it to the edge of the cliff. I came out of my paralysis and shut the door.

'Memsahib, whyfore you do that?' Kutthalingam cried. He was still grasping her arm. My mother did not reply for a second. Then she raked his hand with her nails, and an absurd tremulous scream burst from her.

'Take your hands off me, you black swine.'

Kutthalingam took his hand off her arm very quickly, and put it back on the wheel. We drove home very slowly and in utter silence.

A few days later Kutthalingam took me back to Mount Lavinia. We walked on the beach, and in the deep azure pools amidst the rocks I discovered an immense number of small, incredibly beautiful fish. They were all in gay paintbox colours, almost unnaturally brilliant: and wove in and out of the wreathed weed, flickers of peacock blue, turquoise, vermilion, rose madder. I was enchanted. Kutthalingam fetched me a bottle, and very carefully I scooped a few fish into the bottle, put some weeds in the water, and returned to the car.

But as we drove home, and I peered at the bottle and cradled it in my hands, one by one the beautiful fish, milling in the water, lost their brilliance. The colours died like sunset on their scales, and then they died, floating belly upward to the surface, ugly, whitish little corpses. Only one remained alive when we reached home, and within a few minutes that too was dead.

My mother was not silent and tearful any more. She had suddenly started to have astonishing fits of fury. They exploded at any time, and for no reason: I would hear that terrible bansheelike scream, and the crash of thrown objects. Vincent, the driver, the other servants, and most of all my father, suffered these furies, but I was immune. For some reason, however, she decided that I should witness it all: wherever I was, she would at some point rush in, shrieking, breaking china, her hair standing up around her head like a fright wig, her eyes rolling. Visitors no longer came to the house, the servants lived in terror, and I myself became so nervous that any noise made me jump. The doctors prescribed sedatives for my mother but they appeared to have no effect.

My father, meanwhile, was in a quandary. For some reason I cannot remember, there was no place for me in a day school, and he didn't want me to be a boarder. But he didn't want to leave me with my mother. What he did, therefore, was to take me with him to his office, in order to keep me out of my mother's way.

This involved a great deal of planning. My mother had become inordinately possessive towards me, and when not throwing fits was constantly (to my dismay) with me. She objected violently if I went for a walk with Kumar: I must stay indoors, she said, there were people who wanted to kidnap me. When, therefore, my father first tried to take me to the office with him, my mother produced so violent a scene as to decide him that my removal could only be effected if she didn't know.

This meant that every morning Vincent had to keep watch on my mother, while my father sat outside in the car. As soon as the coast was clear, Vincent sent me rapidly downstairs and out, Kutthalingam started the car, and we shot off. We later had to change this plan, because my mother started to watch until my father had actually left. What then happened was that Kutthalingam parked a little way up the road, and at a favourable moment I slipped out of the house and joined them.

I must have been a considerable embarrassment to my father. I sat in his office all day reading, while his staff, his contributors, and his proprietors came in and out. Eventually, I suppose, people found out the reason why I was always there, but I am told it caused a great deal of comment, not unnaturally, at the time.

I didn't worry. I loved to read, I loved to be with my father, now the only parent I could trust, and after home the busy office seemed like a rest camp. Moreover, I particularly liked lunchtime. We lunched always in one of the large hotels, and my father always allowed me to choose what I wanted. I discovered that restaurant food tasted better than food at home, and, chomping some leathery chop, would exult in the knowledge that the idea of it had originated in my mind, been transmitted by me through the waiter to the chef, and by the chef through the waiter back to me.

My days with my father, however, produced an unfortunate effect on my mother. She had previously believed that she was protecting herself and me against a world that sought to entrap us both. Since I obviously accompanied my father from choice, she had apparently started to believe that the other side had corrupted me. Her tirades now included me.

One morning my mother discovered me getting into the car with my father. A hysterical scene followed, at the end of which I stayed, nervous and sulky, at home. My mother was in a very excitable mood. I locked myself in my rood, and listened as she rushed about the rest of the house, screaming at the servants. Then she started to throw things. I had, even then, a great respect for objects. A glass, an ashtray, any shaped object, seemed to me intact, like a person, and inviolate. To see or hear them hurled about, abused, angered me. I unlocked my door and went down, discovered my mother about to throw a small bronze statue through a window and caught her arm.

Her reaction was very rapid. She wrenched free, then deliberately threw the bronze through the window, in a crash and tinkle of glass, then rushed out of the room. A moment later she reappeared, with a large kitchen knife in her hand. She came at me with it, like something out of a nightmare. I dodged rapidly round her, raced upstairs to my room, and locked the door. A moment later my mother started to hammer at it, ordering me, in a hoarse shout, to open it. I wouldn't. Meanwhile Vincent ran upstairs, and I heard a scuffle outside the door, then silence.

Vincent had tried to take the knife away from my mother, received a cut on the hand, and gone to telephone my father. My mother had retired to her room and locked herself in. In my own locked room I sat in the vast silence, trying with shaking hands to read a book. Finally I heard my father's voice at my door, and opened it. He stood there, very grave, and put his arm round me. The staircase was crowded with people in white coats.

'Come on,' my father said quietly with his arm round me, my head pressed with comforting discomfort against the buttons of his suit, 'let's go to the office.'

We went downstairs. As we reached the front door, there was an outcry, and my mother came rushing after us, hair and eyes wild. 'You're not to go out,' she shrieked at me, 'you're not to go out.'

The doctor, with two women in white, was behind her. He gave a resigned little shrug, and nodded to the women. They moved efficiently forward and pinioned my mother's arms. My father swept me out into the car.

As Kutthalingam was about to start it, my mother appeared at the front door. Both her arms were held, and she was struggling violently, so that she appeared to be on a cross. In her eyes was terror and a sort of sanity. Her eyes met my father's, and she called in a voice like her old loved voice, 'Help me, Frank, help me.'

My father's face went grey. He leant forward and said to Kutthalingam, in almost a shout, 'Drive to the office.'

The house was now full of nurses. They stood like policewomen outside the door of my mother's room, where she lay under heavy sedation. The doctors made daily visits. They recommended that my father authorize electric shock treatment. At this time the treatment was very new, at least in Asia: my father telephoned my mother's relatives in Bombay, and presently they flew in to Colombo, and made the house even more crowded than it already was. There were long family conferences as to whether or not my mother should be given the treatment, but it was eventually decided that she should.

During all this, I spent a great deal of time in Vincent's pantry. Like Kutthalingam, he had children in India, and he knew how to entertain them. He told me folktales from Mangalore, his birthplace, and sang me small birdlike songs. We frequently groomed Kumar, Vincent whistled between his teeth as he brushed the thick golden coat, and once remarked, 'He'll be a champion if we put him in the dog show.' I inquired if he really thought so. 'Oh, yes,' said Vincent. 'When your Mummy's better, we'll put him in for it, and you'll see.'

As a result of this, the dog show was much more on my mind than my mother, whom in any case I scarcely saw nowadays, when one day my father told me that she was to receive her treatment that evening. 'I want you,' he said, 'to go and spend the evening at Negombo with Kutthalingam and Vincent.' In the monstrous way of children, I was delighted. That evening my aunts and uncles arrived; the doctors came, and brought complicated boxes of apparatus with them: for some reason, the treatment was to be done at home. The doctors set up a long trestle, like a coffin, in the study, next to the drawing room: cobwebs of wires filled every corner.

I was ready to leave for Negombo when my father, looking very worried, came up and told me that my mother refused to have any treatment unless I was there. 'I'm sorry, son,' he said, 'I don't want you to stay, hut I'm afraid you'll have to.' This upset me considerably. However, I sat down with an uncle and aunt and began to tell him about my hopes for the dog show. He listened inattentively, and presently started up: the nurses had led my mother, pallid and wild-eyed, into the room.

I was terrified of my mother, and I resented her: she had stopped my evening out. To the natural cruelty of a child I had added in adult sophistication, through being so much with adults. As my mother started across the room towards me, I turned to the aunt on my far side and continued my disquisition on the dog show. She said indignantly, 'How can you talk about dogs when your mother's ill?' and in an odd hysterical jerk, not even knowing I knew the words, I said, 'Because my mother's a poisonous bitch.' There was a frozen silence, and when I looked up I saw the doctors leading my mother away, to the coffinlike trestle in the study.

There was a lot of rustling and whispering, flexing of wires, creaking, as, unseen, they laid my mother on the trestle. Eventually, all the lights went out. The creaking and rustling went on in the darkness. Then a loud lilting Ceylonese voice said, 'Are you ready, Doctor?' and another voice said, 'Yes, ready.'

Then came an extraordinary crashing whistle, and with it, raised jerkily in ululation, a voice I knew must be my mother's. Without any pause for breath, this ululation went on. It went on and on, then stopped, and the lights went up.

Everyone was very breathless and shaky. Later I was allowed into the room where my mother lay wanly amongst pillows. She looked very small. She blinked up at me, then said in a whispery but natural voice, 'Oh, darling, how nice to see you,' and I wept.

Of course, it didn't work. My mother became less violent, but she also became more hazy. The consultants consulted, not for the first time, and recommended that my father try insulin treatment. This could only be obtained in Bombay. So my father sent my mother back to Bombay, and I entered Kumar for the dog show.

For days before the show started, Vincent and I attempted to instruct Kumar in the rudiments of obedience. Though he was a gentle as well as a handsome animal, with the melancholy ears and eyes of his breed, he was unused to the idea of going to heel, or of sitting or lying down when being told to. I, therefore, felt rather unconfident about the whole affair, but Vincent was adamant. 'Of course he will win,' he said. 'He is an Indian dog, none of your Ceylonese pariahs.'

On the day, we drove out to the park where the show was held.

Kumar, burnished and beautiful, was carried from the car by Kutthalingam, so that he shouldn't muddy his paws. We watched flotillas of pedigree dogs, all unremittingly obedient, performing: then my name was called for the Novice Exhibitors class. 'Remember,' hissed Vincent, 'if he won't sit when you tell him, kick his backside.' With this advice in my ears I advanced into the ring with Kumar. There were about twenty other nervous young people, each with a dog. We shuffled dustily round in a circle, while a megaphone blared and the crowd pressed closely in on the ringside. Then each of us had to take his dog round alone. Kumar, fortunately, ambled around without accident. 'Shabash, baba,' beamed Kutthalingam, as I moved into line with the others. He was standing close behind me, so was Vincent.

The judges started to move down the line. The owners were supposed to make their dogs sit, and let the judges examine their teeth. My terror increased as they advanced towards me. Finally, they reached me, offered me kindly smiles, and asked me to make my dog sit.

'Sit,' I croaked. Kumar yawned and wagged his tail. 'Sit,' I repeated. He didn't sit. At that moment wily Vincent, from the close press behind me, shot out a foot and brought it down hard on Kumar's hindquarters. Kumar yelped, but sat and the judges examined his teeth. Five minutes later, the megaphone announced that I was the best novice exhibitor.

Emboldened by this, Kumar and I went on, and he won the prize for the best novice exhibit and the best maiden exhibit. Clinking with cups and rosettes, the car rolled back through the cool, flowered evening to 'Salcombe'.

'What did I tell you?' exulted Vincent, fingering the cups. 'I told you we would win.'

'But in the first competition, it was you who made Kumar sit. That wasn't fair.'

'Fair, what is fair?' answered Vincent. 'The only thing is to win.'

'Yes, yes, you speak true,' said Kutthalingam. 'What is fair?'

This was not as my father had endeavoured to teach me, but I accepted it.

Now that the house was at peace, I did what I had always done, read all day. I read children's books, by Arthur Ransome and Hugh Lofting, and even by Enid Blyton, but I also read adult novels, memoirs, and political books from my father's library. In his library I also came upon Swinburne, and those thunderous rocking-horse lines intoxicated me. Sometimes I tried to write poems like this, but could never make the words fit into the lines, though I rhymed in a fairly facile way. However, I wrote a biography, six pages long, misleadingly titled 'The Epic of Gandhi', and in a hideously twee way wrote and edited a weekly magazine on the affairs of the household, which I presented to my father every Friday morning.

Vincent did not approve of all this. 'You,' he said sagely, 'are a boy. Boys should play games. I shall buy you a football.'

He bought me a football, but his efforts to instruct me proved wholly abortive. He therefore made me a fishing rod. 'Go and fish,' he said.

'But where?'

'Kutthalingam will drive you to Mount Lavinia. Fish in the rock pools.'

'But the fish in the rock pools die if you take them out.'

'They are supposed to die,' said Vincent, exasperated.

'Well, I don't want them to.'

'Toba, toba! Oh my Lord Jesus!' said Christian Vincent, and made me a fishing net.

On my walks with Kumar, I discovered what, since like most small children I lived in a small area of contact, I had not previously known: that near the house was the racecourse, and that on Saturdays there was racing there. Just behind the course was a field full of rough shrubbery. I took to walking Kumar through this field on Saturdays. When we reached the white painted rails, I lay down, with Kumar palpitating impatiently in my arms, and looked towards the grandstand, where the horses tittupped, straddled by jockeys in silks as vari-coloured and beautiful as the fish in the rock pool. Presently when the race started, I clutched close into the earth. The tall centaurs came hammering round the curve, and were suddenly upon me: the great hooves, as they struck, raising clouds with a cluck of sound, glossy vast flanks matted with sweat, the whips flying with a mosquito noise as they passed. I lay out of harm's way with my dog, but in that second of passage I had the illusion of becoming them, twenty tall centaurs, their horse, leather, and sweat smell, their eighty hooves. For a sedentary boy, it was a curious pleasure.

Rooting round the tussocky field one day when there were no races, I came upon a stream, hidden in the bushes. It was about three feet wide, and perhaps a foot deep, and ran from a drain to a drain, but the water was clear, and tiny fish and weeds wavered together in the water. The fish were silvery brown, with red and yellow dots on their sides. I hung, absorbed, by the edge of this shallow trickle, my Amazon, watching this sealed, frozen other life for hours. Presently I remembered my fishing net. With great labour and wetness, I captured some of the fish Vincent found me a capacious glass jar, which I filled with mud, weeds, and water, and I kept the fish in that. They weren't very beautiful, but I liked to watch them.

Later, burrowing in the drain, I saw what I had taken to be a round stone move, and poke out a slowly weaving, wrinkled, yellow head. I scooped it up. It was a mud turtle, with a smooth yellowish carapace to which moss and slime adhered in copious quantities. I took it home in triumph. There was a water tank in the yard, about sixteen square feet. I filled this with mud and water, dropped in some weeds, and erected a pyramid of stones so that the turtle could sun itself if it so wished. Then I introduced it to its new home.

At first it behaved very well, coming up from the bottom with a slow flail of blunt limbs to peck up breadcrumbs which I dropped in. Kutthalingam, however, didn't like it. For one thing, the tank it occupied was the tank from which he washed the car.

For another, it was just under the window of his quarters, and as time passed and the sun blazed, a greenish slime formed on the surface of the tank, and a stench of turtle rose from it. 'Baba,' he said despairingly, 'throw it away.' Being a spoilt little boy, I utterly refused. Then came the monsoon. On the first morning after the rain, I went out to see to the turtle. It wasn't there; Kutthalingam emerged from the garage, looking very pleased with life. 'Baba,' he said, 'last night it raining, tank overflowing, and turtle going away.' I pointed out that the tank was only half full. 'Baba, what anyone can doing?' he said piously. 'These things God's animals, they going back to God.'

We had now been in Ceylon for some while, but I didn't really know anything about the country, beyond Colombo. I could see how the Sinhalese were different from the people in India: they had gold skins and small bones: the men had lilting feminine voices, but the women's voices were rather more husky. The servants called their employers Master instead of Sahib, and the food was different from Indian food: our cook, for example, despite Vincent's imprecations, almost daily produced a rice pancake called a hopper, with a people, despite Kutthalingam, whose countrymen, the Tamils' mush of rice and salt fish, wrapped and baked in leaves, called a lumfry. I rather liked the food, despite Vincent, and the people, despite Kutthalingam, whose countrymen, the Tamils' from south India who came to Ceylon as labourers, have always suffered oppression from the Sinhalese.

But my father, anxious because I wasn't at school, had determined to educate me. When his yearly leave came round, he told me, very gravely, that he had plans for us. Was I aware that Ceylon was littered with interesting ruins? It was time I learnt something about Ceylonese history. We would drive round the island, looking at ruins. Some of them, he added, were deep in the jungle.

This fired my enthusiasm. I had carried my ichthyological research a step further, had filled the house, to Vincent's annoyance, with bottles full of earth and ants, and now subscribed to the magazine published by the Ceylon Natural History Society. In this I had discovered with joy that Ceylon was populated, apart from humans, by elephants, leopards, antelope, wild boar, buffalo, and monkeys. I yearned to see them outside the zoo. Moreover, Ceylon had a Missing Link: a legendary man-monkey that walked and talked, but was elusive and ferocious. It was called the Nittaewo, and no authoritative naturalist had ever seen it. I was determined to be the first one.

The house was shut up, the servants sent on leave, and Kumar lodged with the same family that had had him before. Early one morning my father, Kutthalingam, and I drove off round the coast, past Mount Lavinia, down a road filled with traffic, to Galle, a seaport town that had once been the capital. Here my father led me, disinterested, round the old Portuguese fort, and other antiquities.

Next day, however, beyond Galle, we came to the jungle. The road narrowed, and arrowed down between aisles of trees whose heavy green crowns were alive with blackfaced, greycoated langur monkeys. It was dusky between the trees, and into this dusk I peered intently as we sped by, looking for the Nittaewo. I did not see him, but was pleased enough to see a few jackals, dusty scuttlers, and on a turn of the road a tame elephant, a garland of red flowers round its head, rather pointlessly pulling along a small log. My excitement increased when that night at Hambantota, where we slept, I heard during dinner a sputtering cough like a motorcycle exhaust, and was informed by an impressively casual hotel keeper that it was a leopard that hung round the hotel in order to dine out of the dustbins when everyone was asleep.

We progressed along the coast, through jungle and towns, till we reached Batticaloa, where we had an introduction to a local naturalist. He was a tall, white-haired Sinhalese with magnificent whiskers, and immensely gratified me by presenting me with the tusks of a wild boar he had recently shot. He also offered to take us out into the bay to listen to the fish singing. These musical fish constitute Batticaloa's main claim to fame.

So in the night full of crickets, we paddled out into the bay. The rowboat moved in a chain of splashes through a sea so dark and shiny it seemed pliable, under a vast constellation of glittering stars. Behind us, like fallen stars, the kerosene lamps of Batticaloa glittered in the arm of the bay. In the cool still air, the plangent music of a radio set floated to us over the water. The tall naturalist let a metal pole down into the sea, and we applied our ears to the top end, and presently heard, spiralled up from the warm undersea of coral and ocean flowers, a sequence of thin, splintery chirps. Over us hung a very yellow sickle moon. 'They sing best at the full moon,' said the naturalist in a low voice, and we rowed slowly back. Between the sea and the stars we were alone and I realized for the first time the otherness of nature.

In the morning we breakfasted at the naturalist's house. His wife, a fat, greying woman like a badger, with curious patches of whiskers on her cheeks, which seemed a blurred mirror image of his, fed us egg hoppers, salt fish, and sweets, frequently patted me on the head, and chuckled at every remark anyone made. The naturalist uttered measured words on the probable existence of the Nittaewo. As we were about to leave, however, a young man bicycled up to the sunny verandah where we sat, and announced in a dramatic voice, 'Ponniah has passed away!'

'That is very sad,' said the naturalist. His wife's reaction was more violent. She flung her sari over her head in a gesture of mourning, and began to rock to and fro, wailing 'Aiyo! Aiyo! Ponniah has passed away.'

'Do not be so distressed, my dear,' said the naturalist. 'We were not well acquainted with the good fellow. But how did he die?'

'He was struck by a bullock cart yesterday,' said the young man, 'and being very aged, could not sustain the shock, and passed away this morning.'

The naturalist began to express his sympathy in a measured Victorian way, but his wife rocked to and fro with increasing violence. Tears poured down her cheeks and dripped from her whiskers, her massive body shook with sobs, and in a loud bleating voice she cried, 'Aiyo! Aiyo! Ponniah has passed away. It will come to us all. Aiyo! Aiyo! Why? Why?'

My father and I said hasty goodbyes and departed. Once in the car, we were convulsed with shared laughter. The comedy of it was obvious: but years later, the scene, forgotten all that while, returned to me, and without mirth I remembered the fat whiskery woman crying and rocking on the verandah in Batticaloa, demanding why anyone had to die.

After Batticaloa we swung inland, and drove into the true jungle, the heartland of Ceylon. Kutthalingam plotted our daily course. In the early morning, with multicoloured birds whistling wetly in the trees, we would leave the resthouse where we had spent the night. The laden branches shook down langur monkeys which bounded like kangaroos across the road, or, playfully, alongside the car. They hooted like owls as they went. The morning earth smelt herbal and moist, before the great sun had swelled to full power. We passed occasional forest villagers, skittering like mice down the road, with poles across their shoulders on which dead birds hung suspended.

Early day was the best time to see the larger animals. A leopard stood frozen, once, in a dry watercourse, one paw raised like a tabby. Another time a large brown beast scooted out of the forest, crashed into the bumper of the car, ricocheted, and was gone. 'That be wild pig,' Kutthalingam explained dispassionately. I looked desperately for the Nittaewo, but didn't find him.

Later in the day, the gonged sun almost audibly roared as it poured down heat. The jungle, so rich a few hours before, became motionless and ashen. The animals slept, except for the monkeys.

In dry watercourses I saw crocodiles, squatting on ridiculous bowed legs, that yawned like antique colonels in the sun. As afternoon passed, the shadows lay down quietly in the forest. At evening a small wind moved the trees, they grew green, and rustled, and the animals began to appear.

In the midst of this twined, entrenched woodland, with its separate life of animals, birds, reptiles, insects, plants, rocks, we came to the abandoned kingdoms of Anuradhapura and Polonnaruwa, capitals of the first Sinhalese kings. Their temples had been burst open by vines, trees grew through their thick stone walls. Hidden in a clearing, with langurs whooping round, an immense fractured Buddha lay on his side, sealed eyes calm. At this time the ruins were not as well cared for as they are now: at Sigiriya, a great forested rock on whose summit was a cave full of decayed frescoes, immense brown beehives, like enlarged pinecones, hung by the spiral iron stairway to the top, and the air was full of a sound like the thunder of a distant war.

Yet to see these fallen monuments, invaded by the jungle, inhabited by beasts, made me aware of history. They were more alive to me because though the human life in them was dead, another, prehistoric life had taken over. History to me was the way a spindly shoot sprouted through Buddha's stone eye.

In a reserved area of the forest, a government man introduced us to some Veddahs. They are the original inhabitants of Ceylon, a stone-age people, who fled to the depths of the forest when the Sinhalese first came. They still live there. The government man brought half a dozen men up to the verandah of the resthouse where we were staying. They were ugly: diminutive, very dark, and scruffily bearded. Their thin, naked bodies were smeared with ash. From them had come the Sinhalese legends of gnomes and elves, but they were unaware of it: stood shifting their splayed toes uncomfortably in the courtyard dust. They offered my father birds' eggs and a dead pheasant. My father explained through the government man that he didn't want them, but gave the Veddahs some money. They seemed puzzled, kept offering the eggs and the bird to my father, but he wouldn't accept them and eventually the Veddahs disappeared. They left behind them an acrid smell of ash, leaves, and bark. Later that evening, the resthouse keeper brought my father the pheasant and the eggs. They had been left on the steps of the resthouse. Later, the memory of these people invaded some of my poetry.

We drove on as far as the arid yellow sands of Jaffna on the northern tip of the island, then swivelled down the west coast back to Colombo. Just after we passed Mihintale, where hundreds of steps led up to a rather scruffy temple, my long search for the Nittaewo was rewarded. At a curious lopsided run, an animal moved through the undergrowth at the side of the road. It was reddish in colour, and as it moved it kept lifting its head and emitting a plaintive human cry. I made Kutthalingam stop the car, but by the time I had walked back to where I had seen it, the Nittaewo had disappeared.

When we returned to Colombo, I wrote a very graphic account and sent it to the editor of the natural history magazine. In due course I received a kind letter back from him. 'What you saw may of course have been a Nittaewo,' he wrote, 'but I do not myself think so. However, yours is the most vivid description I have ever read of a lame monkey.'

For that short while in Ceylon I was a happy child. Letters arrived weekly from my mother, but these irritated and confused me. They offered me a responsibility of love that I did not want to accept. Around me were the responsibilities I had chosen. Besides Kumar, I had now acquired a mournful liver and white spaniel bitch called Judy. They had produced a litter of handsome puppies which were inexplicably black. Racked along the wall were the books I had collected, my library. In the verandah outside my room was a long, roomy mesh cage in which I bred budgerigars: at morning I woke to their soft, interested lisping, as the sun rose. In the verandah also were tanks which contained butterfly-shaped Angel Fish, and Siamese Fighters, green and purple, like torpedoes with veils. I knew the nature and habits of every one of my birds, animals, and fish. I did not want to leave them. My father used to take me to the local amateur theatre now and then. One February night, we were about to set off when the telephone chirped insistently. 'It's the office,' Vincent said. My father went to the phone. When he came back, he was taking his dinner jacket off. 'We'll have to cancel the theatre,' he told me.

'Why?'

'Gandhi's dead,' said my father. 'Someone shot him.'

I couldn't believe it. The name was part of my childhood mythology. What the name meant was more than the little kind man I had once met at Juhu, and I mourned the name and the man as separate things.

My father, who enjoyed practising his editorial phrases on me, said, 'It's the end of an era.'

3

But even then I was as cold as stone
Sinking among the ripples of the crowd
And now all my desire is to atone
For an unfriendly springtime, webbed in cloud.
—'Autobiography' from *A Beginning* (1957)

In a garden in Bombay, I lived my own life. In the trim suburban house whose garden it was, my mother lived hers with her sister and her sister's family. I ate and slept in the house, but at every free moment slipped into the garden with an armful of books. A tree overhung the garden wall, the bole of which formed a smooth flat platform. On this platform, the rough bark pressed to my back, enclosed by a shimmery wavery tent of leaves, I lay all day and read.

Ceylon was all over. My mother's weekly letters had been supplemented by letters from her relatives, which pointed out that she was pining for me and that the treatment she was receiving would be hopeless unless I was there. My father broke the news to me one evening. It would only, he said, be for a short while. He had been offered the editorship of his old paper, the *Times of India,* but this would take a few months to finalize. When it was finalized, he would come back to Bombay and we would all live together once more. I was by no means sure that I wanted to live with my mother, but my father seemed to want me to. So I agreed to go back to her in Bombay, and there await his arrival.

My father and I flew to Bombay. Kutthalingam and Vincent, both very upset, saw us off at the airport. They promised to look after the menagerie, and bring it safely back to India. I said a tearful goodbye, but my tears stopped once we were in the plane. It was the first time I had flown, and the paraphernalia of air travel fascinated me: the seat belts, the life jackets, the transparent swirl of the propellers as we rode high above the slow fluff of clouds. I enjoyed having lunch above these clouds, and I was sorry when we eventually landed.

I was even more sorry when I saw my mother, wan and untidy, her eyes huge in her wax face, at the airport, flanked by her sister, her sister's husband, a large hirsute salesman with a bellowing laugh, who called my father 'old boy', and their four noisy and spirited children. It sank into my mind that I was to live the next few months with these people, without my father, Vincent, Kutthalingam, or the dogs, and those months seemed endless and menacing.

My mother was much more normal than before, but she would scarcely speak to my father, and in her caresses I felt a fawning quality which repelled me. I didn't want to be left with her, and before my father departed next day, I begged him to let me return with him. He said I couldn't, that I must try and be a good boy, and that he would be back soon. I remember when I kissed him goodbye I noticed for the first time that his temples were stippled with grey hair.

Now I began the life of a refugee. My aunt's family was large, friendly, and normal, but I suppose I was not a very normal boy. The more overtures the other children made, the more I shrank into myself. My uncle decided that if I did not want to play, I should be forced to play. Accordingly, he encouraged his children to drag me into their nursery and flourish toy trains and tricycles at me. This only made me worse. My mother, colourless and withdrawn, petted me whenever she saw me, but I did not see her very often, and moreover, with my memories I didn't want her to pet me. However, as my father had taught me, I tried to be civil.

A short while after my arrival, I was sitting with the family in the parlour at evening. The set-up in my aunt's house, as in many Indian Christian houses, was Victorian: the parlour, full of rubber plants and antimacassars, was where one sat, and as one sat there one drank tea. The patriarch, my uncle, occupied the best chair, a little apart: the women of the house sewed in their corner, brawled round by their progeny. I sat stiffly in my chair, hating the other children's flat, rhythmless voices. One of them, the eldest, in an excess of zeal, rushed over to his father and began to belabour him with a newspaper.

My uncle straightened up, a heavy, moustached man, and in a deep bull-bellow declared: 'If you don't stop that, I'll give you such a clout—'

I was appalled and paralysed: in all my life the only person I had known who shouted like that was my mother, and my mother was supposed to be mad. The errant child, however, was not appalled: he went on belabouring his father, and suddenly my uncle's large, hairy hand shot out, and he hit his son across the mouth. The stinging crack of the blow was followed by a storm of blubberings and howls: the boy fell to the floor, and lay there producing his ugly, undignified sounds, while his father, slowly rubbing his hand on his sleeve, said with satisfaction, 'I told you that would happen,' and returned to his paper.

I found myself standing up, saying furiously, 'My father wouldn't do that. Why don't you behave like people? You behave like animals.'

My uncle looked up slowly, stupefied. Then he said, 'Don't be cheeky, young man, or you'll get some of the same.'

I was so angry I was crying. It was not the physical threat that shook me but the insult to my dignity. Nobody had ever spoken to me like that before.

'Go to bed at once,' said my mother.

'Don't worry, I will,' I said, and did.

After that I lived my own life. Nobody knew where I spent my day, and nobody really seemed to care. Only sometimes the raucous children would rush into the garden, shouting my name and demanding that I come and play. High up with my books in my leafy tent, I pretended I was not there.

The suburb of Bombay where these people lived was called Santa Cruz. As the name suggests, it was inhabited mainly by Christians, middle-class people, who lived in ugly houses of pink or white stucco. The centre of the place was the church, a peeling edifice in which monstrous saints and virgins brooded over a plaster altar. One of the indignities I suffered was that, though I protested my disbelief, I was hauled off to this church every Sunday. 'We'll have no pagans in the family,' my uncle said.

My paternal grandfather also lived in Santa Cruz. He had been a successful engineer, and had bred a number of children, mainly daughters. All these daughters had been widowed, and they and their children lived with my grandfather in his large house, where at one time (he was a noted hunter) he kept a leopard cub in the backyard.

He was a staunch Catholic. His greatest pride was that one of his daughters, Lily, a beautiful girl who according to the official biography was at nineteen 'devoted to frivolity and pretty dresses', had been persuaded to become a nun, performed various cures and made various prophecies, contracted tuberculosis, and died in the odour of sanctity at the age of twenty-one. The house was full of pictures of Lily and Jesus Christ, and there were phials of Lourdes water everywhere.

My grandfather had been opposed to my father's marriage. He objected to it firstly, on the ground that my mother came from a different Christian community, and secondly, because she was frivolous. Though nobody could now have called my mother frivolous, my grandfather's initial objection remained. He, therefore, scrupulously ignored my aunt and her family, though they lived only a few doors away.

However, when I arrived in Santa Cruz, my grandfather found it impossible to ignore me. I had, after all, some of his blood. Soon after my arrival, therefore, he limped slowly up the garden path to my aunt's front door. He was a small neat man, then in his seventies, with a white moustache and a faint look of my father. I was up in my tree when he arrived, but this look, and the knowledge of our relationship, brought me scrambling down in haste. To me he seemed a symbol of liberty. I rushed up to him and hugged him enthusiastically.

In a thin, rather harsh voice he said, 'Let me go at once, boy. You will dirty my suit.' I released him, and he stared at me and demanded where my mother was.

My mother came to the door. 'Hullo,' she said in her bemused way. 'Do come in.'

'No,' said my grandfather. 'I will not come in. I only came to say that I will teach Frank's son Latin. It is not necessary,' he said, looking with disfavour at the tousled heads of my aunt's children, peering round my mother, 'for every child to be brought up like a savage. Let him come to me tomorrow morning.'

I was delighted. My small, arthritic grandfather became, suddenly, a stable tower in an unpleasant and tottery world. I looked forward eagerly to our lessons. Every morning thereafter, I made as careful a toilet as possible in a house with very primitive arrangements, and then dashed round to Crossville, which was what my grandfather's house was called. There I was always fed cake and made much of by my father's widowed sisters, who scuttered round on tiptoe downstairs, and presently I went upstairs. Flanked by a picture of Jesus and a picture of Lily, my grandfather lay on a chaise longue, his legs stretched out. He suffered from eczema as well as arthritis, so his trousers were rolled to the knee, as though he were about to go paddling. His dark, scrawny legs were taut-skinned, shiny, and hairless, and were covered in pink sores. I looked at them with love and pity, and settled down to my Latin.

I was a quick learner, and moreover, I was trying very hard to please my grandfather, and at first I did well. My grandfather, however, never praised me. Sometimes I caught him looking at me in a peculiar way, his lips curled a little, his eyes narrowed behind his spectacles. One day, when I came up to him to hand over my day's exercise, he waved me away.

'Do not come near me! I have put up with this long enough. You stink, boy. Have you no sense of cleanliness? Do you never have a bath?'

I felt myself turn to ice and water, but said, 'I'm sorry. You see, there is no bath in the house.'

'Faugh! Look at your hair. When did you brush it last? Why are your shoes so dirty? Boy, your mother is bringing you up to live like a pig.'

After that I did not return to my grandfather's house any more.

Occasionally, my mother made trips to the city, for her treatment. Generally she left me behind, but once some old friends asked her to tea, and offered to look after me while she was at the specialist's. So we took a taxi into Bombay. I hadn't left Santa Cruz since my arrival there, so it was my first look at Bombay for two years. The rush of traffic, the teeming streets, excited me: when we passed our old flat, and the park where my early childhood had passed, I felt positively euphoric. We arrived at the house where I was to be left, on Malabar Hill, above the sea. Aunt Pilly (she was no relation, but an old friend) came out to welcome us. She was cool and lovely in a white sari and her lips felt cool when she kissed me. When we went through the front door, it was cool and dark out of the sun. There were books everywhere, paintings on the wall, all I craved for. My mother sat silent as usual, but Aunt Pilly wisely left her alone. Instead she concentrated on me. We talked about books I had read, had a delicious tea, with cucumber sandwiches, and laughed a lot. When my mother left for her appointment, Aunt Pilly asked me how she was, which made me feel adult, something I had not felt since I last saw my father. Then the bearer brought in lemonade for me and gin for Aunt Pilly, and we went out to the terrace to see the sun disappear in a blare of colours. Aunt Pilly had a soft voice which I liked, not like the voices in Santa Cruz. She showed me the pool on her terrace, where bright little fish fluttered and spun.

'Your father said you bred fish. Do you know what these are?'

I picked out the various sorts of fish in the pool, and finally said raptly, 'That's the loveliest Midnight Molly I've ever seen.'

'Do you really think so? I'm sure that's an expert opinion. Would you like it?'

'To keep? I couldn't really.'

'Of course you could,' and then seeing me reluctant but yearning, 'to keep for me till your father comes back and brings all your own fish with him.'

We had a splashy but pleasant time catching the Molly. Aunt Pilly presented me with a fishbowl, and the Molly swam free in his new home. He was velvety black, and lazy as a panther, hanging in the water for moments before a leisurely flick of his tail shot him around the bowl. 'You must come back whenever you want to,' Aunt Pilly said, 'and tell me how he is.'

'I will,' I said happily.

When my mother returned Aunt Pilly sent us home in her car. I held the fishbowl carefully on my knees. It was not only that I cherished the Molly but that it represented a bridge between me and Aunt Pilly, a bridge to the life I seemed to have lost. I talked away about my day, which was unusual when I was with my mother, but as usual she was silent and didn't seem to hear.

The car drew up outside my aunt's house. The chauffeur opened the door and we got out. My aunt's children stood gaping at the gate, and at once surrounded me, saying in their flat nasal voices, 'Ooh, aren't you grand? Coming home in a car. What's in that bowl?'

'Nothing.'

'Come on, be a sport, let's have a look.'

I panicked, backed away, clutching the bowl hard. One of the children snatched at it. It slipped from my arms and fell on the concrete path. I heard the thin noise as it broke.

I ran into the house, found a torch and a cup of water, and ran back. It was pitch dark, and a hoarse bird was making eerie noises. I shone the torch up and down the path, and eventually found the Molly, lying amidst splinters of glass. Someone had trodden on it. The black velvety body, so poised in its element, the strong shovel of the tail, were a smear of red and white. Only the square head was intact.

'Here's a broom,' called my mother behind me. 'Sweep that mess off the path.'

I swept my broken bridge off the path, into the rank grass.

I had never been absolutely confined to one place before. In Ceylon, if I felt like it, I could always ask Kutthalingam to drive me to Mount Lavinia, or the zoo, or somewhere. Here, since I was not allowed on buses or trains by myself, I was stuck. The proximity of my aunt, my uncle, and my cousins bored and irritated me, and I developed a habit of loneliness. However, it was not very consistent: whenever visitors arrived I would rush into the parlour, hopeful of a break in the tedium. There never was one. When visitors came to our house in Colombo, I was allowed to sit in the drawing room, to listen to conversations which were sometimes fascinating, and even to interpolate comments of my own. But the visitors in my aunt's house were different. They were all exactly the same as my aunt and uncle, and their talk was exactly as dull. The children, moreover, if they were permitted in the parlour at all, were not supposed to say a word.

So after a while I gave up trying to entertain myself with the visitors. There was only one exception. This was another aunt, a relation by marriage, who came over about once a month. Whenever she was there, I sat religiously in the parlour with the others. This was not in order to listen to her conversation, for she had none, contributing only a placid, expressionless smile. But I liked to look at her.

At this time I was ten years old. Aunt E. was, I suppose, about thirty. She would have been a beautiful woman in any country. She had the tranquil face of a madonna, and in fact, with her smooth olive skin, looked rather Italian. She also had magnificent breasts, like large exotic fruit, and though a sari conceals most things about a woman's figure, it could not conceal Aunt E.'s bust. She tended to wear rather low-cut blouses, so that a certain amount of her gently quivering, golden breasts and the crease between them, was visible. I could not take my eyes off this vista. I had no idea why I couldn't, but, looking at it, I felt a vague yet intense pleasure.

In pursuit of happiness, I proceeded to what I suppose was a courtship of Aunt E., like my courtship of Miss James a few years before. I wandered around collecting bedraggled posies which I presented to her, and when she was there for tea, leapt forward like an antelope in order to be able to hand her a cup. She may have been rather puzzled by my assiduousness, for like most very beautiful and placid-natured women, she was stupid. But she rewarded me with kisses which sent an extraordinary quiver down my spine. Sometimes she put her arm round me, and, my head pressed to a splendid, pneumatic breast, I inhaled the light musky scent she wore, faintly flavoured with armpits in the summer heat, and became faint with joy.

One evening, the children were sent to bed early, because the adults were off to a party. Aunt E. was to pick my aunt and uncle up in her car. Knowing that she was to arrive, I made desperate excuses to stay up, but was forbidden to do so. Sulkily, I went to bed. I heard Aunt E. arrive, and presently heard her low, rather musical voice on the stairs. My mother was with her.

'I haven't changed,' said Aunt E. 'Is there somewhere where I can?'

'Go into our bedroom,' said my mother. 'The boy's asleep.'

The light went on. I was about to sit up and surprise Aunt E. when something decided me not to. So I lay still. Aunt E. came into the room, closed the door, and then, to my great surprise, started to take off her sari. I watched through half-closed eyes. She had a pink petticoat on, and a blouse, and while my beelike eyes hovered, she sighed, unzipped her blouse and took it off. Under it she wore what I now think must have been a very utilitarian pink brassiere; I looked at the three pink straps intersecting on her golden shoulders and back, and began to tremble. Then she turned, her large silky breasts overflowing the laden pink cups and suddenly I felt as though my whole body were made of liquid honey, and closed my eyes. By the time I opened them again, Aunt E. was dressed. The light went out, and I lay in the tousled darkness, aware that in some extraordinary way I had changed.

Next day I went foraging in the laundry basket, and extracted several brassieres belonging to my mother and her sister, from it. I examined them carefully, but they failed to give me the faintest flutter of emotion. On the other hand, every time Aunt E. came back on a visit, I trembled, and prowled round her, craning down her low-cut blouse, anxious somehow to see not only her breasts but her brassiere.

I considered writing to my father to ask what had happened to me, but thought better of it. It was not, I reflected, something that could be said in a letter.

But my father was on his way. He wrote to me, saying he was on his way. He had acquired a new flat in Bombay, which we were about to move into. He couldn't bring the birds and fish, he said, but we could always buy new ones: and Vincent and Kutthalingam were coming by train, and bringing the dogs.

It now became a matter for me of counting the days. I forgot completely about Aunt E. and her brassieres, my constant preoccupation for weeks, and instead ticked off the time before my father's arrival minute by minute. A minute in a child's world is a long time.

But the minutes ran together, became hours, became days, and soon I was standing on the flat roof of the Bombay airport, the sun beating down watching my father's plane drop steeply from the sky. It slid down the runway to a halt. I watched intently, and when my father emerged I shouted as loud as I could, 'Daddy!'

He couldn't hear me, but it didn't matter, he'd be through Customs in a minute. I turned excitedly and found my uncle smiling down at me. 'Well, old boy,' he said, 'you're glad to see your Dad, aren't you, eh?' The hairy ogre of the past months vanished: I saw instead a vulgar jovial man, a man who genuinely wished to be kind, too clumsy to achieve his aim.

'Thank you very much,' I said, 'for looking after me.'

Then my father was there, and I was hugging him, feeling the bumpy places in his suit, and he was saying I'd got a lot taller. My mother stood a little apart, looking wan. My father kissed her.

'We're staying at the Ambassador,' he said, 'till the flat's ready. It should only be about a week. Kutthalingam and Vincent will be here tomorrow with the dogs.'

'I don't want to stay at the Ambassador,' my mother said uncertainly. 'The boy and I will stay where we are. We're happy where we are.' 'I'm not happy where I am,' I said vehemently. 'I want to stay at the Ambassador. You can stay where you like.'

A curious blurred look came to my mother's face. I had seen it often before, and was to see it often again, but I didn't know what it was, because then I didn't know how much I hurt her. 'All right,' she said, in a tired voice, 'we'll stay at the Ambassador.'

So we stayed at the Ambassador. Next day I met Kutthalingam and Vincent off the train. They grinned down happily at me, while the dogs leapt and licked: now even months without them were worth it, because it was so marvellous to see them once more. Then we all went to look at the new flat. It was spacious and handsome, in a block on Malabar Hill, over the sea, quite near Aunt Pilly. In the grounds stood a swimming pool. I resolved to learn to swim.

'This is home, then, Daddy?' I asked my father in a businesslike way.

'Yes, son,' he said. 'It's home.'

The swimming pool proved to be a flop. I enjoyed sitting in a deckchair, looking at the pretty women in their bathing suits, but when Vincent tried to coax me into the water I declined to move. I was not confident of my physical prowess, and was desperately afraid I would make a fool of myself.

'What shall we do with you?' said Vincent in despair. 'You won't play football, you won't swim, all you do is sit and read. What kind of life is that for a boy?'

'I like it,' I said.

Then my father took me to a cricket match. I was fascinated. Though I did not really know what it was all about, I liked the formality and slowness of the whole affair, and the movements of the players were more graceful and aloof, more physically self-contained, than the sailings and scamperings of swimmers and footballers.

I promptly did as I had done when, after starting to keep fish, I had read avidly about natural history, and when, after finding the ruined cities in the forest, I had read about human history and archaeology. I started to read books about cricket, and to follow the cricket scores in the newspaper. The result of this was that very shortly I knew an immense amount about the game and the players, without ever having touched a bat or ball. I watched local cricket matches with considerable aesthetic pleasure, but when Vincent tried to induce me to actually play, I refused.

'I don't know,' lamented Vincent, 'I don't know. What is there in your head except dreams? What shall we do with you?'

I didn't care.

During these early months at the flat I saw little of Mother. She kept to her own room, where, palely, she said endless rosaries. She was visited by priests and nuns, whom I avoided because they were connected with her. Vincent, a good Catholic, was very respectful to all these fathers and sisters, but Kutthalingam, who had to drive them to and from their various churches and convents was very bitter about them. From time to time my mother asked me to come and talk to some priest or other, but I always refused. 'I'm going to the park with Vincent,' I said, or 'I'm going to a cricket match with Vincent.'

My mother became sadder and paler. She had stopped having treatment now, but she was neither as beautiful nor as gay as my first memories of her. My father tried frequently to take her out, to parties or concerts, but she wouldn't go. Then quite suddenly, she ceased to be quiet and pale, and ordered the *galère* of clergy out of the house. Pale and terrible, like the plague walking, she started a daily stalk from room to room. In every room she would pause, before a bowl of flowers, or a picture, stare at it fixedly for a few moments, then with a slow deliberate sweep of her arm smash it on the floor. She never spoke during this period, but having completed her mission of destruction would return to her room and her rosary. At mealtimes she would fix Vincent with a strange intense look, and, as he served, suddenly knock the dishes from his hand, or throw a plate or knife at him. Her terrible silence filled the flat. The only sound in it seemed to be the splinter and tinkle of broken objects.

After some weeks of this, Vincent came to me and said, 'I'm going to leave.'

Terrified, I said, 'But you can't leave. Why must you leave?'

'If things go on like this,' Vincent said, 'I shall go mad myself. I'll go away for a little while and give your mother time to become calm. Then I will come back. But I thought I should tell you first.'

My father tried to dissuade him too, but not unnaturally, Vincent was adamant. 'It is me she does not like,' he said. 'If I leave, it will be good for her also. I will come back when she is better.'

So, very unobtrusively, he left. At dinner that evening, served by the hamal, my mother spoke for the first time in days. 'Thank God,' she said, 'that man has gone.'

I said defiantly, 'He's coming back soon.'

My mother was smoking a cigarette. She leant across the table and very carefully ground the burning end into the back of my left hand. There was a tiny sputtering sound, and a peculiar smell, but through defiance and fury I did not move my hand or speak. It did not actually hurt me very much at the time, but I still bear the scar.

Presently, my mother took the cigarette away, dropped it in an ashtray, and said, 'He'll never come back.'

He never did. Years later, on a visit to India, I was told by my father that he had had a letter from Vincent asking for money. My father sent it. Later he received another letter from Vincent's wife. He had contracted tuberculosis, and died in his native Mangalore, aged about forty. His wife thanked my father for the money. It had come in handy for the funeral.

4

> … the girl at Hanoi with her white
> Hands and dog's eyes, dripping with amber light:
> Have these things shaped me for the craft of verse?
> — 'Autobiography' from *A Beginning* (1957)

I was on a ship, with my parents. We were going to Australia. It was my father's first leave since he had started to edit the *Times of India,* and, since he had never been to Australia, he had chosen it for our holiday. I knew nothing about Australia except that from it came cricketers, kangaroos, and the duck-billed platypus, but the idea of travel pleased me. The great liner pleased me, an organized complex city borne on dark waters: mealtimes, when in the huge chandeliered saloon I looked through the long menu, and deliberately chose: bedtime, in an austere but comfortable bunk cleated to the wall. The motion pleased me: the thunderous run of the engine, the slow surge forward, the ploughed white field of the wake, with flying fishes flittering like daytime bats over the waves. The only thing I disliked was that there were so many other children aboard, but once it was established that I was not expected to play with them, that was a fact I could disregard.

We stopped at Colombo, where old friends came to see us: then came the long landless plod south, and the ship became an isolated community. Because of my mother, it was difficult to meet people: but they gravitated to my father nonetheless, and our table in the bar was always crowded. I sipped lemonade and prayed that my mother, sitting waxen amidst the talking faces, would not start a scene. She never did, but whenever we were with someone else my nerves fluttered like butterflies.

We started off under bald blue skies: but after Colombo grey squalls raked down across the sea, spattering the decks and portholes, and the ship rolled wildly, so that at meals the stewards had to cleat the plates down. One morning, with garish violets and reds in the thick clouds, and rain and wind flying over the decks, the engines slowed. From the deck we were able to see a clump of islands, very green, but hazed in cloud and mist, rainbeaten, remote: these were the Cocos Islands, and the ship was to deliver and collect the mail.

Presently two small boats put out from the nearest island, and hesitated towards us over the heaving sea. The waves lifted high over them, then burst down on them in spray: they disappeared repeatedly, then reappeared, streaming with water, but determined. As they neared the ship the sailors tilted black oil into the sea: it stippled the grey viscous water, slipping from the crests to the troughs of the waves. The little boats edged over it, but when they were nearly alongside, the sea lifted suddenly in a huge wave, and both boats floated belly up in the oil and water, with heads bobbing all round. The sailors dropped rope ladders: one by one the heads materialized as dripping Englishmen, helped on deck by vicariously excited passengers.

Later, the dripping men materialized as dry men, bronzed, with ragged beards and hair, drinking beer in the bar. A tornado was blowing up, which meant that they would have to come to Australia with us. I eyed them with awe. I had read my *Robinson Crusoe*. My awe increased when I was told that one of them, the only clean-shaven one, was the king of the Cocos Islands. When, once, he spoke to me (making some such observation as 'Hullo, son') I was so overcome that I could not reply. As the voyage continued, however, the glamour started to fade.

One of the shipwrecked islanders had a drink at our table, a speechless, bearded young man, who seemed not to understand a word anyone said. Though silent, he was obviously not strong, in fact he was positively weedy. I tried to imagine him killing tigers, snakes, sharks, and hostile natives, which was what I thought the king and his lieutenants probably did daily, but even my imagination was incapable of the effort. I was bitterly disappointed. People, I decided wisely, were never what they seemed to be.

We were supposed to disembark at Melbourne, but before that the ship stopped at Perth and Adelaide, where we wandered around. A nervous child, I hated to be conspicuous, and I had been terrified that my brown skin, in a country of red ones, would make me so, but I needn't have worried. Everyone was tremendously friendly. I was puzzled when taxi drivers called my father 'mate', told him all about their lives, and invited him into bars for 'a brace of ice colds', but it was obviously well meant, though I myself objected to being called 'nipper'.

I didn't like Melbourne quite so much. A hot, very dusty wind seemed always to be working down the grey, towering streets, blowing people before it. Sydney was better, with the sea filled with swimmers and sharks, a blue field dotted with foam-flowers, and the green arms of the land reaching into the bay, where the bridge like an eloquent bow tied in steel pronounced its epiphanies of traffic. The rush and racket of the city was more intense than that of Melbourne, and therefore, more sympathetic: and in Romano's I ate my first oysters.

Canberra was even better. At that time it was a prefabricated kind of city, full of temporary-looking red brick bungalows. But the Indian high commissioner there was K.S. Duleepsinhji, the cricketer, a plump, gentle man, with a pleasantly cracked, husky, whispery voice. He showed me how to bowl, persuaded me to bowl him a few deliveries on the lawn of his house, allowed me to bowl him, and in token of my triumph, presented me with his Cambridge Blue scarf, which I cherished for years.

From Canberra we went north. I was trying to keep a journal of our trip, and worked at it every night, while my parents were at dinner. Into this journal came bits of verse which I seemed to produce without much effort, and which read like it. I did not really know why I wrote these verses, except that I had a vague yearning to shape and say my experiences in a more complete way than I could do in prose. I cannot remember now what they were about. We were mainly in cities, and the people I met with my father were generally politicians: W.M. Hughes, the First World War premier, the originator of the White Australia policy, a shrivelled old man who swore frequently and colourfully, Menzies, Chifley, and Evatt.

Eventually we drove into the Blue Mountains (which produced a spate of verse) and then went further north, to the Queensland cane country around Mackay and Toowoomba. It was very hot here, with a sticky quality in the air, like the thick warm ooze of the canes. At one plantation, as we were inspecting a dully rustling canefield, a small black man in dungarees shuffled up and asked my father for a cigarette. The overseer waved him impatiently away. 'Don't take any notice of him,' he advised my father. 'He's one of the abos, Abo Charlie, scrounges all he can get.'

But the small man shuffled closer, and said to my father, 'You from India, eh? I too. I from Jhelum side, bloody fine country that. You gotta cigarette?'

My father said in incredulous tones, 'He's an Indian.'

'Is he, by Christ,' said the overseer. 'Never knew that.'

It turned out that Charlie (his real name was Chauhan) had come to Australia before the Great War as a camel driver. When the utility of camels in the Australian desert ended, he hadn't enough money to return home. He had made a living through casual labour for thirty years, had married an Australian wife, and had several children. His one regret was that he could not get his wife to cook Punjabi food.

He was terrible: he begged my father for cigarettes, for whisky, for money to buy them with. The overseer looked disapprovingly on, but eventually my father presented Charlie with a pound. He took it with a lifting of his clasped hands to his forehead in thanks, which after forty years in Australia was still purely Indian.

He was the first expatriate I had ever met, and I eyed him with a wary kind of scorn, not knowing that in a few years I should be one myself, in a country that didn't want me.

In Brisbane, a town of shanty houses and palm trees, rusted by the sun, I was introduced to an old man named Roger Hartigan, who forty years before had made a hundred runs against England. This was his only claim to fame as a cricketer, though he had since become a prosperous businessman. He had very white hair and very pink skin: a kind, rather equine face with bright blue eyes. In spite of the dust and heat, he was always immaculately clad in a suit, and he moved his highly polished shoes with precision, keeping them exactly parallel as he walked. Whenever he came to our hotel, he brought my mother a bunch of flowers or a box of chocolates.

The press officer who was arranging my father's interviews had produced him when I asked if I could meet some cricketers. Mr Hartigan was apparently the only cricketer left in Brisbane: all the others were away. It was true, said the press officer apologetically, that he wasn't a very famous cricketer: but he was a cricketer.

It made no odds to me whether the press officer thought Mr Hartigan famous or not. He had played in a Test match and made a hundred, and anyone who had done that was famous so far as I was concerned. My awed silence when I met him obviously puzzled Mr Hartigan, for it must have been some decades since schoolboys sought his autograph. Equally obvious, it must have pleased him. He paid us a daily call, arriving punctiliously at ten every morning. He would hand my mother her flowers and chocolates, stand my father a drink, and then take me on a slow, processional walk round the dusty pavements of Brisbane, talking about all the people he had played cricket with. At first I drank it all in, but later it started to bore me a little. The attention that had been riveted to him during our first walks began to wander to people, to houses, to trees, and the sky. Mr Hartigan eventually noticed this. As we walked along one day, he said, in his courteous and elaborate way, 'I hope I am not boring you?'

I liked Mr Hartigan very much, but I wanted to be truthful. 'No, not exactly,' I said, 'but I was thinking of something else.'

'Ah,' said Mr Hartigan. He escorted me back to the hotel, bowed to my mother, bought my father a drink, patted me on the head, and walked off, keeping his highly polished shoes precisely parallel. That was the last time I saw him.

In New Zealand I remember the boiling mudholes at Rotorua, the shiny brown mud turning itself over and over in its bestial trench, bubbling and rumbling, sometimes with a suck drawing its own viscous self down into itself: the gulping power of the earth, greedy for us all. It seemed a mysterious country: behind trees and rocks, in a mountain shadow, I glimpsed shapes that weren't there, speaking or moving shapes. I became aware in New Zealand of being in some sense separate from my body. Looking at the mud boiling, or at a lake shivered by fish, in which I glimpsed indeterminate shadows under the skin of the water, I seemed to look down at myself looking down, from a long way away. I would repeat my name, and it meant nothing, it had no connection with what I was. In certain types of landscape, these symptoms have recurred in me ever since.

Perhaps it was because I was now aware of my parents as separate people, no longer flesh of my flesh. I had become more and more abstracted, and sought my loneliness deliberately, speaking less, and at the same time writing more. My journal had spread into several volumes, and the passages of verse had become very frequent now. I knew that I wanted to be a writer, and like an athlete, but quite unconsciously, I was going into training.

When we flew back to Sydney from New Zealand (in a seaplane, landing in a bounce and flurry of spray which, as it flew, rainbowed in the sun, so that it was as though slow constellations of meteors fell past my window), a message was waiting for my father. The Indian government wanted him to tour Southeast Asia and prepare a confidential report about the press relations in the various countries. My father drew up a list of places: Djakarta, Singapore, Saigon, Bangkok, Rangoon: the names delighted me, and I made a sort of litany of them, which I chanted softly to myself.

My mother was less pleased. She wanted to go home, she had had enough of travel. Throughout the trip she had been subdued, though not unhappy, but now the excitable hysterical mood which signalled one of her storms was on her. Surprisingly, it was Duleepsinhji who calmed her: he flew to Sydney, and told her it was a government mission that took us through Asia, important to the country: memories of her nationalist youth stirred in my mother, and she agreed to come.

We flew from Sydney to Darwin, landing at midnight on a barren airstrip loud with mosquitoes. Skeleton shapes showed in the bush beyond. It was suffocatingly hot, and in small cubicles, with fans siphoning humid air over us, we slept uneasily till dawn. Then we headed northward. Below us Australia petered out in a morass of khaki headlands and creeks, and the aeroplane lumbered steadily over a powdery blue sea towards Djakarta. The hostess brought round the morning papers, coffee, and biscuits. We were on our way.

Eventually the sea faded into land, sprawling away in forest and hill below. We landed at Djakarta at dusk. The Indian ambassador, an affable old man from the south, was there to meet us. We drove to his house through the warm and redolent night, down roads lined with shacks, past glistening dark canals. His wife welcomed us, and I was sent to bed, where I lay awake wondering what it was like outside.

Next day the ambassador's wife took my mother and me for a drive. Djakarta was beautiful in the strong whitish sunshine, with broad avenues lined with trees, the trees all in extraordinary, explosive flower, and canals in which, to my great interest, women were bathing, their figlike dark nippled breasts bare. We drove to a beach where a white clubhouse, formerly reserved for the Dutch, stood, and ate rijstaffel, and drove back at evening, with the Javanese in bright colours fluttering among many kindled lamps.

To my surprise, my mother made friends with the ambassador's wife. She was a small, very neat old lady, with silver hair and spectacles, and had had several children. Her gentleness was visible in all her movements, even in the movements of her hands when she sewed, which was all the time. I was surprised because my mother seemed neither to expect nor require friends: she had dropped all her old friends in Bombay, and in Australia had withdrawn so completely as to make friendship with her impossible.

She took to the ambassador's wife completely, however, and since I think the ambassador's wife was herself rather lonely, they tended to spend the whole day together, talking. This meant I was free to move about as I pleased. I accompanied my father on several of his interviews, listening to fat, dejected Dutchmen who talked about the extortionist policies of Sukarno's government, and bespectacled Javanese, until recently terrorists, who talked of Sukarno as though he were the risen Christ. In consequence, I saw quite a lot of Djakarta.

My father obtained an interview with Sukarno. I went with him in the car to the President's palace, and then the chauffeur drove me around the city for an hour. My eyes drank it in, the flowers in the trees and the hair of the people, the ramshackle bungalows of the old colonists, the spruce white houses of the modern Dutch, many of them now requisitioned by Sukarno. The small-boned, golden, cat-faced Javanese struck me as the most beautiful nation I had seen.

We returned to the palace and waited for a while, and eventually my father and Sukarno, followed by two bodyguards came down the steps. Sukarno was short and fanatically neat, in white ducks with a Muslim fez. As my father limbed into the car he leant forward, shot out his arm in a Hitler salute, and shouted, 'Jai Hind!'* My father looked baffled for a moment, then responded, 'Merdeka'† I echoed him feebly, Sukarno once more shot out his arm and shouted, 'Jai Hind!' We again murmured, 'Merdeka!' Fortunately the chauffeur started the car at this point, thus obviating the necessity for any further exchanges.

On the day before we left, the ambassador's wife called me into her reception room. She was sitting on the sofa, sewing. She patted the sofa beside her and I sat down. She blinked at me over her spectacles like a kind little owl.

'I have been talking a lot to your mother,' she said. 'You're a big boy, so you know that she has been ill. She is still very troubled in her mind, and it is mostly about you. She feels that you are not in contact with her. She is afraid she will lose you. You know, you must be very patient with her.'

'She hasn't been very patient with me.'

'But she loves you very much,' said the ambassador's wife. 'You must know that.'

'Well, I don't love her.'

'You may not think you do,' said the ambassador's wife, 'but some time, perhaps very soon, perhaps in many years' time, you will find that you are wrong.'

Singapore was hot, teeming, and filled with muddled rumours of terrorist activity. We stayed in the Raffles Hotel, under mosquito nets and fans. At night, while a Eurasian dance band blared, the local magnates, English, Chinese, and Indian, moved round the

---

* Long live India—Indian nationalist slogan.

† Freedom—Indonesian nationalist slogan.

ballroom in slow, inelegant rhythms. The blotchy shoulders of the planters' wives, revealed by their ill-chosen decolletages, and their raucous and confident voices, revolted me. I refused to go down to dinner, and had it sent up instead.

A Chinese millionaire friend of my father's invited us to his house. Hiis garden was full of plastic deer, emblems of the salve from which he had made his money. In his drawing room, two obscenely fat Cupids pissed whisky and soda respectively at the turn of a tap. Puritanically I decided that Singapore was an entirely vulgar place, and not to be borne.

As usual, however, I accompanied my father on his interviews, which included one with Malcolm Macdonald, whom I was to meet years later under different circumstances. In this way I heard a lot about the terrorists who were then busy on the mainland, and about Malayan independence. I had an excellent memory, and could remember a poem by heart, for instance, as soon as I had written or read it, so I remembered most of what I heard.

My parents were asked to an evening party, and the host said I could come too. So we went. It was in a pretty house, shadowed with bougainvillaea, by the sea, with enormous gardens which were soon alive with adulterous couples. I wandered about for a while, and presently, in a corner of the garden, came on an Indian police officer smoking a cigar. He said hullo, we introduced ourselves, and after a few remarks about the night's beauty, I started to ask him questions about the terrorists. He had just returned from the mainland, and knew quite a lot about them, and I was delighted at the thought that I would be able to retail some first-hand information to my father. So I went on asking, he went on replying, we strolled across the garden, and presently reached my father, surrounded by a group of people.

'I say, Mr Moraes,' said my friend the police officer, 'I must congratulate you upon your son. How intelligent are the questions he has asked me about the terrorists! How profound is his knowledge of the situation! A remarkable boy altogether!'

My father smiled, and I saw that he was pleased. Flushed with triumph, and by the proximity of an audience, I promptly started to ask more questions. They were mostly rather pointless, and the policeman, now surrounded by adults, was soon visibly bored.

On the way home my father said grimly, 'There's a lesson you must learn, and that is, not to show off. If you'd left well alone when you should have, you'd have made a wonderful impression. But by asking all those other silly questions, you simply made a fool of yourself. That tends to happen when you show off. D'you understand?'

'Yes,' I said meekly, but looking out of the car window at the crowded and noisy streets, felt more than ever confirmed in my belief that Singapore was a nasty and vulgar place.

The day before we arrived in Saigon someone had thrown a bomb at a café in the Rue Catinat. From the high window of our room in the Metropole Hotel, I could see the scorched pavement, and the splintered glass of the café window. Nobody seemed to care. The other café on the boulevard were doing a roaring trade: sitting under gaily striped umbrellas, ex-SS men from the Legion were drinking pastis and making passes at every woman who went by. It was their night off. 'It would be better not to go out,' said a harassed-looking first secretary from the Indian embassy, 'till the Legionaires have gone.'

They went about an hour later, cuffed and kicked into a lorry by a roaring bull of a sergeant. When we ventured out, a smell of cordite still hung in the air round the bombed café. We dined in a place full of French officers and Vietnamese whisperers. 'Full of spies,' said the first secretary. 'It's a curious place, Saigon.' He was loose with wine and murmured, 'A very curious place. Either you get a nervous breakdown if you live here, or you come to treat explosions like the chimes of a clock.' All this talk excited me: I longed for an explosion like a sunburst in the window, or for rifles to spit in the street. I thought of them purely as themselves—not as the causes of death.

We drove about the city for the next few days, while my father interviewed people, but I heard no explosions, saw no shots fired, only the spruce French officers and the small, cool Vietnamese, drinking, buying, and selling in the shadows of the street. Then one night we went to a cabaret, where a troupe from, of all places, England, was dancing the can-can. My heart pounded wildly at every kick, every flurry of lace, as stout pink legs flew into the air, and turned into the flashing spokes of a wheel. By now I knew exactly what my emotions in this matter were about, and was in the process of selecting the prettiest dancer to dream of, when abruptly the lights went out. There was a loud stuttering noise outside, and several sharper sounds, like sticks snapping. My father pushed my mother and me under the table. I crouched there, my head pressed uncomfortably against my father's knee, till a shout from the door brought the lights up once more.

'Just a small incident up the road,' said the first secretary affably. 'A patrol must have run into some Viet Minh.' I was deeply disappointed. I had missed the firing, and now I missed the dancers as well, for they didn't reappear.

After a week in Saigon we flew to Dalat, where my father was to interview Bao Dai, the puppet ruler set up by the French. Dalat was in the mountains, with thick forest all round: I saw three naked, dwarfish Sakai aborigines, with bows and arrows, flit away from the kitchens of the luxurious hotel where we stayed. A waiter told me they had come to sell game. The hotel stood by a lake, blue as an eye, on the far side of which Bao Dai's palace stood.

At this hotel I ate snails for the first time. It was my sole cause for excitement. My father refused to let me come to see Bao Dai, since he had been threatened with assassination a few days back, and the attempt was likely to take place at any minute. In point of fact the attempt, which failed, was made the day after we left Dalat, which seemed to be a shame.

After Dalat we travelled north to Hanoi. It was a ramshackle, far-flung town, and across the Red River, a brown snake that lay still in the grassflats on the outskirts, we heard, like a large door slammed with monotonous regularity, the reverberations of French howitzers. The house of the Indian consul vibrated gently at each reverberation, but he seemed unmoved. Attended by a pretty Vietnamese maidservant, he sat on a chair, his bare feet tucked unaffectedly under him, complaining of the shortage of whisky in Hanoi. 'Tomorrow,' he told my father, 'you and I will drive to a French post. It is forty kilometres. But today we shall drink, and what is there to drink? Pah, only rice wine.'

'Can't I come, too?' I asked.

'Bah, it is no place for a boy,' Kutty said. 'There may be shooting on the road.'

'I'd like to come,' I said, glad that we had left my mother, who wanted to shop, in Saigon.

'If you want to come,' said my father gravely, 'come.'

Kutty shrugged his shoulders. 'It is your responsibility. Now, since there is only rice wine, let us drink rice wine.' So they did.

Next day a jeep with a Vietnamese driver stood at the door. Kutty climbed into the front, and my father and I into the back. Then we rattled out of Hanoi. Outside the town inundated paddy fields lay on either side, an endless vista of muddy water, with occasional green shoots poking through, till a faint blue haze of hills broke the horizon. Along the road, at regular intervals, were French sentry posts, concrete pillboxes with slots for windows.

'Sometimes,' said Kutty, 'the Viet Minh lie down in the fields, under water, and breathe through straws, till a French convoy passes. Then—zzt! No convoy.' He laughed heartily. 'They may be there now.' We passed a ditched truck, its bullnose twisted hopelessly to one side. Some of the pillboxes, I noticed, had caved in at the side. 'Grenades,' said the all-explanatory Kutty. He began to talk about the French casualties. I no longer felt the zest with which I had started the day. The casualties Kutty enumerated had made a leap from statistics into actuality.

The landscape stayed the same, flat fields flooded with muddy water, across which in wind a slow ripple occasionally passed. In the distance the blue haze of mountains and along the road the pillboxes, so often violated and sad, their slotted eyes staring vacantly. So we came to the French post. It was an assembly of prefab huts and tents thrown roughly together on high ground, and surrounded by thick tangles of barbed wire. Sentries demanded our passes. One of them chucked me under the chin. We squelched through a hundred yards of mud to the commandant's hut, where Kutty introduced us. The commandant, who had a blue chin but friendly eyes, handed me a bon-bon. Though I felt rather too old for it, I accepted it with thanks.

The interview started. My father's French was limited, so Kutty acted as interpreter. The commandant put his muddy boots on the table, tilted back his chair, and emitted guttural replies to the questions. They had had an engagement with infiltrators, he said, two nights before, and had driven them back. All the while that he spoke he appeared to be listening to something outside the hut.

Eventually he offered to take us round the post. We squelched round with him, staring in an embarrassed way at the soldiers, who, stripped to the waist, many with crucifixes round their necks, whistled, played cards, and stared back. I noticed with a strange sick feeling two crosses in the field behind the post. In the hospital tent several men were lying, bandaged and worn-looking. One of them had rusty stains of blood on his bandage, but they all seemed quite cheerful.

The commandant asked if we would like to see the prisoners taken in the skirmish two days before. They were brought out by two tough-looking Germans with sten guns tucked under their arms: half a dozen tiny young men, skinny, clad in dark brown tunics and trousers. I never discovered whether this was the Viet Minh uniform or the uniform for prisoners. They were lined up, and my father, through Kutty, asked one a question. The Vietnamese looked back with the rolling eyes of a frightened pony. His upper lip was shaking uncontrollably, and soon his thin shoulders also began to shake. He didn't answer. At this the commandant, with a smiling, rather complacent look, slapped him three or four times across the face. They were not very hard slaps, lazy almost, the slaps a cat might give a kitten, but the Vietnamese staggered and nearly fell. At this my father hastily said that he thought he had asked enough questions, and we squelched back to the jeep.

As we started off, I said to my father, 'Why didn't you stop him hitting that man?'

'How could I have stopped him?' inquired my father, and Kutty chuckled. 'The commandant may be having some friends who were killed by that fellow's friends also. What you can do? War is war.'

That evening we went to visit a Vietnamese professor who was a Viet Minh sympathizer. He had been educated at the Sorbonne, and had married a French wife. They made a very handsome couple, in a large drawing room looking over a garden from which the scent of magnolia floated. From an inner room came the sound of a violin. Presently this ceased, and a girl came in. She was about fifteen, two or three years older than I, slim, and very beautiful, with a soft face in which the almond eyes of her father and the rather full, smiling lips of her mother blended. 'This is my daughter Jacqueline,' said the professor. 'Jacqueline, show this young man the garden. You can practise your English at the same time.'

The girl and I went into the garden. The rustle of her dress sent a hundred tiny needles through me, and we stopped under the magnolia tree, still pouring its heavy odour into the air. It was dark now, till the southern sky lit up with the crump of an explosion.

I asked her about her school and her future plans, and she answered in a quiet, husky voice, which seemed to me doomed and therefore, beautiful. After a while I ran out of conversation. We stood under the magnolia tree. She leant on it, crumbling the waxy white petals between her fingers, and letting them fall. Her thick dark hair framed her face which was waxy and white, like the petals that she crumbled. I could not speak, yet the silence in which we stood became as intense as though I spoke and she listened. Then lights shone in the doorway to the garden, and our parents came through.

Bangkok is mad and lovely: I thought so even as a child, walking amidst its pagodas in the rain, or boating on the muddy Chao Phraya, which runs through the city, cluttered with houseboats and floating shops. The golden, dotty people, with their insipid, delicious-looking food, their hours-long dances to a thin inaudible music, appealed to me then, and still do. One of them, who during the war had been imprisoned and tortured by the Japanese, and, chained foodless in a dungeon, made a diet of cockroaches, offered to take us to the best restaurant in town, run by a Chinaman. We took a taxi through a filthy cobweb of streets near the river, then walked for some distance. Finally we reached a bolted door. 'This restaurant,' said our Thai friend, 'is known only to a favoured few. It seems to be closed, but so'—he disappeared into an alleyway, and emerged with an ill-favoured Chinese who had been sleeping there—'so we will gain entry.'

The Chinese, who seemed by no means pleased at being awakened, unbolted the door and we entered a very small room which contained a kerosene lamp, a deal table, and some chairs. Our friend and the Chinese whispered together, and the Chinese disappeared into the shadows. 'Now,' said our friend, 'we will have a meal fit for some kings. When I was a Japanese prisoner I used to dream of meals such as this.'

We sat in the flickering and odorous light of the lamp till the Chinese reappeared with a dish which contained our first course. The Thai told us what it was.

'Fried rice?' said my father dubiously, peering into the dish.

'No, no,' said our friend, indignant. 'I told you this place was special. Fried mice.'

Several years later, in a hotel bar in Bangkok, a Thai girl on the next stool asked me to buy her a drink, and since she was very pretty I agreed. We went on to dinner, and presently she asked me what I did. 'I'm a writer,' I said, 'what do you do?' She leaned towards me and whispered, 'Don't tell anyone. I'm a spy.'

From Bangkok we flew to Rangoon, a dull unsightly city, apart from the Shwedagon Pagoda, and from Rangoon to Calcutta. We had been away six months. When we arrived in Bombay, however, Kutthalingam was beaming at the airport, and at home the dogs went wild. A natural Judas, like most children, I had forgotten Vincent already.

5

Your eyes are like mine...
When I last looked in them
I saw my whole country,
A defeated dream,
Hiding itself in prayers...
—'Letter to My Mother' from *Poems* (1955–1965)

Back in Bombay, I dreamed frequently of Jacqueline in the garden in Hanoi. The arid sky of the city, where kites and vultures floated in a hypnotized stillness, melted back for me into that other velvety sky, erupted into by abrupt flames, under which the held vision of the garden stayed, heavy with the smell of magnolia. I wrote verse nearly all the time, but every new attempt was a similar kind of failure. My idea of what poetry was like was derived from what I had read in my father's library: volumes of Swinburne and early Yeats, or anthologies like the *Golden Treasury* and *Poems of Today.* But somehow this kind of verse had started to dissatisfy me. Inhabiting as I now did the intense, lurid colours and thunderous visions of adolescence, I discovered an anthology (compiled by, of all people, Somerset Maugham) which included work by Eliot, Auden, and Spender. It excited me immensely, I seemed to see for the first time how to write verse.

The verse I now wrote varied in style between the verse of these three poets. An adolescent reaction to Eliot filled my own poems with a cosmic despair: from the early work of Auden and Spender I took a crude Marxism. I struck these attitudes in three different styles, one day pouring out imitation *Waste Lands*, on the next curt, mysterious sonnets full of spies and frontiers, and the day after invoking young men and young comrades in the early Spender manner. I wrote all day, and produced not only half a dozen poems a day, but also short stories rather like Saroyan, and a book about my travels. Eventually, a short story was published in a local newspaper. This brought me luck. Hitherto my father's more artistic friends had tended to ignore me: I was an inarticulate thirteen, and do not blame them. Now, however, Mulk Raj Anand, a novelist who had some fame in England in the 1930s, congratulated me on my story. So did G.V. Desani, who had returned from London after publishing a novel which Eliot had praised. The soft, husky voices of Anand and Desani, their large, vague eyes, long fingers, and high foreheads, awed me. They had published books, and had met writers who were myths to me. It was necessary, I thought, to look like them if one was to be a writer. I brushed my hair upward a dozen times a day in an attempt to broaden my brow, and constantly pulled at my fingers, to make them longer.

A little while later, there was a writer's conference in the city. Auden and Spender flew to Bombay to attend. I went to hear them read, and could not believe it: there they actually were, physically present: Auden with a lined, expressive face, grave and heavy, Spender tall and stooped, with a white cloud of hair and large, intent blue eyes. I had thought of them as very young men, and was surprised: then a new idea of the poet came to me, the poet dedicated, apart, carrying his work on through a lifetime, wrapped in a vatic cloak. Afterwards, my father introduced me to Spender. I was too awestruck to speak, and stood gaping raptly up at him while he stared at me in a kind, rather puzzled way. At last I blurted out the words, 'I want to be a poet.' Spender began to laugh, then stopped and said gently, 'Perhaps you are one.'

This innocent remark intoxicated me: in it I saw a recognition of one poet by another, transcending all barriers, and under this gratifying illusion doubled my output of verse.

I was leading a kind of double life. Though immersed in poetry, I still liked cricket, and for the first time had started to play it. I was now old enough to be allowed out by myself, which was fortunate, since because of my mother I could have met nobody otherwise. My mother wasn't violent now, but had developed an embarrassing habit of talking all the time, recompense perhaps for her years of silence, and when visitors were there she tended to insult them, if she did not like them, for hours on end, in a monotonous rapid voice punctuated by wild bursts of laughter. Fewer and fewer people, therefore, came to see us. At evening, however, I strolled down the seafront with the dogs, looking at the sunset producing effects of great violence above a pallid, crinkled sea, which had drawn back like a very old man's lips from gapped, black, smelly rocks. Here I met other adolescents with their dogs. They generally approached me with remarks about pedigrees: some of them invited me to play cricket, and soon I was a member of a team of local boys, which was called, because we wore red caps, the Cardinals. I turned out, to my surprise, to be a good bowler and fieldsman.

The difference between my two lives was very marked. At home I was the hermit poet, alone, who read when he didn't write. I furrowed my brow over poems, or Kierkegaard (since I had read somewhere that he had influenced Auden), or Henry James. But in the cricket field all this fell away from me. With other tall, pimply boys (my first crop of acne was just flowering) I talked about cricket, or, crudely, about sex, or about films. Because I played well, I was accepted by the others, but it embarrassed me sometimes when they spoke in Hindi, the language they mostly used at home, and I was unable to comprehend or reply.

However, I liked our matches. We played mostly against local schools or clubs, sometimes in the oval park of my childhood. Here there were pitches for hire, and also tents, in which the batting side sat in a hot smell of grass and bat oil. I was not a good batsman, but when we fielded, and I held catches or took wickets, I felt for the only time in my life complete confidence in my own body and my physical skills.

But there was something nervous in me that dreamt of death, which my cricket friends never did. Through bowling so much, I developed a callus on my finger. This I displayed to my father. 'I think,' I said, 'I have cancer.'

My father examined it, looked at me in a peculiar way, and said, 'Do you really think so?' I did, and affirmed that I did. 'Perhaps it's too late already,' I said sombrely, 'but perhaps the finger can be amputated in time.' My father, with a small, tolerant shrug, sent me to the doctor. I showed him my finger and informed him of my diagnosis. He was very kind, gave me some ointment, and told me not to worry: but for weeks after I studied the entry on cancer in the encyclopaedia very closely, checked my symptoms, and wrote poems about death.

Meanwhile, however, between poems and stories, I wrote essays about cricket. One day I showed some of these to a publisher friend of the family's. 'Do you know,' he said in amazement, having read them, 'I think these may sell.' A few months later the essays were published in a small, green-covered book, which I touched with excitement and pleasure. It didn't last: I am now desperately embarrassed and irritated when I see a copy of this volume, which I sometimes do because over the last decade and a half, the stray copies which float into London have become collectors' items.

Among the occasional visitors who still came to the flat was a small, grey-haired man in shorts, called Tendulkar, a particular friend of mine. He had mild, shiny eyes, and a very gentle voice, listening to which sometimes almost hypnotized me, creating worlds to listen to within its own echo. Tendulkar had spent some years in Russia, and had been a Communist, but when he returned to India, Gandhi had reconverted him. He had since occupied all his time compiling a biography of Gandhi, an immense work in eight thick volumes. Tendulkar was fastidious about the design and printing of books, and listening to his conversation I first became aware of the intricate way in which books are physically made. He also told me a lot about Russian literature, and lent me hundreds of volumes from his library. Because I developed such a taste for Turgenev and Gorky, he called me Domski, and it is him calling me that which I most remember: the soft voice nearly singing, as it split the nickname into two spaced syllables, a lilt of affection that always touched me and moved me.

Though he was a favourite of Nehru's, and his Gandhi biography was published by the government, Tendulkar was very poor. He lived in a one-room hovel in Kalbadevi, where sometimes I went to visit him. One had to climb several flights of rickety stairs, smudged with betel and excrement, for he lived at the top of his tenement. His room contained a charpoy on which he slept, but no other furniture except for the shelves lining every wall, which contained his large library, and two cases in which he kept a collection of delicate ivories and antique bronzes, collected over the years. He would lift them from the cases, in small delicate fingers, and display them to me, turning them over with love: 'Look, Domski, is not this configuration beautiful?' Or would take a piece of bright handwoven cloth off his charpoy, his fingers moving slowly over the warp of it: 'Look, Domski, at the run of the threads. Things made with the hands are always beautiful.'

Together we walked through the city. Ancient monuments fascinated Tendulkar, he loved to visit the caves and temples around Bombay, but equally he was fascinated by the life of the city. We stopped to look at the huddled hovels, festooned with washing, where people lived sometimes ten to a room, at shops run by stout smilers, where minuscule quantities of rice and pulses were purchased by scraggy housewives: and the beggars who seemed to be everywhere, crawling and wailing in the summer dust and the monsoon puddles, ageless and homeless. 'Look, Domski, look. That is the way people live in our country. They should not live like that. Men should not live like that.' And, fervently, his eyes lit up and looking, 'Some day we will have justice, and freedom.'

I had never known what life in Bombay was really like, until Tendulkar showed me. The instincts of socialism fostered in me by the work of people like Gorky and the Thirties' poets flared up. I went into the city by myself, distributing my pocket money amongst the beggars. But there were so many of them it was impossible: the money ran out quickly, and I was always left stranded in a tide of beggars, lapping at my shoes with thin dry hands, whimpering and crying for more.

In a paradoxical, typical way, I was taken on most of these expeditions by Kutthalingam in the car. He was astounded by my strange new behaviour. 'These worthless fellows,' he said, 'rascals, no got any jobs, why my young master wanting give them money?' Democratically I would say, 'I'm not your young master, I'm your friend.' 'Yes, yes, you my friend, sure,' Kutthalingam would say, wagging his head with maddening omniscience, 'but also you my young master.'

Manishi Dey was a painter. When I was still very small, my father had commissioned a picture from him. He produced one of girls in a garden, which was beautiful, till one day arriving drunk at our flat when my parents were out, he adorned it with an immense blue sun. Later, repentant, he took the sun out, but in due course a large dark stain showed up where it had been. The picture, stain and all, still hung in our flat. The story of the sun had been a legend of my childhood. So when we came back to Bombay I was particularly interested to meet the main character. Manishi was a fat affable man with a baby face, dressed always in flowing Bengali robes. He flippered about in loose slippers, flapping his hands, and crooning and cooing with a dove's delight whenever he met a friend. He had no money ever, and was often at our flat for meals and drinks, drinks in particular, since he consumed a lot of those.

When, shyly, I told him I wrote poetry, he was enchanted. Producing those strange dovelike noises which are my main memory of him, he demanded to see them. He read them with coos of pleasure. 'I must illustrate these poems,' he said, 'so beautiful they are...yes, yes, definitely.' He illustrated them in pen and ink, returning to the flat every week to read my new verses and illustrate those. In this way I collected a considerable portfolio of poems and sketches, which I had bound: one of my sorrows is that I lost it years ago.

He had a habit of turning up in a taxi for which my father had to pay. It became normal procedure for the bearer on Thursdays, when he usually called, to be given a small sum of money in order to settle Manishi's taxifare. One Thursday, however, the bearer, came to my father in some alarm.

'Sahib, Dey sahib is outside in a taxi, and has no money to pay.'

'Well, you pay.'

'Sahib, I cannot. Dey sahib is asleep, and the taximan says the fare is 120 rupees.'*

My father was obviously startled. However, 'Bring the taximan here,' he told the bearer. The taximan came in. 'Sahib,' he said, in an embarrassed way, 'I picked the fat sahib up today, and he told me to drive him to a bar. When we reached there, he asked me to loan him ten rupees and wait. He came out when I had waited for an hour, and told me to drive to another bar and loan him another ten rupees. Sahib, we have been to eight bars now, and the fare is as I say.'

My father paid, and the bearer and he assisted Manishi into the flat. He rolled from side to side, cooing softly, with streaks of

* About £10.

drink and sick all down the front of his robes. Owlish, his large bloodshot eyes blinked round the room. When he saw me, he lurched forward, and dropped to his knees beside me, fumbling in his pockets.

'Look, look, I have been very bad, I am a badmash, a rascal, but I remembered to keep the drawings safe.'

He handed me a little sheaf of sketches, dry, clean, and uncrumpled. 'I kept them safe,' Manishi repeated, and then noisily passed out.

He was the first Bohemian I ever met, and he died in Calcutta a few years back, in poverty and alone.

I had known most of these people long before, when I was still a child. They had all been family friends. I now met another, whom neither my parents nor I had met for some years, during which time he had lived in the wilds of Central India. This was Verrier Elwin, an Englishman who had been at Oxford with my father. There he had obtained a double first, but had abandoned a fellowship offered him at All Souls' to become an Anglican minister. He had been sent to India as a missionary, but had soon become much too interested in politics for the government. When he started to support Gandhi, he was deported to England, and told he would not be allowed to return unless he swore not to interfere in politics. He swore he wouldn't, quit the Church, and came back to India to try and help anyone who needed help. He soon found an aboriginal tribe, the Gonds, living in the forests of Central India, who were dying off rapidly through exploitation and disease. For the next twenty years he lived with the Gonds, and in fact, married one. He translated their sung poetry and published volumes about their tribal customs which earned him fame as an anthropologist. Most of all, he was able to stop the exploitation of the tribe by moneylenders and officials, which was rapidly killing it off. After Indian independence he became an Indian citizen. When I met him, Nehru had just appointed him officer-in-charge of the rebellious Naga tribesmen in Assam. Verrier spent much of his time burrowing into the Assam forests, making friends with the tribesmen: but occasionally he came to Bombay on leave.

He was very tall, and stooped, with an ungainly scholar's body which never seemed to fit into a city suit. His white hair wisped up above a strangely birdlike, amused face, with large spectacles, and he spoke in a don's deliberate voice. To me he spoke about poetry, which he loved and in a way lived. He introduced me to the work of Dylan Thomas, David Gascoyne, and other modem poets, and also to the work of the recent poet I think he most admired, Sidney Keyes. In Keyes, who was killed in the war, aged twenty-one, he seemed to admire something English and fated, in rather the same way as the generation that went to the First World War admired Rupert Brooke. Indeed, for a man who had scarcely revisited England in thirty years, his taste was peculiarly, wistfully English: the great poet of all time, to him, was Wordsworth, whom I did not know. In fact, I had read no classical English poetry, outside the *Golden Treasury.* Apart from recommending me to contemporary poets whom he liked, Verrier sent me to the Metaphysicals, to *Don Juan,* and to Wordsworth. 'You must know poetry,' he said, 'if you want to be a poet.' He opened his knowledge to me, and tentatively I entered. My shyness faded when he praised my own work: perhaps too kindly, but he confirmed me in my belief that I was a poet. No poem I ever wrote pleased me: once I had finished one, an itchy agony of frustration drove me on to the next, and so endlessly forward. I saw the faults in my verse, and did not really believe a word of Verrier's praise: but strangely, the very fact that he treated me seriously, even though I did not accept his praise, encouraged me. From the jungle his long, badly typed letters crossed the thousands of miles to Bombay. They spoke of arduous trips and of fever, but only briefly: otherwise, as though he were writing them from rooms in All Souls', they discussed poetry, and, on occasion, life.

I devoured the bits about poetry: but, at fifteen, the bits about life bored me intensely.

My brindled bitch, Judy, was operated on for a gallstone in 1952, and died. This left me with only one dog, Kumar: I had given the puppies away. Golden and sedate, he became my constant care. He puffed a little as he climbed to the foot of my bed every night, and there slept.

He was the remains of my childhood: I took him for walks, soliloquized to him, read my poems aloud while he curled, snoring faintly, at my feet. It was not surprising that my mother became resentful of this attachment. The stage I had reached was a stage when I despised and criticized my parents. I told my father how despicable journalists were, and how I would never be one, and though it was his ambition for me, he received my remarks with his usual aplomb. With my mother it was different. She had herself driven her friends away, but was lonely, and loved me with a dry, consuming love. She obviously wanted to talk to me. But when we met in the drawing room, and she began her tentative, sad advances, speaking of the weather or the headlines in the newspapers, I was silent, and withdrew to my own room with Kumar, to spend the day there. My mother's attempts to recover her lost son became a little desperate. She began to give me breakfast in bed, and she would cook and fetch it herself. She had always had a cook, so her eggs and bacon weren't very well made, and I took every advantage of this. I told her how horrible her breakfasts were, and refused to eat them. I realized I had the power to hurt her, and a cold sort of cruelty rose in me as I exploited my power. Simultaneously however, I felt deep helpless sorrow, for the circumstances that had fetched us to this ridiculous pass, for my inability not to be cruel, and for my mother's obvious pain. Sometimes I made efforts to be kind, but always before the end something in me forced me to say a cutting and hurtful sentence, and leave her sitting there with her hurt.

I now think that this was the main reason for the relapse she suffered. She continued to be very talkative, but her violent spells occasionally recurred: she threw plates about and screamed at everyone except me: when, during one of her spells, she passed me, she rushed by with averted head, as though she knew she was only confirming my opinion of her, but was as helpless to stop it as I was to stop my coldness towards her.

Another monsoon came, splashing thunder and rain into the sea outside our windows. Kumar fell ill. He had become very corpulent and wheezy, and he was old: one day he simply collapsed, and lay there breathing heavily, unable to rise. I was in a terrible, hysterical state of distress. I put Kumar in a basket in my room, and rang the vet. When he arrived, however, my mother refused to allow him into the flat. He carried germs, she said, from the animals he treated, and so violent was the scene she made that I left Kumar where he was, since he could obviously not be moved, and went to the vet's surgery myself. Here I described the symptoms, collected some medicine and ampoules, and a syringe for injections, and returned home.

When I arrived back I discovered that my mother had had Kumar removed to the front balcony. It was raining fiercely, with a seawind driving clouds of spray over the balcony. He was soaked through, but when he saw me made an effort to wag his tail. Furiously, I confronted my mother.

But she was in one of those strange wild moods that always led to explosions. She refused to allow Kumar in the flat, because she said he would infect us all. When I tried to carry him back to my room, she rushed to prevent me, and a short, undignified scuffle followed. I was helpless. My father was away in Delhi, and the servants lived in too much terror of my mother to obey me instead of her.

So for a day and a night, an absurd figure with an umbrella and raincoat, I sat on the verandah, endeavouring to protect both the dog and myself from the rain that lashed down from the sky.

I talked to him about the old days, the dog show we had won, and how he would soon be better: at first he seemed grateful for the sound of my voice, feebly wagged his tail, or licked my hand: later he lay still, wheezing terribly, or in a fitful, whimpering sleep. On the second morning he was asleep. I had a streaming cold and was very tired. I left him, and went to lie down. I had been asleep a few minutes when the bearer woke me and said, 'Sahib, kuttha mar gaya,' the dog is dead.

He was lying on the balcony, his eyes wide and staring, as though he had looked round for me as he died. His tongue protruded from his mouth. On the wet floor a train of black ants had appeared from nowhere, and the first one had already reached his protruding, helpless tongue. I brushed the ants away and carried his body down to the car. Kutthalingam and I found a place by the sea, and there, together, we buried him, and the last of my childhood.

After this I lived a lot of my life outside the flat. I played cricket, but this was the only time I really sought company. Mostly I took long solitary walks, or sat in restaurants by myself, drinking coffee and reading. What I needed most, I suppose, was a girlfriend, but at fifteen I was too shy and pimply to make advances to anyone. Verrier was away in the forests, Tendulkar and Manishi had ceased to come to the flat because of my mother, and my father was often in Delhi on business. So I had nobody to really talk to, for though at cricket I was surrounded by other adolescents, there I conformed to them, and became somebody else.

The magazine which had published my first story, *The Illustrated Weekly of India,* now published some of my poems as well. The editor, Shaun Mandy, a large, benevolent Irishman, praised the ones he published: the ones he did not, he sent back with one-word comments blue-pencilled on the margins. He liked long words: 'elliptical', he would write, or 'rebarbative', and generally I had to look them up in the dictionary. However,

Shaun Mandy was very kind: one day he asked me to have a drink with him, in his house by the sea. It was the first time we had met, and his bearer had mixed a quantity of Tom Collinses. I accepted six of these gratefully. Though they were the first spirits I had drunk (my father occasionally allowed me a beer) they had no effect on me, except to make me more talkative than usual. I told Mandy my problems. 'Well,' he said, 'my assistant editor, Nissim Ezekiel, is a poet. You ought to get together with him. He's quite young. And by the way,' he added, 'how old are you?' I told him, and he seemed stunned. 'Do you have much experience of drinking?' he inquired. Not wishing to seem backward, I implied that I was never off the bottle. He said dazedly, 'I had heard that young people were now more advanced than they used to be, but, my God.'

A few days later I received a letter from Nissim Ezekiel. I had read some of his poems in the *Illustrated Weekly*, and, even at my uncritical age, could see that they were a lot better than anything else there. Moreover, he had published a volume of verse in England. I was deeply honoured when he asked me to have a coffee with him, and went to the rendezvous with a large folder full of carefully typed poems.

He was a slight young man, pale-skinned and bespectacled. He turned my poems over in long, somehow disdainful fingers. 'These are not poetry yet,' he said, his words penetrating icily to my heart, 'but,' he added, 'they show some talent. Let us take a short walk.'

We walked by the seafront. To walk there at evening, alone, made me dizzy and electric, when I inhaled the smell off the withdrawn waters, mingled with the occasional scent of a woman passing by, and looked at the glistening tearful rocks and the final streaks of sunset in the sky. To walk there with an actual poet, even though he did not consider me to be one, made each moment terrible and joyful. When Ezekiel spoke to me of his views on poetry, it was as though he had unlocked a box full of unheard whispers. 'Naturally, people in India will praise you,' he said in his dry and cryptic voice. 'There are no good critics here. The critical standards are appalling. Don't accept praise easily. You must work on your verse.'

Though his words shrivelled my confidence, they increased my desire to write well. The further this secret, this mystery, floated away from me, the harder I pursued it. My meetings with Ezekiel became weekly, and always followed an identical pattern: we had coffee in a seafront café, when I showed him my new work, and then walked along the front, and he would discuss it. That is to say, he would scissor it softly to pieces: then, into my dismay he would drop the two words of hope: 'Work harder.' So long as he did not despair of me, neither did I. I worked harder. I read the poets he recommended, and critical books which he lent me. I mostly found the latter very dull, except the essays of Pound and Eliot, and some of the early work of Leavis. But I ploughed through them. Ezekiel had introduced me to the idea that mine was not merely a gift that had floated down on the wind, but a craft I must study, and know intimately, before I could do it well.

'As Yeats said,' Ezekiel would remark cryptically, as we paced our darkened shore, 'we must labour to be beautiful.'

My grandfather died. I remembered what he had once said to me, but no longer resented it: however, I had had no real contact with him for years. Sometimes we drove down to Santa Cruz on Sunday for lunch. This was a contrast to home because there we ate English food, roast beef on Sundays: at my grandfather's house the old Indian Christian life remained, and his daughters cooked dishes which had perhaps once been Portuguese, before the Indian proselytes touched them with spices: black sausages, rather similar to a Spanish chorizo, but much hotter, pork curries, and sweetmeats made with cinnamon and coconut. My grandfather, at the head of the table, said Grace before and after meals, with my father and I standing rather embarrassingly apart.

I neither liked nor disliked my grandfather, and felt no emotion at all when I heard of his death. It came suddenly, through a heart attack, in the night. Next morning my father and I drove down to Santa Cruz (my mother, who hated my grandfather, would not come) and found all the shutters drawn at Crossville. Inside the whole household was gathered in the main room, all weeping, the women occasionally emitting high, strident cries. Upstairs my grandfather lay, tiny and withered, on the bed where he had died. He looked nearly the same as usual, except for a bandage round his chin, which kept his mouth closed.

I was repelled by the wild cries downstairs, but not by the fact of death. At last something private and mysterious had enveloped my grandfather. I was not distressed, but was moved by the privacy around him. The funeral was next day, and my father sent me post-haste back to town to buy a black suit.

Next day my grandfather was buried in the local churchyard, near my grandmother. I remember afterwards my father and I stood at the churchyard gate, receiving the condolences of the mourners. It was muddy underfoot and cloudy overhead. I kept hitching up the trousers of my new suit, which were rather long, so that they shouldn't be marked by the mud under which my ancestor lay. The people coming up were mournful in appearance, and clasped the right hands of my father and myself with both theirs, staring tearfully into our eyes as they muttered, 'A tragedy. Sincerely sorry…sincerely…'

I was not sorry that my grandfather was dead. He had achieved dignity, after years of age and eczema. In a dreamy mood, I felt sorry for these people who clasped my hand and appeared so sad. As they clasped my hand therefore, and said how sorry they were, I smiled at them reassuringly, and said in tones of equal sincerity, 'Don't worry about it. It's really quite all right.'

The mourners gathered in knots on the road, whispering to each other, and staring back at me. Though I was unaware of the fact, it was the first time I had justified the reputation for madness which was to follow me through the Catholic community in India.

On my sixteenth birthday, my father took me out to dinner. I ate frogs' legs and chicken supreme in a large hotel. 'The best frogs, sahib,' the waiter said. 'They coming from a well in the courtyard.' I didn't care where they came from: chewing them, in evening dress, like my father, I felt my maturity had arrived. It hadn't quite. I eyed the girls in the cabaret with a sad lust: not only had I never slept with, but I had never had a relationship with any girl ever.

'We'll have to think of what you're going to do,' my father said. 'In a few years you'll have to earn your own living.' Importantly I said yes, I was going to be a poet. Ezekiel had introduced me to Rimbaud, I had read all his poetry, and the Starkie biography, and I intended to be like Rimbaud, *maudit,* at the age of twenty giving it all up with a gesture to sell guns and slaves in exotic places.

'For a start,' said my father, 'you ought to go to Oxford.'

Rimbaud hadn't been, but lots of poets had. 'Okay,' I said.

'You'll have to pass exams to do that. Will you try?'

'Okay,' I said. 'I'd like to study French.'

'There's an Alliance Française here. You can go to that. But you'll have to go to school as well.'

The poet was willing: smiling wryly and cynically, as Rimbaud must have smiled, he lifted a glass of what, in prohibition Bombay, was unfortunately only lemonade, to his lips and murmured, 'Very well.'

So a couple of weeks later, I commenced lessons at the Alliance Française. I had private lessons, from the wife of the director. She was young and pretty, blonde, and her name was Colette. I immediately fell in love with her.

I started my lessons with a curious amount of knowledge. Though I was totally ignorant of spoken French, I had acquired a French dictionary and with it had been deciphering the original versions of poems by Rimbaud, Verlaine, and Apollinaire. My first appeal to Colette was for help with the poems of Laforgue and Corbière, but she was adamant in her wish that I should learn the parts of speech, grammatical constructions, etcetera, before I attempted more specialized flights. I learnt quickly, however, impelled partly by a desire to read French poetry, and partly to please Colette.

We sat on a sofa in the Alliance office, with books spread out on a low table before us. Sometimes, when she leant towards me to emphasize a point, her fair, coarse hair brushed my face. Her blonde smell excited me, but in a manner by no means lustful. She was the first woman I had seen much of who was not a relative: the flexibility and softness of a woman's hands and skin at close quarters filled me with a sort of baffled adoration. Through her I yearned towards the entire sex, marvellous and unattainable.

She was an amateur of the arts, typical, though I did not know this, of a certain kind of woman. She acted in plays put on by the Alliance, and in her adolescence, she told me, had written poetry. I showed her my poems, and together we translated some of them into French. This made me feel very close to her.

Eventually I wrote a poem called 'French Lesson', which was about her. It explained to me what I did not know: that we didn't understand each other. Most of my poems hitherto were written on a sort of insistent impulse, a rhythm that sang itself in my head and wanted to be fleshed out with words. I threw the words down on paper quickly, trying to fix the rhythm before it left me.

But with this poem it was not merely that. I fixed my words down like butterflies with delicacy and care, and felt the object that was being made by my hands. The shaping and polishing of the object outlasted the first impulse, so that I worked a long while on it. Moreover, whereas normally before my poems rose from other poems I had recently read, in this one I tried to express my own emotions with precision. When I showed it to Ezekiel, I got a reaction that amazed me, the reaction I had always wanted from him. He read it carefully several times, and nodded his pale intellectual head. 'Congratulations,' he said. 'This is a good poem. It's the first poem you've ever written.'

It surprised me then, though it would not surprise me now, that having written this poem for Colette, my emotions towards her first cooled and then froze, and I stopped my lessons at the Alliance.

Since the death of Kumar, I had gone deliberately out of my way to hurt my mother. It was seldom that I addressed a civil word to her. I would abuse the Catholic Church, and she, a rosary in her hands, would beg me to stop. Or else, more hurtful to her still, I would tell her of my plans to study abroad. She must have been aware that eventually she would lose me physically, as already she had lost me mentally, but it was a knowledge she resisted. I was the apple of her eye, and my very presence in the flat, even when I wouldn't speak to her or was rude, made her happy.

The impending threat of my departure, and my constant harping on it, triggered off all the suppressed illness left in my mother. Daily she grew worse. My father awoke one night to find her standing over his bed, a knife in her hand. After that he always locked his bedroom door. She blamed him for intending to send me abroad, and was intolerable when he was at home. She also attacked the servants several times. The flat resounded once more to the sound of shouts and breakages. I shut myself away from it, and wrote.

One still, burning afternoon, I was at work when I heard my mother scream hysterically outside, and then the crash of crockery. I heard the frightened voices of the servants, then a succession of thunderous sounds, as of furniture being overturned. As always when my mother's attacks started, I felt utter terror take hold of me, and then a fierce, almost impersonal anger. Objects and people were not to be treated like this. I unlocked the door and went out.

In the drawing room my mother stood, hair flying, eyes rolling, the image of my childhood ogre of Ceylon. She clutched a knife in her left hand, and was brandishing it in the faces of the terrified servants, who stood in a line before her. With her free hand she slapped out indiscriminately at them, while they tried helplessly to shelter themselves from the blows. Around her on the floor were the fragments of every breakable object in the room, and furniture overturned in an unsymmetrical, brutal way. My terror and anger twisted in me, and my anger rose above my terror. It was the terror of the servants which made this happen. They were poor and helpless, they depended on us, that was the only reason they suffered this so tamely, and confusedly I thought my mother must know this. I stepped up to her and pulled the knife out of her hand. In doing this I gashed my fingers, but didn't notice. My mother turned with a loud, chilling cry, and flew at me with her nails.

As I wrestled with her, I breathlessly ordered the servants back to the kitchen. They fled. I remained locked with my mother, swaying obscenely across the wrecked room. Her strength was terrifying, but more terrifying was the fact that she seemed incapable of speech: she simply shrieked, and struggled. Finally I broke free of her, and stepped back. She stood before me, a wild, frantic figure, still shrieking. A vague idea of stopping hysterics mixed with my anger and disgust, and my hand swung out of its own volition and hit her very hard across the face.

At the moment I did this I felt, as I had often felt in moments of complete calm, that I was separate from my name and body, a spectator of all this. My mother's head snapped sideways from my slap, and blood appeared on her face. It was my own blood, but this I did not know. We stood rigid, and she stared at me with absolutely normal eyes, which dilated slowly and overflowed with tears.

I knew in that instant that something final had happened. Pity for my mother flooded my whole body. I stepped forward, intending, I think, to put my arms round her, but, still trembling with sobs, she swung away and ran out of the room.

I had just become aware of the pain of my cut hand when from the back of the flat I heard another scream and a really appalling crash. When I got to my mother's bedroom I discovered that she had picked up a large chair and thrown it through the window. She was now lifting another. When I rushed up she turned. Her face, terribly distorted, was covered with blood and tears, and there was foam on her lips. Her eyes were totally impersonal: they seemed to look at me with a faint curiosity, as at something they had not seen before. She tossed the heavy chair over the verandah rail, and I ran to the telephone and called my father.

While I explained to him what had happened, the flat echoed with crashes. My mother had ceased to scream, but she was throwing every movable object, systematically, one by one, out of the window. As I finished my call, she appeared by the telephone, breathing heavily, her staring eyes appearing now not to see me at all. She grasped the telephone and pulled it completely out of the wall.

Then I spoke to her, but she seemed not to hear. So I obeyed my father's instructions. I went into the kitchen, where the terrified servants were huddled, and told them to leave the flat. After that I left it myself. My whole body shook uncontrollably, as though I was very cold. Downstairs, a large crowd stood and stared up at our windows. From them, every few minutes, like deformed birds, a chair or table would erupt, and crash to the hot concrete beneath. The crowd turned a hundred heads and stared at me, and I stood there shaking, and stared back. Then our car came flying up the drive. My father and two doctors stepped out, paused to reassure themselves I was safe, and ran upstairs. The known familiar arm of Kutthalingam enclosed my shoulders. He was nearly in tears. He led me, hiccupping, to the car, and made me sit down. I wept, and the crowd stared in through the windows.

My father came back. He stood abstractedly by the car door, biting his nails.

'She's locked the doors. She won't open them. They're trying to persuade her now.'

One of the doctors ran downstairs.

'This is no use. She will not open the doors. There is only one thing to do. We must certify her insane. Then we will break down the door, and tomorrow she can be committed to an institution.'

My father brushed his hand indecisively across his brow. Then, in a shaky voice, he said, 'I swore once I would never do that. I have never done it, all these years.'

Irritably, the doctor said, 'What is the alternative? She is a public menace at present. The police will be here soon. Besides, reflect...it is very likely that she will do herself some injury.'

The argument continued. The furniture had ceased to fall. The crowd buzzed and stared alternately at the windows and at us. Angry neighbours came up. 'We shall telephone the police,' they said. After twenty minutes, my father's lips twitched a little, as though they were dry. He said to the doctors, 'Very well.'

'It would be better if you went away now,' they said, suddenly kind. 'Your presence will only excite her.'

We drove to friends nearby. Their quiet flat filled with their solicitude. They fussed over me, while my father intermittently used the telephone. It told him what had happened, hour by hour. My mother, under heavy sedation, was in a clinic. She had been certified insane, and found a place as a private patient in the Bangalore mental home, the best in the country. The doctors were to fly her there the next day.

It was as though she had become inanimate, like a parcel or letter, to be sent from place to place, to be controlled by the authorities. She had been detached from my life. Yet vivid in my mind was the moment I had slapped her that afternoon, when above the smeared blood on her face, the eyes of a hurt person stared back at me and filled with tears. My own unshed tears were for that face, which stood clear in my mind, and brought with it the first ache of the guilt that I feel still.

6

> The towers of the unwashed hospital,
> The black house in which everyone is sick,
> Throw shadows in the courtyard where the tall
> Fidgety prince still paces with his book.
> —'Melancholy Prince' from *John Nobody* (1965)

I was now at school. It was a Catholic missionary school, a large grey barracks patrolled by Jesuits, with arid stretches of playing field. By the gates stood an ugly church. A monsoon wind had blown the steeple off, and it was never replaced in my time.

Most of the boys in this school were Catholics. I was prejudiced against them. Partly this was because of the associations the religion had for me with my mother and other members of the family, partly because these boys had an unquestioning attitude, not only towards their faith but towards everything, conservatives at fifteen and sixteen. The priests walked affectionately through their flocks, laying hands on first one, then another, christened head. Towards the non-Christian boys their attitude was more ambivalent.

I found to my dismay that I had to attend Catechism classes. There was no escape from this, it was my first collision with institutional discipline: so I had to sit daily through an inexplicable half hour in which the teacher explained to us that our unchristened schoolmates were pagans, and would go to hell, unless we converted them. He urged us to speak to them constantly on the subject of religion, and attempt to fetch them to church services, so that they could see how splendid Catholicism was. Once I queried the necessity for this, and thereafter, the stock witticism from the teacher was to urge my classmates to perform the same service for me as they were supposed to for the pagans. Some of them actually did: with pious faces, they talked to me about religion, and tried to lend me Catholic books. Finally I determined to register a protest. I was just starting to read Marx, a man whom the teacher assured us was at that very moment roasting unhappily in hell. At the next Catechism class, I opened a copy of *Das Kapital,* and propped it on my desk, the cover turned towards the teacher. He noticed it at once, and his face reddened fiercely, as though at an affront to his modesty. 'I shall *confiscate* that book,' he said, snatching it from my desk, 'and I shall *burn* it.' The burning of books confirmed my opinion that religion was uncivilized, but I felt I had made my gesture.

Eventually I made friends with two 'pagan' boys. These were Mickey, a Muslim, and Satish, a Hindu. We began to go about together, and one day one of the priests, a Spaniard, called me aside after class. 'Why is it' he demanded, 'that you have not made friends with some good Catholic boy?'

'I prefer the friends I have.'

'They are pagans, my son,' he said gravely.

'They are more intelligent than the Catholics.'

He gave me a look, a sorrowful, missionary look. 'You are mad, my son,' he informed me, and swished away, harnessed like a camel into his white cassock. I have an idea that it was my supposed unbalance that saved me from expulsion.

Meanwhile I worked on my poetry harder than ever. My head was full of unresolved words and lines which, like someone constructing a puzzle, I fitted into poems till they worked. After the boredom and dust of a day at school, I felt a vibration of pure power when I sat down at my desk. Here the words and I were equal masters: like a wrestler, I bent back and let the words take me, then with a twist of the wrist I was on top, forcing them slowly into place. I was still seldom satisfied with anything I wrote, but I occasionally felt that tremor of excitement which meant I had succeeded, to me still the most potent excitement in the world. Even Ezekiel was sometimes pleased and he now talked to me on equal terms, as one poet to another.

Stephen Spender came back to India on a visit. Ever since I had met him, years before, he had become a hero of mine. He had been the first person ever to tell me that perhaps I was a poet, and I attached considerable importance to this. When he arrived in Bombay, I left a folder of poems at his hotel, with a request that he read them. The next few days passed in a frenzy of anticipation, yet when his reply came I could hardly believe it. It said he had liked the poems very much, and invited me to breakfast next day.

I arrived at the hotel early, and sat in the car with Kutthalingam for the best part of an hour, feverishly consulting my watch every few minutes. Kutthalingam laughed gently at my impatience, and inquired who the gentleman was. A poet, I said, he wrote poetry, but it was no use: he didn't understand the English word.

Presently it was time: I rushed into the hotel and demanded Mr Spender from the desk clerk. The minutes it took him to come down in the lift seemed endless, then suddenly he was there, immensely tall, white-haired, with large sea-coloured eyes looking down out of a very pink face. Over breakfast, while I sat in silence, he talked in a gentle, rather precise voice about poetry. 'Writing it,' he said, 'is like looking into a mirror, and after a while the face in the mirror becomes terrible.' I did not understand what he meant, but agreed that I had often felt this myself. He looked at me rather quizzically.

After a while I was emboldened to ask him about other English poets I admired. He knew them all, and talked of them, sometimes with little barbs of amused, fraternal malice. At these moments his face flushed deeply, and broke into an enormous, astonished smile. The idea that poets, the godlike ones who sat on mountains, were people like myself was new to me. I rather liked it.

He spoke of my own poetry. 'It's very influenced by Rimbaud,' he said, 'isn't it? And the symbolists? You'll write a different kind of poetry when you're older.' And, reflectively over his coffee, 'What do you want to do? Besides write poetry, I mean?'

I told him about my plans for Oxford, and then fell silent. I had no idea what I wanted to do afterwards. I had always imagined that I would live by poetry, but this, he said, was impossible. There was no money in it. However, money for me had always been something that was there, quantities of it, lying so thickly in the bank that nobody knew what to do with it all. I imagined it must be easy to obtain. I would obtain it somehow. I told Spender this. Also I said I wanted to settle in England. I had never really reflected on this before, but as I said it, it seemed to become true. England, for me, was where the poets were. The poets were my people. I had no real consciousness of a nationality, for I did not speak the languages of my countrymen, and therefore, had no soil for roots. Such Indian society as I had seen seemed to me narrow and provincial, and I wanted to escape it. As I spoke to Spender, reasons wheeled and fell into place around me, and I convinced myself.

Spender said, very kindly, that if I needed any help in England, he would help me. I thanked him very much and left the hotel, my feet airborne. After that I met him twice or thrice, and, speechless with excitement, saw him off at the airport. As he was saying goodbye, I asked if he remembered meeting me as a small boy, a few years before, and saying that perhaps I was a poet.

To my disillusionment, he said he didn't remember.

Spender's encouragement gave me a feeling of exhilarated power, which I took into the decrepit grey barracks of the school with me. I came top of the class, and entered for an essay competition sponsored by the government, the prize for which was a trip to America. My essay was declared to be the best, but the government turned me down because I did not speak Hindi. A baffled, cheated feeling came over me. Now positively, I did not want to stay in India.

But in the meantime, with my friends, Satish and Mickey, I started a school magazine unoriginally called *The Monthly Review.* The headmaster agreed to have it cyclostyled on the school machine, which from his point of view was a mistake. The first issue contained an article on sex, several obscure and sexual poems by me, and a study of Auden which applauded his support of the Republicans in the Spanish war. The headmaster, himself a Spaniard, was particularly annoyed by the last. The three of us received a furious lecture in his study, and permission for the magazine was withdrawn. By this time, however, we had circulated it throughout the school. It gave us great pleasure to see groups of small boys poring over the text in the playing fields, till an irate Jesuit, cassock fluttering, snatched their copies away.

We next launched a production of *Julius Caesar.* The headmaster agreed to let us perform it on Speech Day. I directed it, being too shy to appear in a toga. We rehearsed in the gymnasium, and I organized battle scenes on a technicolour scale. On the day, however, we discovered that the actual stage w'as about a quarter the size of the rehearsal room. It was too late to do anything about it: watched by a bored horde of parents, the battles raged, and centurions dropped like flies. Once Brutus had impaled himself, the stage was packed solid wnth corpses. Mark Antony and his friends, waiting for their final entrance in the wings, asked me for instructions. 'Walk over them,' I said, so they did. But the dead rose, with cries of pain, when stepped on, and the curtain dropped on a stage filled with resurrected corpses struggling with their slayers.

In between all this, Mickey, Satish, and myself wandered through the day looking for entertainment. At lunchtimes we repaired to a filthy little café across the road and smoked cigarettes. The café had a small balcony, which contained a stained, chipped wooden table and some chairs, and we made this our own. Here we sat, Mickey with a cherubic face and curly hair, Satish, who had European blood, fair-haired and pale-eyed, myself with a Byronic haircut, all three with incipient acne, blowing the smoke of cheap cigarettes inexpertly across the table as we talked of religion and sex. We felt entirely adult at such moments.

It didn't last: when school broke up all three of us lounged about, casually, outside the western gateway. None of us ever spoke of why we were there, but all of us knew: it was through this gateway that the female staff of the school passed on their way home. Some of the teachers were young and pretty: under lowered lids, we brooded over their breasts, their neat waggly bottoms: when the last one had left we lounged away. The dust of the trampled playing fields was white on our shoes and brown on our white trousers.

The School Certificate examinations came and went: slowly, in a long hot room filled with the scratchy sound of pens and the shuffled shoes of invigilators. I obtained the six distinctions I required to qualify me for Oxford. But the road was not yet fully opened. I still had to find a college to take me. A long triangular correspondence started between my father in Bombay, Stephen Spender in London, and Nevill Coghill, to whom Spender had recommended me, in Oxford.

While all this was resolved, I remained footloose. The empty flat seemed enormous, and I sat in it and wrote, and sometimes thought of my mother. She seemed smaller and more remote as the months passed, but I thought of her now as she had been in my earliest childhood, and was filled with love and piety. Neither my father nor I were allowed to visit her: she was making a good recovery, the doctors said, and to see us would be a setback.

Mickey and Satish were also free, and bored with freedom. We visited one another. They were both to go up to Bombay

University shortly. Satish used to frequent the grounds of his prospective college, trying to pick up girl students, but had singularly little luck. 'Three's better than one,' he said hopefully, and tried to persuade us to come too, but having less confidence in our charms than he, we wouldn't.

We ate ice cream at Bombelli's, or walked by the sea: there was nothing to do, it seemed, but to wait for our imminent adulthood. It palled. One day I met Tendulkar, and complained about it to him. 'You must not waste your time, Domski,' he said. 'For you time is precious. Go and look at some of the old caves and temples. There are many, many of those, perhaps you will learn something there.' I looked up a list of ancient monuments around Bombay and discovered that there were some Buddhist caves at a place called Kanheri, quite close.

On a burning blue day, Mickey, Satish and I set out by train for the nearest station to Kanheri. We arrived at our station at midday: it was an outer suburb of the city, cluttered with matchboard shacks between which slaty buffaloes moaned and excreted. There was a stench of cattle everywhere, so we walked quickly away, down the road to Kanheri. At a certain point the road petered out into a pebbled dirt track: the track dipped into a valley, and from the lip of the valley we looked down at a scrubby, dusty plain of red earth, sprawled out to a ring of hairy hills.

We started out across the valley. It was blindingly hot: sweat ran down into our eyes and mouths, and soaked our shirts. By the time we reached the Kanheri hill, we were exhausted, and sat in the shadow of a clump of trees, unable to speak, but the trees and the shade climbed the hill, and presently we climbed with them, emerging on a rock flat, among the caves.

There was nothing much in the caves. A couple of giant Buddhas sat in one, their blank faces staring out over the arid valley to the further hills. In others, stone couches had been cut out of the wall, the cells of the monks who had lived here sixteen hundred years before. Drains had been channelled in the rock, where the grass had been dried by the sun to the coarseness of pubic hair. Otherwise there was nothing but an immense emptiness, an odour of absence. High up in the glaring sky indolent hawks wheeled on the axis of their hunger, and miles away across the burnt land we could see the pallid film of the sea. There was nobody anywhere except us: it was as though we had been the first to come on these caves, so long vacated. While Mickey and Satish were exploring, I stood in the shadow of a cave, looking towards the miles-off sea. The familiar eerie sense of separation from my body came over me, more strongly than it ever had before. Root and rock, plant and man, today and every day ever, linked themselves in me, and looking towards the sea I seemed to look into and through all the years ahead. The moment passed: my friends returned, and we squatted under the mute feet of Buddha and ate our sandwiches. Later in the evening coolness we walked back across the valley, seven miles to the station.

After this I returned to Kanheri often, alone. I found I could dispense with the long walk by hiring a bullock cart at the station: it bumped and swayed me across the plain to the caves. I climbed to them and sat and looked at the sea. Sometimes, thus alone among the caves, enormous echoes seemed to explode around me, created purely by the utter silence. Surrounded by statues, echoes, hawks, the forest and the sea, I tried to write. It was impossible, of course, but back at home, comfortable at my desk, the grasshopper fan whirring and clicking overhead, I produced several poems, about the caves and their environs, which were published in my first book of verse, and later much anthologized.

Sex was very much on my mind at sixteen. Anything to do with women had the power to excite me, but Aunt E. undressing was still vivid in my memory, and a brassiere outlined under a thin blouse, or seen in a shop window, made my mouth dry and drained my breath. Aunt E. in fact, remained the centre of my diffused lust. She was the only woman I have ever met whom

I thought of purely as a sexual object. For six years I had been staring intently at her magnificent bosom. I thought of her less as a person than a pair of breasts.

After my mother went to hospital, Aunt E. came several times to the flat to help pack and store away her jewellery and clothes. Visually, this was a godsend to me. The process of packing demands that one bend over a good deal, and every time Aunt E. did so, my eyes flew down her neckline and settled between the ample doves of her breasts, nested tremulously in a pink nylon brassiere. This happened so often that one day it became too much for me to bear. Looking down at her as she packed, I suddenly found myself saying, 'Do you know Keyt's translation of the Krishna poems?'

Aunt E., somewhat to my disappointment, straightened up. She said she didn't.

'Well, it says,' I babbled on rather hysterically, 'that Radha's breasts are like melons shaking in the wind. Your breasts.'

It was the first thing remotely resembling a pass I had ever made, and it went down very badly. Aunt E's splendid bosom swelled out still further, and she said, with precisely the correct mixture of dignity and reproof, 'It's disgusting that a boy of your age should have a mind like that.' Then she went home.

I find this episode now rather funny, but at the time it shattered the little sexual confidence I had. For days after, I burned with shame at the memory. Carefully, I examined my face in the mirror, to find out if I was as hideous as I seemed to myself. On the whole, I felt that I was.

My references to the mirror were interrupted one evening by a visitor. She was a family friend who had not called for some time, a woman of about forty, handsome in a tired way. My father was out, as I explained to her, pouring out his beer for myself meanwhile, and my mother was in hospital. She raised her eyebrows, a habit of hers. She had not heard about this. So I told her about it while she studied me with hooded, rather alcoholic eyes. 'Poor boy,' she said, 'poor boy,' and laid her thin leaf-veined hand on my hand. 'You must come and see me,' she said, and her hand fluttered to my knee. 'Come and have a drink with me tomorrow.' Her eyebrows rose as though in surprise at herself.

Next day, in her flat, she seduced me, or tried to. My recollections are not very clear, but it was not a success at all. Still, I was grateful to her. Now, to add to my other neuroses, I had fears about my virility, but another part of my confidence had been restored. I no longer felt that I was totally undesirable.

Suddenly I started to move towards life. Mr Christie, the principal of Jesus College, wrote to say he would give me a place provided I passed the college entrance paper in English, and the university entrance paper in Latin. I hadn't done Latin in school, and he suggested that I come to London at once and attend a crammer there. It was settled swiftly, and my passage by sea was booked for August of that year, 1955.

There was still a few months left, but already I felt in transit. Wherever I went in Bombay I experienced an ache of nostalgia, as though this was the last time I would ever visit this particular place. The brown-skinned people of whom I was one swirled past me like the sea outside the window. I had separated myself, to stand on the unknown mournful rocks left when the tide had passed.

I developed what I had not had before: a strange detached love for the country of my birth, the love one might have for a former mistress. I realized that I hadn't really seen much of India, and decided to remedy this. My father was all for it. 'From now on,' he said, 'you'll have to rely on yourself, so you might as well get used to it.' Put like this, the idea gave me a hollow and apprehensive feeling.

I travelled north to Kashmir, which I loved. Srinagar, with its blue lakes and waterways filled with houseboats: a shikara* at night moving on the smooth water, the smelly boatmen whistling

* A small punt.

and murmuring like an aviary, the lights of other boats dimly hinted at across the lake: these filled my notebook with poems, till I rode up into the mountains on a pony, slept in a tent by a glacier, and contracted pneumonia. My remaining memories of Kashmir are of the smell of illness. Eventually I was flown back to Bombay and put to bed at home. My first essay at relying on myself had not been wholly successful.

When I recovered, I set off for the south. I stopped at Aurangabad, from which I made excursions to the Ajanta caves and the temple at Ellora. The Ajanta frescoes and the Ellora temple, which, hewn from the hillside rock, appeared to hang and float in the midge-shimmered air, brought me an awareness of what it was I intended to leave. The frescoes and the temple were beautiful, but they were not alive. The sun had blared down on them, the rain had eroded them for centuries and sun and rain had shrunk the people, scratching the earth with wooden ploughs in the fields around. There was death in India which was not yet complete, because there seemed to be no definite past or future. The two were mixed, like the people, as in a dream. The talent I had was not a talent that could wake this country, so my duty to my talent exceeded my duty to the country. What my talent wanted was a defined tradition, hard outlines, soil for its roots. It wanted to move from dream to reality.

Further south, when I drove from Mysore to Hallebidu and Belur, abandoned temples erected before Christ, I grew even more conscious of this. The temples, carrying on their sails of stone a profusion of carved lovers, monkeys, fruit, and leaves, stood amidst a dull, scrubby waste, beaten by the sun. Near each was a teeming village, where dogs and children nosed one another outside the shabby huts. At Belur I inquired where I could go to the lavatory: they showed me to a courtyard behind the village. The whole floor was a sea of human excrement, several inches thick, of different colours and textures. Bare footprints on the surface showed where the last person had entered, and a thunder of flies filled the air. Through my disgust and shock a sudden fury rose. I remembered Tendulkar: 'Domski, they should not live like that. Men should not live like that.' My fury was directed not at the government or the people but the whole country which, locked in its dream, had sucked them all, passive, back to the dream's womb.

My father said, 'You must go and see your mother.'

It was July. In a few days it would be my seventeenth birthday, and a few days beyond that, the ship that was to take me to England would sail. I had been thinking of my mother for weeks, but did not know what I could do for her: the doctors still felt that we ought not to visit her. I reminded my father of this. 'They've agreed to let you visit her,' he said. 'So we'd better fly down to Bangalore.'

We arrived in Bangalore on my birthday. It is a cantonment town, to which colonels retired in the British days: a kind of Indian Cheltenham. Except for the strong sun and the powdery dust, it has an English look about it. I didn't see much of it, however, since I was expected at the hospital. Before I departed, my father said, 'The doctors say not to tell your mother you're leaving for England. They say it will excite her.' I nodded, climbed into the hired car and drove to the hospital.

We entered through a gateway, which had to be unlocked by a turbaned servant, and drove to the main building. Here I met a brisk doctor. 'Ah, yes, yes,' he said. 'Your mother is expecting you. She is all agog, by heavens! But please do not excite her. Her condition is very fine at the present, but she is sometimes excited.'

We walked through the grounds, full of dusty trees, to a small white cottage that stood by itself. 'Her own residence she has, you see,' the doctor explained proudly. As we approached, the door opened, and my mother flew out. She hugged me almost desperately. I had not remembered she was so small, and she had become very thin, but her enormous eyes were alive in her pale heart-shaped face.

'Look at my son, Doctor. Isn't he tall? He's the most intelligent boy—'

She took my hand, as though I were still a child, and led me into the cottage, chattering away as we went. The cottage had two rather sparse rooms, and a bathroom. In the front room a taciturn woman in a white sari folded her hands in welcome. 'This is Mary,' my mother explained, 'my ayah. She looks after me very well, don't you, Mary?' Ayahs were things only children had: somehow, though, my small fragile mother had now the air of a child. She sat me down in the best chair, and began to ask me if I was eating properly, if I was happy, and if I had fully recovered from my pneumonia. I answered all these questions in the affirmative: when I said I was happy, however, a strange lost look crossed my mother's pale face.

Then she began to talk about herself. She was allowed to do a little pathological work in the hospital laboratory, which pleased her, and the other day, she said, she had actually been permitted to drive into town with Mary and have tea with Sir Mirza Ismail, an old friend, She was full of the joys of this expedition, and again I was reminded of a child: the simple fact of having had tea out of a Georgian silver teapot seemed to have delighted her beyond measure. In this situation, I felt myself to be the parent: she my responsibility: I felt an ache in my chest, of sorrow and loss, as a parent must when parting from an only child.

Presently my mother said gaily, 'Oh, here's lunch. I ordered you a special birthday lunch, darling. The food here is wonderful, really top notch, and I told the cook to make a special effort.' A hand trolley, pulled by Mary, had appeared, and she laid lunch out on the small table in the corner. The food was terrible, a thick, lumpy soup, a segment of fried fish, some tough chicken, and peas. I ate it all, however, with expressions of delight. My mother perched birdlike on the chair opposite, watching me eat with a rapt and pleased expression. She herself pecked at some bread and butter and a bowl of yoghurt. When I pressed her to eat she giggled and said, 'I'm watching my figure.' I looked at her thin arms folded on the table and did not reply.

Finally my mother went to a cupboard and produced a small piece of Gruyère cheese. 'You always used to like this,' she said, 'when you were little; and now you're a big boy I thought you could have cheese after lunch. So when I went to tea with Sir Mirza the other week, I bought this to keep until you came.'

At that moment I found myself in tears. My mother put her thin arm round me. 'Don't cry, darling,' she said quietly, 'what's the matter? I'm quite happy here, really.' I couldn't stop for a long while, and she stood by me, holding my head against her. At length I blew my nose and, silently, ate the cheese.

Through the afternoon we talked. My mother seemed determined to show she was happy: she laughed, and told funny stories, about her girlhood and her courtship with my father, and my childhood. For the first time I saw her as a person, who thought, felt, had lived and loved and borne a child, and was now carried by the trajectory of her life into this sparse cottage in the grounds of a madhouse. The unbearable quality in this was that I felt that I was responsible for her presence here. I sat in a dull silence, till suddenly she said, 'You'll be leaving for England soon, won't you?'

I forgot that I was not supposed to tell her. I could not have lied. 'Yes. Next month.'

'Well, you mustn't forget to stock up with warm clothes. English winters are very treacherous, you know, and you have a weak chest. I had bronchitis when I was there in 1926. You won't forget to buy some sweaters, will you?'

I shook my head. She said, abruptly jocular, 'And look out for those English girls. They'll all be running after you.' She stroked my hair almost ruefully. 'You'll be a handsome man, like your father.' Suddenly she said, 'You'll be coming back, won't you?'

'Oh, well, yes.'

'You promise?' she said, and looked at me intently with her enormous eyes. I saw the grey streaks in her hair. One last betrayal: I said, 'I promise.'

'Then that's all right,' she said with perfect innocence. 'I couldn't have borne to lose you forever, you know. But you've got to be educated.' Then she asked Mary to make some tea, and we drank it.

After tea, the doctor arrived. 'Well, young man,' he said, 'it is time for you to leave. Say your adieux to your good mother.'

'I'll come to the gate with you,' my mother said, and then laughed in an embarrassed way. 'Oh, I can't. I'm not allowed that far.'

I took her skimpy body in my arms, kissed her very hard, and then stumbled after the doctor without looking back.

When I got back to the hotel, Manishi, who was then domiciled in Bangalore, was having a drink with my father. He greeted me with delighted coos, but I did not feel communicative. Then my father said, 'How was she? Was she excitable?'

'Quite the opposite,' I said, and in dry outline sketched the day. Manishi blundered up from his chair and flapped over to me. He put his plump arms round me and hugged me hard. 'Oh, my poor young poet,' he said. 'My poor, poor young poet.'

After So Many Deaths

After so many deaths, I live and write;
I once more smell the dew and rain,
And relish versing: O, my only light,
It cannot be
That I am he
On whom thy tempests fell all night.

—George Herbert

7

> At sixteen I came here to start again,
> An infant's trip, where many knew to walk.
> I stumbled dumbly through the English rain,
> The literature, the drink, the talk, talk, talk…
>
> —'A Letter' from *Poems* (1960)

Once more I was on a ship. It was a sister of the one that had sailed us to Australia, but this time it was going the other way, my journey was irrevocable, and I was alone. In the blue and lazy dooryard of the sea, during the first days out, I brooded over books. They were designed to inform me about England. They were books of pastoral verse, by Clare, Blunden, Andrew Young. I read about badgers, flowers, and village life with pleasure, but, eyeing the English people around me, also with disbelief. This was perhaps fortunate. It's silly to have too many illusions.

The days before my departure had been full of visitors, who were full of advice. A solicitous old man told me how to befriend my future landlady. I must invite her, he said, to the pictures once a week, and after the pictures buy her quantities of fish and chips. 'It is the common habit,' he informed me. In this way all English landladies expect to be treated.' But I didn't intend to spend my time with landladies. I intended to be with poets, and, if lucky, with a beautiful woman or three. Yet in a sense I was grateful to the stream of visitors: each one postponed for a little my realization of imminent departure.

On the day, therefore, I was unprepared. At breakfast it occurred to me that I would not again sit at table with my father for some considerable while to come. It did not affect me at once because I could not realize it to be true. After breakfast, saying goodbye to the servants, it affected me rather more. By the time we drove to the docks, however, the familiar spectacle of Kutthalingam's plump uniformed shoulders and bald head in front had become painful to look at. While my father talked nervously, I maintained a tremulous silence.

It was only broken at the end. My father saw me to my cabin and tipped the steward. Then he conducted me to the restaurant, and tipped the head waiter. 'Find my son a good table, will you?' he said, and the head waiter said effusively, 'Don't you worry, sir, I will.' Then the last bells went, and we emerged on deck. There Kutthalingam stood, weeping, and put his arms round me. 'My young master,' he wept, '*my* young master. You coming back quickly. I waiting for you.' Then he disappeared, and in a blur I saw friends' faces, and shook hands mechanically with several people. Out of the blur my father's face came suddenly clear. He put an awkward hand up and cuffed my ear lightly. 'Goodbye, son,' he said very abruptly. 'Be a good boy.' I broke my silence. 'Don't go,' I said, but he had gone.

I stood at the rail of the ship, and willed myself not to cry. Things blurred over once more. But the noise of the people around me intensified, and when I looked down, a gulf of blue water lapped between the quay and the ship. I went down to my cabin, and intently, as though trying to hypnotize myself, read a chapter of a detective story. Then I felt better. The lunch bell hummed sonorously and I climbed to the restaurant. The effusive head waiter nodded coolly when he saw me. 'You're over there, young man,' he said, and waved me to a small and crowded table behind a pillar in the corner.

The first class passengers, who now formed the community I lived in, could roughly be divided into three kinds: English people going home, Indian businessmen and students, and a few Australians on visits to the Old Country. I didn't like what I saw of any of them, and was in any case too shy to approach people. So in the first three days out I spoke to nobody except my cabin steward. He was a young man called Milton, who talked to me endlessly about London as he made the bed. 'You'll like it, you'll see,' he said. 'There's nowhere like it. It's bloody marvellous.' My shyness appeared to astonish him. 'It's full of birds, up on the passenger decks. Why don't you go and pick one up? Don't do you any good sitting down here reading. Go on, pick a bird up, bloody marvellous.' His expostulations eventually drove me up on deck, where I sat eyeing the flying fish as they darted over the rough blue waves. An unread book fluttered gently on my knee. I was lonely.

Amongst the other passengers who strolled past my solitary deckchair were an English mother and daughter whom my eye picked out frequently and sadly. They were blonde and beautiful, the mother a svelte woman in her late thirties, the cornsilk daughter about fifteen. The daughter fell madly in love with me in my fantasies, but in actuality she never spoke to me, nor could I ever really hope that she would. One afternoon, however, there was a knock on my cabin door. I opened it to find the blonde mother outside.

'Oh,' she said, 'the boy with the book. I've noticed you on deck. If you're who I think you are, I knew your parents years back, in Bombay.'

I stammered for a while, but she cut me short and said, 'Do have a drink with us tonight. I'm with my daughter, and she's about your age.' So, unbelieving, I said I would. That night, in the bar, I met the daughter for the first time. Seen close to, she was even more beautiful than I had imagined. She was also even more unattainable than I had imagined: for though I yearned at her sadly, she ignored me from the start.

She continued to ignore me. The ship was full of boisterous young people who swam, played deck tennis, and organized fancy dress parties. It was, in fact, an idyllic place for Celia: she was always bounding off to some new entertainment, and the only times she ever seemed bored were when she was with her mother and me. Then, like a small cat, she would curl in a chair, her pink mouth widening in the most unostentatious of yawns. I suffered.

Alice said, 'It takes a long while to get to know my daughter.' I didn't believe her. It seemed to take the lively young men on the sports deck a very short while to get to know Celia. 'It's only me,' I said dispiritedly. 'I'm hopeless when I meet people.' Alice's blue eyes dwelt on me a moment, amused yet sympathetic: then she began to talk about literature.

This, indeed, was a constant topic with her. She had vague literary ambitions, and had been writing a novel, apparently, for several years. She knew a number of writers, of whom she spoke with an unaffectedness that delighted me. Her marriage had not been a success: she was on her way home to divorce her husband. When she spoke, in a rather wistful way, about her hopes for Celia, I experienced a flutter of tenderness and excitement, partly because she was talking about Celia, partly because in her I saw normal motherhood in operation, which was new to me. Rubbing salt into my wound, I talked to her often of Celia. We passed a lot of the day together, for to my surprise she seemed to find me likeable. I showed her my poems, which she duly admired, and told her about my hopes, which she duly encouraged. After dinner, feeling very masculine, I led her to the bar for a drink to wind up the day.

One morning Milton, making my bed, remarked, 'Still waters run deep. Coo-er, you quiet ones are the worst. I hear you've picked up the best bird aboard, and her only twice your age. Bloody marvellous.'

He startled me. When I thought about it, I realized he had told me a fact I had not really known. I was not in love with Celia at all, I was in love with Alice.

The ship nosed further north. It moved now on a dull sea, under a dreary sky. After Marseilles, when I set foot in Europe for the first time and failed to find it extraordinary, pullovers appeared, and shortly after that everyone assumed coats like identities. Alice and I paced the deck and talked about England. She obviously looked forward to it eagerly, to her friends and the places she had not been to for a long while: as the ship leant into the Channel her nostrils flickered like those of some intelligent dog, scenting home. Though to her I was a shipboard acquaintance, the young son of friends, to me she had become much more. I felt that I was being abandoned, especially since she was going up to Scotland at once: but then in a subconscious way I supposed I wanted to be abandoned. In a poem written during this time there is a line, 'I am in love and long to be unhappy.' It expressed my feelings perfectly, at seventeen.

However, she was staying in London overnight, so I arranged to meet her for dinner. She gave me a telephone number, and then disappeared from my life for the last day of the voyage. She was packing. I tipped Milton, and he packed for me. I had not, at this time, ever packed a suitcase for myself.

The night before we docked, I lay awake, looking up through the porthole at the cold foreign stars. I was full of apprehension and of love. With half my mind I thought of Alice, the other half filled slowly with fear of the unknown. It disappeared when the next day was flooded with sunshine, through which, over a shrunken sea, the scrubby flat coast of Essex came into view, and slowly, groaning and hooting, while the decks filled with excited people, the ship pushed into the Tilbury docks. We had arrived.

I was met by Mulgaokar, the London correspondent of the *Times of India.* He was an amiable, languid man, a friend of my father's. We sat together in a train that roared through vista upon vista of ugly prefabricated houses, laundry flapping sadly in the backyards. The occasional housewife glimpsed as we flashed by looked pale and scruffy. I felt a slight shock, I hadn't realized that there were poor people in England, and looked back from the window at Mulgaokar's quizzical and friendly eyes.

'I've found you some digs,' he said. 'At least my secretary found them. We'd better go and look at them first.'

I nodded, a little frightened at the prospect of digs. The train snorted its way into St Pancras, shuddered fastidiously and stopped. We took a taxi to Earl's Court, where a sleazy landlady showed us to a barren cubicle on the top floor. 'It's nice and clean,' she said, 'and only three pounds a week.' Net curtains fluttered drearily in the windows. Mulgaokar fixed an appalled eye on them. 'No, no, no, no,' he said, 'this won't do. You'd better come and stay with me till we find you somewhere.'

He lived, in the Edwardian style that was somehow part of him, in a bachelor flat in Jermyn Street. Here I established myself in the spare room. Mulgaokar had work to do. He drew me a rough map of where we were and despatched me into the unknown city.

So I walked to Piccadilly Circus, where I had my first meal in London, at a Chinese restaurant. Then I wandered about till I came to the Odeon at Marble Arch. There I watched a film about Ulysses. Afterwards, not being quite sure where Mulgaokar lived, I took a taxi back. I was very pleased I remember, when the driver called me 'Sir'. This was the first of a sequence of taxis: since travel on a bus or tube involved so many inquiries, I preferred to travel everywhere by taxi. The habit, formed then, still persists.

Back at Mulgaokar's, I found he had finished work. He yawned, which he often did, in order to belie the acute efficient mind behind his mask, and said, 'I'll buy you dinner. What sort of food do you like?' 'Thanks awfully,' I said, 'but I'm supposed to take someone out to dinner myself.'

'Oh,' said Mulgaokar, with quizzical brows. 'Oh, really?'

I inquired if there was a good restaurant in the vicinity. 'The Ritz,' he yawned amusedly, 'is just round the corner.' I had heard of the Ritz.

I telephoned Alice and asked her to meet me there. There was a rather puzzled pause, then she asked if I were serious. 'Of course,' I said, indignant.

We met at the Ritz, and had an excellent, if expensive dinner. I was tremendously happy, and talked well, and felt I was a Londoner already. Afterwards I took her back in a taxi to the house where she was staying.

I had drunk a lot of wine at dinner, and as we passed St George's Hospital, I muttered, 'I love you.' The lights of the hospital illumined her pale shocked face as she turned it to me: 'What did you say?' Tentatively, I repeated it. As we jolted on, the lights of the hospital fell alternately on her face and mine, so that I had the sensation of being in the middle of a slowed film. 'No, no,' she said. 'It's absurd.' The lights fell on my face. She looked at me, then said very gently, 'It's not absurd, of course not. I'm very flattered. But, you know, I'm in love with someone already.'

'Oh, Alice,' I heard my own horrified voice saying, and I fell forward, pushing my face into her cloudy, scented hair, and, my mouth full of it, muttering rather inarticulately, 'Alice, Alice, Alice.'

'Dear boy,' she said a little absently, and stroked my hair. I went on muttering, 'Alice, Alice, Alice,' but somehow the hand on my hair was very soothing, and it was as though the name Alice was somehow my mother's name.

I returned home shattered, yet elated to know that I was capable of such unhappiness. Mulgaokar, when he saw me, grinned, and said dryly, 'You have lipstick on your collar.' 'I know,' I said, proud, remote, melancholy, and then I went to bed.

That was my first day in London.

My father had always had a curious habit, which I could never understand, of consulting astrologers. As a child I remembered a very tall, bespectacled man named Shetty, with a loud rather hysterical laugh and a wildly leaping Adam's apple, who came to read his palm. Sometimes he also read mine: I liked this, because he traced the lines with a long skinny forefinger, muttering meanwhile, which had a pleasantly hypnotic effect on me. Shetty reappeared, summoned by my father, shortly before I left for England. However, he declined to read my palm. 'The powers,' he said with his weird laugh, 'the powers are displeased with me. I cannot make them work. However, sir, I will give you the name of a remarkable, yes, a most remarkable woman, the consultant of several Maharajahs. She will foretell your son's future.' My father made an appointment with this sorceress. She lived in a cottage in the grounds of a Maharajah's house. We arrived there one evening, and were shown into a room filled with white-clad devotees. The room smelt of incense and oil; in the centre of it the sorceress, a plump, matronly woman in a sari, sat primly on a chair. Nothing happened for a while. Then the sorceress suddenly began to sway to and fro, and, presently, to emit a low crooning sound. She shook her head, and her hair, which was done up in a bun, came loose with a scatter of hairpins, and fell snakily round her shoulders. She crooned and swayed on, and suddenly her face appeared to become grey with ash, which is what reputedly holy people in India spread over their bodies. A gasp of awe went up from the devotees, no wonder: she was now a really awesome figure, with long snaky locks, ash-covered face and arms, and closed eyes. The crooning continued for a while, then stopped. In the ensuing silence, the sorceress plaited a lock of her hair in her fingers, then ran them down it, and a quantity of sandalwood paste fell from it into a platter obligingly held in position by a disciple. She continued silently to milk her hair, and sandalwood paste continued to drop in a soundless shower, overflowing several platters. There was something mad about it, but impressively mad.

Eventually the torrent of sandalwood paste ceased. The devotees gathered round the platters, taking pinches of the paste as talismans.

The sorceress sat rock-still in her chair, her eyes closed. A devotee led my father and me up to her chair. 'Do not,' he whispered, 'ask any questions. She will tell you what you want to know.'

We stood and looked at the sorceress. Her face, streaky with ash, was swollen and puffy, and her eyes remained shut. However, she turned this blind, puffy face towards my father, and began to speak in Marathi, which the disciple translated. Then she turned to me and did the same. 'She says,' explained the disciple, 'that you will soon travel across the black waters. All your life you will travel. In three years you will be famous. What you want to do, you will do, but you will never live in India.'

Having told me what I most wanted to hear, the sorceress scraped through her hair once more and filled, first my hands, then my father's, with sandalwood paste. When we were outside, my father said, puzzled, 'Look,' and from the yellow heap of powder in his palm, fished a small silver effigy of what appeared to be St Christopher.

I believed all that she had said implicitly, for I needed to believe it. My faith in the supernatural was slightly shaken when we discovered a partially scraped off 'Made in Hong Kong' engraved on St Christopher's foot: still, when I came to England, I repeated the prophecy to myself every day. I had little else to believe in. My London life was questing and empty.

Mulgaokar was very kind to me. He took me around London, explained tubes, buses, the scale of tips, how to use a telephone box, and so forth, simple but essential pieces of information: then he found me a small flat in Knightsbridge, and, after I was installed there, asked me to lunch once or twice a week. He was, however, the only friend I had. Stephen Spender was abroad: Alice was in Scotland. Friends of my father's, to whom he had written, occasionally took me to dinner or the theatre, and, their duties discharged, dropped me. I was unrewardingly inarticulate.

I had three weeks to kill before I went to the crammer's. They passed like aeons. I had thought I might work, but found myself utterly unable to concentrate. I moved through my small attic flat, touching objects, to reassure myself that I existed. My mind, turning over slow and lonely as a mill wheel, was empty of verse. Its emptiness drove me out into London as soon as I awoke.

It was autumn, the gutters and parks of the city were populated with dead leaves. A shrunken sun occasionally squinted out of a cloudy sky. I had nowhere to go, and nobody to go with. I had never learned to cook: so when I awoke I would go to a place in Sloane Street, breakfast there, and read the papers. Then I walked to the park, and squelched my way to the Serpentine. There I stared at the willows that wept by the water for a long time. Afterwards I went to a coffee bar, till the pubs opened. I had a local, in which I sat apart, reading, drinking, and sometimes lunching, from opening time till closing time. I think it was at this period that I developed a habit of heavy alcoholic consumption which I have never quite lost. There was nothing else to do: besides, it cheered me up, and made me more confident. After lunch I usually went to the British Museum. Wandering round, amongst other silent people, looking at things, soothed me: also, the first time I went there, I stood and stared at one of the large pharaonic heads in the Egyptian room, and presently saw, rising from a crouching position of scrutiny on the floor beside it, an intent man whom I recognized as Henry Moore. It confirmed a fact I had started to doubt: artists did inhabit London.

In the evening I usually went to a cinema, then had dinner, and then went home to bed. There was nothing of my own in the flat, except a few books, and my unused typewriter. It was the typewriter my father had had in Burma, in the war, and it gave me a sense of connection. Before I fell asleep I wondered what my father was up to in Bombay, and Kutthalingam and the servants: what my mother was thinking of in her cottage in Bangalore: and I longed for the sun.

At last it was time for the crammer's. I was glad of something to do. The establishment was in a large handsome house in

West London. Somebody had lived there once, but now it was split into classrooms, in which the more stupid children of the wealthy sat and imbibed instruction designed to squeeze them into university. I was anxious to make friends, but was too shy to approach anyone, and nobody approached me. The other boys split up into cliques, each drawn from the same public school: they talked of sports cars, girls, and parties: I was too ignorant to interpret this type of conversation as a kind of insecurity. The girls, some of whom were very beautiful, swept scornfully in and out of the cliques: their high confident voices terrorized me at the time, but I now suppose they were rather silly too.

However, I was as isolated as before. I had private tuition from the Latin coach: he was fairly young, but aged by the subacademic world he lived in: a balding, shabby man, the shoulders of his coat snowy with dandruff. As he spoke a discoloured saliva oozed from the corners of his mouth, and was licked back, so that he gave the impression that he was constantly chewing a thick grey blanket. He repelled me, but long practice had made him a good teacher of his kind: he knew exactly what the Oxford examiners wanted for Latin Responsions, and he fed it to me (like a grey blanket) for several hours a day. By this time Oxford seemed so far away that I did not greatly care whether I got there or not, but I worked hard at my Latin because, at least, it gave me something to do. It was not interesting: poetry didn't come into it, nor indeed literature: grammar was all. Still, I worked at it, because I had nothing else to do, and lived my boredom hard. Then Spender returned to London, and the doors opened.

The *Encounter* office was much smaller than I expected. It was tucked into a little street off the Haymarket, and ascending in the lift I felt a tremor of nerves, wondering which contributor might not be there: Edwin Muir perhaps or Koestler? Or perhaps (with another tremor) even Auden?

There was nobody there, except a nice secretary. 'Oh, is Stephen expecting you?' she asked. 'Just go through there, his office is on the left.' I crept down a short passage, and found Spender in a room full of books and paintings. He loomed up from a chair to shake my hand, and inquired how I found London. 'Everybody seems to be in an awful hurry,' I said. He laughed, and made me less nervous. I showed him some poems, and was delighted beyond measure when he said, 'We must publish some of them. A page of them, perhaps.' Then he said, 'Who would you like to meet?' There were so many people I wanted to meet I couldn't decide, but he solved my problem by saying, 'You ought to meet Morgan Forster.' He wrote out a letter of introduction, and handed it to me. I looked at it with awe, a passport to a country beyond the crammer's.

I despatched Spender's letter to Cambridge, and a few days later received a note from Forster asking me to tea at the Reform Club. It was a dank, cold afternoon when I arrived there, but I was warm with excitement, and entered the hallway pouring with sweat. The porter showed me to where Forster sat, in a sea of tables and sofas. He rose, shook hands, and said, 'Don't you find it cold outside?' Wiping my brow I told him that I found it very hot outside. He looked at me in a rather perplexed way, and I sat down beside him.

He was a small, comfortably plump man, with a grey moustache in a face which, like that of some intelligent hare, was both inquisitive and withdrawn. His gentleness, which was extreme, calmed me, and I failed to feel, as usual, my lack of conversation: for he had evidently noticed this lack, and at first he talked and I listened. He talked about India, then about Cambridge: then I felt confident enough to speak myself. I asked him questions about D.H. Lawrence and Virginia Woolf, his friends, but at once he appeared to withdraw. So I stopped. Our game of advance and retreat stopped too: he became talkative and so did I. I talked about my poetry and my going up to Oxford. He listened attentively, like an old wise hare, sitting up on the grass-coloured sofa. He said, 'Why do you not see a little of Europe? I go to Greece, myself, in the winter, and sometimes Provence. There are still places in Provence which are beautiful, if you know where to go. It would be useful if you went to Europe, before you go up to university.'

He saw me off, helping me courteously into my overcoat in the hallway. When my coat was on, I asked awkwardly if he would like to read my poems. He withdrew once more. 'I don't,' he said evasively, 'know much about poetry. I couldn't write anything about them.' I felt that he misunderstood me. 'I don't want you to write about them, sir,' I said, 'I only want you to read them.' It was true: I felt that the very fact that a writer like Forster consented to read my work was in itself an accolade.

The day after I met Forster I wrote to my father to ask whether I could travel in Europe before I went up to Oxford. He replied to say that I could, provided my admittance into Jesus was definite for October 1956. My aims had now come clear: savagely I worked at my Latin. The examination day approached, and on the day before it I was to sit for my entrance examination at Jesus. One dingy day of frost and mist, I left London on the Oxford train.

It was the first look I had ever had at the English countryside: beyond Reading the mist lifted, and I saw the green sad fields, so civilized, and the hillsides beyond dotted with scrawny thickets that might still conceal wolves or druids. Then out of the fields the spires rose, and I arrived in Oxford on the first of many trains.

When I reached Jesus, I still had a few minutes before my interview. I wandered through the college, its green quadrangles, its weathered yellow walls, and beyond them a hideous new wing swaddled in scaffolding. I hoped I wouldn't have to live in it. Still, the whole atmosphere elated me. Henry Vaughan had been here once, and had perhaps touched the stones which I now touched. Very cheerful, I burst into the principal's lodgings, where my interview was, and found half a dozen gowned young men standing in the hall. 'Hullo,' I said, 'are you waiting for an interview too?' One of them gave me a dry smile and said, 'In a manner of speaking. We are Fellows of the College, and I believe you are the young man we are to interview.' This dampened my spirits considerably.

Eventually I found myself in the principal's study, facing a line of dons. In the centre the principal, Mr Christie, sat, silver-haired and friendly. He asked me various questions, which I answered, then the other dons took over. One of them asked me in what area, if I had lived in Elizabethan London, I would expect to find Sir John Falstaff drinking. It seemed to me an irrelevant query, but I hazarded Cheapside. 'No,' said my questioner, but Mr Christie smiled benevolently. 'He knows it, obviously,' he said. 'He means Eastcheap.'

Afterwards I was given a question paper to answer, and left in the principal's study to answer it. When I had finished, it was lunchtime. I went into the hall and found an elderly don there.

'Ah, you've finished,' he said. 'The principal told me that the college must pay for your lunch, since we fetched you up today. I haven't dined out much myself recently, but I recommend the Randolph. They do you very well there. Here is some money.'

Ignoring my protests, he handed me a shilling.

I still had to wait for the results of my college entrance and my Latin Responsions. But the time now was not as tedious as it had been. On most Sundays I lunched with the Spenders at their house in St John's Wood. Here I first met Spender's wife, the pianist Natasha Litvin, a tall, beautiful woman whose vigorous brisk manner concealed great sweetness of nature, and their children, Matthew and Lizzie. Inarticulate though I still was, I found myself able to speak to the Spenders: but with other guests I tended to relapse into a beaten silence.

One of these guests was Cyril Connolly. I was so overawed when Natasha told me on the phone, the day before, that he would be at lunch, that I rushed to Simpson's of Piccadilly and bought a new suit. In it, I arrived in St John's Wood in a state of pride and terror. Connolly was already there, with his wife, the writer Barbara Skelton. She lay, languidly beautiful, on the sofa, moving a hand like a lily over the weft of the carpet: he sat in an armchair, under a vivid Ghika. He had an attractive batrachian expression, and a surprisingly soft voice, in which he asked me, 'Where did you buy that suit?'

Very self-conscious, I said, 'At Simpson's.'

'Hm,' said Connolly. 'It doesn't fit you.'

This reduced me to utter silence. Barbara Skelton drifted a few dreamy remarks in my direction, and I mumbled back, aware that I was a bad guest, but incapable of remedying the situation. Finally Stephen produced some of my poems, and showed them to Connolly. Connolly read them with a furious expression, while I shrank back into my chair. Then he raised his head and said very kindly, 'I like them very much; some of them are exquisite.' He then proceeded to shower me with some of the best criticism I have ever had in my life. This reduced me to silence once more, but this time a happy silence. Barbara Skelton read the poems, and handed them back to Stephen, saying absently, 'They're very sexy, aren't they?' I had never thought of them like that before.

After lunch we sat in Stephen's study and listened to music, the *Dies Irae,* and I looked at the shelves full of books and the paintings on the wall and heard the gramophone thunder and eddy, and thought this was how a writer should live. All these people seemed to belong to each other, to the books, the music, and the painting. But I didn't belong. Perhaps, I thought, this was the way a writer shouldn't live. When I looked at Connolly, he was tucked into his chair, his eyes inward to the music, and an expression not of sadness, but of actual sorrow on his face.

At a later time, I met Raymond Chandler at the Spenders'. He was heavy and bespectacled, with a greyish, mottled complexion which I now realize was due to illness, and throughout lunch he fixed me with what seemed to be a stare of fury and hatred. Oversensitive though I was, I had never felt so actively disliked before. Over the cheese, Chandler suddenly barked, 'Nehru's a fool.'

I remained, as usual, silent. Chandler said, 'He's selling out to the Communists everywhere.' He then fixed me with an icy eye and demanded, 'Isn't he?' I replied truthfully that I had no idea. Chandler snorted, and didn't speak to me after that. In a way I felt sorry for him. He lugged his body about like an extra burden, as dying people do, and in some way seemed isolated from it.

These lunches at the Spenders' sophisticated and toughened me. They also introduced me to people I would never otherwise have met at that time: they introduced me to literary life. Yet inwardly somehow I felt that this life was not the life that writers should lead: the pain must be lost, and the hard battle with words, when you wanted a house, a family, friends, love, possessions. I didn't really understand that writers are people, and that one day I should want and have these things myself, and be forced to justify them to the young.

One day Stephen asked me to lunch in town, on a weekday. The other guests were two young poets, both of whom he had published. One was rather fey, and talked throughout lunch of his experiences in a mental hospital. The other was slight, with thick dark hair and an intent triangular face. He did not speak at all.

After lunch, as we dispersed outside the restaurant, the silent poet said to me, 'Care for a drink?' I accepted, and made for the nearest pub, but he caught me by the arm and conducted me across Leicester Square into Soho. 'We're closer to the clubs here,' he explained. 'It's nearly closing time already.'

This young man was called Oliver Bernard. Later, he translated Apollinaire and Rimbaud, but at the time I first met him he lived by occasional teaching, or work in the Post Office. He wrote verse, but not much of it had been published. He told me all this as we stood in a crowded Soho pub, sipping halves of bitter in the few minutes left before closing time. Then he said, 'Shall we go on to a club?'

I agreed. We walked down Dean Street and entered a semi-basement, a long room with a bar in the middle, and chairs and tables along the wall. It was half-lit, which was fortunate, since it contained some of the worst paintings I have ever seen. A small raddled woman called Jenny served us. 'This is Jenny's place,' Oliver explained.

Gradually the bar started to fill. The customers were mostly already drunk, and they were all very scruffy. I was rather appalled, especially when a tall, skinny man with a fine face contorted by alcohol stumbled up and made a pass at me. 'That's Colquhoun,' Oliver said. 'He's a famous painter.' He introduced me to several other people, with an air of pride, like a ringmaster showing off his circus. We drank more and more. The air filled with smoke, raucous voices, and music. Colquhoun kept stumbling back to me and making passes. My stomach filled slowly with sour beer, and I started to feel sick. I took a taxi home.

Next day I had a ghastly hangover. I also had a note from Oliver. He apologized for the chaos of the previous day, and invited me to visit him. He lived in a small flat not far from my crammer's, so I called on him that afternoon. His girlfriend had just left him, and the flat was in disorder. We ate baked beans on toast and, facing each other across a cluttered wooden table, exchanged poems like salutes. Afterwards he suggested we go back to Soho for a drink.

Something about all this began to fascinate me. The disorder of Oliver's flat, the baked beans, the dependence on Soho for a meeting place, the departed mistress, were exactly what I had visualized literary life to be like. Moreover, I was still not able to write, and to be surrounded by people who were writers or painters, as I seemed to be in Soho, gave me the illusion that it didn't matter. Alone or with Oliver, I made forays into Soho every night.

The pungent smell of exotic food and people in the street, the pretty, waiflike girls in the pubs, the sense of inhabiting a village inside a city, intoxicated me. I became friendly with the drunk painter, Robert Colquhoun, and his friend, the painter Robert MacBryde. Once they knew I was not homosexual they did not make any passes. When sober, they were marvellous to be with. Colquhoun was very gentle, with a soft Scottish voice, and very intelligent. He had read a lot, in a scattered way, and talked better about literature than he did about painting. MacBryde was small and elflike, a wicked, Scots elf: he was very funny and malicious: he liked life, and was the housewife of the pair: a cook, a cleaner, a handyman. They both liked children, and were sorry, I think, that they obviously couldn't have any.

When drunk, however, they became intolerable. Colquhoun was terrifying in his cups: his thin body seemed to buckle forward at the hips, while his legs weaved a wild way across the floor. In a thunderous, bullying voice, his eyes unfocused, he would demand to be bought a drink. MacBryde did not bully, he wheedled: drunkenly, tittering, he would ask for a beer, or money to buy beer with, since neither of them ever had any. Occasionally they would physically attack each other, and sometimes appeared festooned with bandages and plaster.

They had come down from Scotland together in the 1940s, and their first exhibitions had been a considerable success. Colquhoun in particular was linked with Vaughan and Minton as part of the romantic movement of the period. But both had sold well, until they began to inhabit Soho. Then, like butterflies, they were pinned to a wheel of alcohol and crapulas. Pinned to the wheel, they made no effort of will. Neither tried to escape. Now neither had painted for years. Nor did they, until at the very end of his life Colquhoun began once more, turning out monotypes and drawings in a rapid, desperate way. At last in 1962 he had a heart attack while working, and died at his easel. MacBryde died in Dublin shortly afterwards. The lives of these two men described the classic parabola of the doomed romantic artist. Though even when I first met them one could see the end of the parabola, I was young then and admired them, and did not think it a waste. Yet though one's death chooses one, one should be able to choose one's life.

I sent Nevill Coghill, who had recommended me to Jesus, some of my poetry. He wrote back to say he liked it, and on my next visit to Oxford I called on him in his rooms at Exeter. He was a tall, rather gawky man, with a handsome and leonine head: sprawled in a red velvet chair, under an old tapestry, he was exactly as I had imagined an Oxford don would be. In a quick, lisping voice, he talked of literature and writers he had known: he had been Auden's tutor, and awed me by producing a notebook which contained the early poems. He recommended me to various poets I hadn't heard of, and presented me with a copy of *Burnt Njal.* We drank China tea out of delicate and beautiful cups.

Later, he came to see me in London. He sprawled over a small chair in my flat exactly as he had sprawled in his armchair at Oxford: a kindness and sympathy came from him that were almost palpable: it was as though you could stretch your arm out and take them from the air around him. He was very worried about my loneliness: 'You must,' he said, 'meet people of your own age.' I told him about Soho, and he seemed shocked. He did not understand, I felt, but with another part of my mind feared that perhaps he did. We had a rather scratch tea at the flat: I was surprised to find that I enjoyed it more than I would have done Soho.

Meanwhile, news came that I had passed both the college and university entrances and that a place had been found for me at Jesus in October 1956. I was pleased, and started to sketch out plans of travel. France, I thought, and Italy, and Greece: perhaps I could go as far as Greece. I read books about these three countries, to decide where I would go in each. When I told Oliver, he was pleased for me: he had just completed a Christmas stint at the

Post Office, and was tired, but his pleasure was wholly unselfish. It was curious, I thought, how different we both were, when we drank together away from Soho: absorbed in poetry, comparing notes, or merely talking: in Soho we were detached, wolfish, we hovered and surveyed the half-lit, stained tapestry of drunk and lost worlds, so different from the antique tapestry with birds, landscapes, and shy, beautiful women that was mounted on Nevill Coghill's wall.

Sometimes, in Soho, rumours of a party spread like tame fire from bar to bar. When this happened, everyone about downed drinks and went, no matter whose party it was. I went to some of these parties, and they always had the same depressive effect on me. They seemed the same: a few smart writers and painters, lots of scruffy writers and painters, red wine and the odd bottle of whisky, a gramophone that wailed through the smoke and triggered off a sudden cloud of couples clutching each other and moving their hips with expressions of languor or ecstasy. At the end these couples would be lying about the place indulging in the preliminaries to copulation. Perhaps it was sheer envy that made me so depressed. I was too inhibited to approach a girl, though the girls at these parties were usually very approachable, and I tended to stand apart, watching couples pair off. Standing there, alone, I would think of poetry, which had after all, brought me to this place and this pass, and realize that I no longer wrote it. It began to feel as if I never would, as though the entire meaning of my life had been taken away, by some unknown force that had begun to operate as soon as I had arrived in London. It seemed ironic, somehow: I felt that I had finished my career in the city where I had hoped to start it.

The day before I was due to leave for the Continent, in an icy January, I met someone in Jenny's who told me he had been asked to a party in Chelsea. 'Why don't you come?' he said. I agreed. We took a taxi to the party, which was exactly like all other parties in one room. In the other room were various other people, including Stephen Spender. I stood with him for a while, but everyone here was much older than I was, and full of gossip which was incomprehensible to me. So I backed off into the other room. By this time everyone I knew there was pleasantly occupied, so after standing miserably around for some time I went and stood in the passage between the two rooms. It struck me that this was an image of my life at present: I was stuck in a passage between two cultures, or two patterns of behaviour. It was an easy image, but I dwelt on it lovingly, till tears of self-pity filled my eyes.

As I stood in the passage, a glass in my hand, Spender came out into it, with another man. 'Oh, hullo,' he said, 'are you going? Perhaps I could give you a lift.' I thanked him and said yes please. He drove rapidly towards Knightsbridge. I sat beside him in the front and the other man sat in the back. They exchanged literary talk, while I brooded in my corner. Suddenly (they came only too easily in those days) I found tears pouring down my cheeks.

Spender noticed them. He slowed the car and said gently, 'What's the matter?' and handed me a handkerchief. Oblivious of the stranger in the back, I told him what the matter was. He listened patiently until I had finished. By this time we had drawn up in front of my flat. In the crisp nocturnal silence, he said, 'Don't worry. Don't worry. You're very young still. You have to find your way, but you'll find it, I'm sure. You ought to be at Oxford, with people of your age. Then you'll settle to what you want to do.'

The shadowy man in the back (I never saw his face) said quietly, 'Stephen's shown me some of your work. You have a real talent. Don't worry. It will take you through this.'

I climbed out of the car. It slid away from me. The night was very cold, and in the black sky overhead the sharp stars stood. I felt inexpressibly thankful and released. While there was faith and charity in people, there was hope in me, permanent as this cold night and these sharp stars.

Next day I felt very cheerful. Oliver came to help me pack, since I was incapable of this by myself. 'My God,' he said, pushing down the lid of my case, 'you'll have to learn, won't you? *And* pretty soon.' I laughed and telephoned a taxi.

The Golden Arrow was standing at the platform at Victoria. I found places for my luggage and myself, and Oliver and I went to the buffet for a drink. It was cold, and little horsetails of mist floated idly through the station. Our breath clouded in the air.

'Well,' said Oliver. 'You'll be in Paris tonight. *Bonne fortune.*'

'And to you,' I said. 'I wish you could come.'

'Yes, it would be nice. Remember to look up David Gascoyne in Paris.'

It was nearly time. I shook hands with Oliver at the barrier. A sudden rush of elation overcame me.

'When I come back, I'll have a suitcase full of poems. The best poems you've ever read in all your life. You'll see…'

When the train coughed and shuffled forward I took my notebook out of my coat pocket, and started to write.

8

It was the winter of my seventeenth
Year when I lost what some call innocence.
Lightly that night the snow fell on Belgrade…
—'John Nobody' from *John Nobody* (1965)

I reached Paris at twilight. At twilight London was shabby and furtive, but Paris wasn't. The bars and cafés were brilliantly lit, and the people in the streets seemed in less of a hurry than Londoners, and also more pleased about their destinations. The city smelt interesting too, especially round the Sorbonne, where, on Oliver's advice, I sought an hotel. When eventually I found one, I was thrilled by its large, comfortable bed and strange lavatory arrangements. Most of that first evening I walked round the quais, dropping into the odd bar, goggling touristically at tarts, gendarmes, and sullen slinky Algerians. From then on, every day, I set off on foot early, and within a fortnight had more or less traversed the city.

After that I developed a working schedule. I awoke at eight, and worked till ten. Then I went to the nearest café and sat there amidst the strong coffee smells and the posters about alcoholism, drinking first coffee then pastis, and continuing to work. What I produced wasn't particularly brilliant, but at least I had the sensation of pursuing my vocation, which I had lost in London.

I didn't talk to many people, though I developed friendships with the concierge at my hotel and the waiter at the café. Through them I developed a knowledge of Parisian argot, which later stood me in good stead. My command of English argot was, I realized, more limited. One night I was in a St Germain café, when a young American at the next table started to stare at me intently. Rather crossly, I stared back. He rose, came over, and demanded in a husky whisper, 'Are you gay?'

I had no wish to be thought depressed, an object for pity. 'Oh, yes,' I said, with a broad smile, 'very gay,' and was much surprised to be invited back to his room. It took me a long while to extricate myself. Many people thought I was homosexual at seventeen. I suppose it was a combination of shyness, large sad eyes, and longish hair. I resented it deeply.

In my last days in Paris I plucked up the courage to telephone David Gascoyne. I had always admired his poetry, and I had introductions to him from Stephen and Oliver. I was also very interested in him because Stephen never ceased to say how much I reminded him of Gascoyne.

We arranged to meet in the Deux Magots. I arrived, eager, an hour early. He arrived an hour late. I was not at all annoyed: why, after all, should he be in a hurry to meet me? When he eventually appeared, I sat and looked at him in respectful silence. He was tall, angular, with a beautiful twitchy face, masked in spectacles, and long hands which he plaited together incessantly. In fact his entire aura was one of such nervousness and sensitivity that, respect apart, I felt almost afraid to speak: it was as though I might upset him if I spoke. This was a pity, because Gascoyne himself seemed neither to intend to speak nor to be able to speak. From time to time he pursed his sensitive mouth, as though about to utter, but no words were ever audible, and I soon realized this was a nervous mannerism.

After about twenty minutes of this, he heaved himself forward in his chair, and with an apparent effort, said, 'This is rather a treat for me. I haven't been out of the house for three weeks.' I inquired if he had been ill. 'No,' he said, and relapsed into silence. At last even I became desperate. I reached into my pocket, fished out some poems, and asked if he would read them. An expression of dismay flickered over his face. 'I don't,' he said, 'read poetry at all now.' Crushed, I put my poems away. After another twenty minutes or so he suddenly rose. 'Goodbye,' he said. He turned away, leaving me feeling dejected and inadequate. I ordered another drink, and was sipping it when Gascoyne suddenly reappeared by my side, as though by some feat of levitation. 'Er, perhaps,' he said, 'you'd like a drink at the flat tomorrow. Six o'clock. Er, goodbye.' He vanished once more, but left me much more cheerful.

At this time Gascoyne had lived in Paris for several years. He had recently written a radio play, *Night Thoughts*, which had been his first work for some time. I resolved to ask him whether he had written anything more since. I arrived at his flat to find him very carefully mixing vodka martinis. Several platefuls of canapés stood on a table. He gravely handed me a martini and inquired if it was too dry. I said it was delicious, it was, and then blurted out my question. Gascoyne looked stricken, and said, 'I can't write poetry any more.' Like most of his statements, it was final: he didn't bother to elaborate, but left it to stand like a No Trespassing sign. He continued to look extremely displeased for some time, but then sat down, and asked me if I knew various friends of his in London. Unfortunately, I didn't, at that time, so the conversation once more came to a halt. I nibbled at the canapés, which were excellent, and finally I said they were. To my amazement, Gascoyne's eyes lit up. He proceeded to explain, in a lively and even witty way, how they were made. This took him a long while, but afterwards he seemed to unbend, and even talked about contemporary English poetry, little of which he seemed to like.

My admiration and affection for Gascoyne have always remained absolute, and for years now I have been trying to discover whether or not he has in fact written new verse. Once, when he was staying with me in London, years after our first meeting, I thought I was on to something. In his luggage was an enormous notebook, of which he took the greatest care, reassuring himself every so often that it was intact and safe. I felt that it must be filled with new poems, and one day I asked him boldly if I could look at it. To my surprise, he consented at once, and with an air of pride. The book was full of recipes for dishes, carefully cut out of French and English magazines, with notes in Gascoyne's own tall poet's hand. 'It's taken me twenty years to collect all those,' Gascoyne said.

In Rome I found a small hotel near the station, devoted a fortnight to exploring the city on foot, as in Paris, and then evolved a new working schedule. It was February, and occasional flutters of snow fell from a dirty sky. This excited me because though I had seen snow lying still on mountains, I had never before actually seen it fall. I started to walk in the snow, working poems out in my head, and I was pleased with the results. The feathery sting of the flakes aroused something rich and bitter in me, which I was able to transmit to paper, to my own satisfaction at least. I was happy in Rome, I was working well, and also I liked the people very much, the elaborate courtesy and occasional vivacity. Armed with a phrase book and a sharp ear, I was able in a short while to pick up enough Italian to get around with.

Stephen had given me an introduction to Marguerite Caetani, who published the massive quarterly, *Botteghe Oscure.* Princess Caetani was an American, who had married into an aristocratic Italian family, and she had been associated with literary magazines for years: in the 1920s she had worked with T.S. Eliot, and most writers of reputation had appeared in *Botteghe Oscure.* A lot of awful writers had too, but Princess Caetani's taste was very catholic.

I sent her some poems, with Stephen's note, and a few days later received a letter in large scrawly handwriting, inviting me to tea. I put on my best suit, and arrived at the palazzo, in the street from which her magazine took its name, exactly on time. The gatekeeper put me into a creaky lift, and I rose slowly through several floors. When the lift stopped, an old lady in a drab dress opened the door. Beyond stood a svelte elderly woman, I stepped up to her, murmured, 'How do you do?' and made to shake her hand. She refused to take it, and waved towards the old lady. 'That is the principessa,' she said, 'I am the maid.'

To my relief, when I turned back, the princess was laughing. She was, I now saw, a very beautiful old lady. There was a girl's laugh inside her laugh. She took my arm and led me firmly into a large room, filled with manuscripts—'before you make any more mistakes'—and there she sat me down on a sofa and sat herself down by me. In the next half hour she took my shyness in her hand and calmly threw it away. She appeared so interested in me, and so enthusiastic about my work, that I started to talk. I talked so much, in fact, that she asked me to stay to dinner. Here I met her husband. The princess was then about eighty, and her husband was some years older. He was grave and courteous, but did not speak much, except to say that he had been in India, for the Durbar in 1902, and to inquire whether I numbered any of the Indian princes he had met then among my friends.

After that I called at the palazzo a good deal. The princess mothered me in a brusque, unfussy way. 'You aren't used to the cold,' she said. 'You must wear a thick sweater,' in that soft voice that had not quite lost its American accent, and next time I arrived she handed me two sweaters which she had bought, and insisted I put one on. She had decided to print a substantial number of my poems, and paid me far more than the normal rate for them. In some curious way she filled me with confidence, and, unfailingly, made me talk as much as any unshy person.

Several young Americans resident in Rome whirred round the palazzo like a circus of tiger moths. They were all writers, who assisted the princess in the production of the magazine. One of them, Eugene Walter, the novelist, infuriated me by always calling me 'Dear Plum-coloured Creature'. But they were all very friendly, and after leaving the palazzo, we tended to drink together through the afternoon. Through the princess I also met Giorgio Bassani, so handsome and polished I could scarcely believe he was real, Moravia, pale and austere, with an impressive limp, and Pier Paolo Pasolini, who, scowling in Italian under a dockworker's cap, deliberately untidy in blue denim, I liked the best of the three.

Through her I met also another American poet on a fleeting visit to Rome. He had taken a flat in the Lungo Tevere, and invited me there for a drink. I arrived to find him already very drunk. He was slumped in a chair, his large, hairy hands hanging slack, his mouth working and producing muffled sounds. One of his friends, a young Italian, shrugged his shoulders expressively. 'What the hell? He's often like this in the evening. Have a drink anyway.' Presently the American lurched slowly to his feet, stared blindly at us, and stumbled off down the passage. 'The trouble is,' said the young Italian, 'he can't write poems any more. What the hell, I say, what is it so marvellous, to write—you have *soldi,* anything you want you can have, me, too, what the hell—but no, no, he can't write, so he drinks like pigs. *Allora...*' and he wrung his slim shoulders out like towels, and flashed his teeth. We had a few more drinks, and he became very comradely. 'Those pigs in there has passed out, what the hell, we go out and find some womans now.' He waved ample curves into the air. 'I like womans better,' he explained.

I asked, at this point, where I could pee. He pointed down the passage. 'At the ends there, I will telephone some womans meanwhile.' I went down the passage, opened the bathroom door and discovered the American seated, naked, on the lavatory seat. He opened his mouth and bubbled at me. I was about to withdraw when I saw that he was holding his hands out towards me, and on each wrist was a sickle-shaped cut, from which blood dripped to the floor. The stippled red and white arms, sliced like pomegranates, waved slowly in the air, as though in appeal. I shouted for the Italian. He arrived and surveyed the scene with a certain disgusted calm. 'This is not the first time, what the hell. You better leave now, I take care of him. No womans tonight,' he said, wrinkling his lips furiously, and took a first-aid kit out of the bathroom cupboard.

I had always known that my vocation was ferocious, but not that it was as ferocious as this. It terrified me when I thought of the years ahead. The wrestle with words was difficult enough, but when that wrestle stopped, the horror happened. Eliot had remarked that anyone once visited by the muse was thereafter haunted by her. What appalling ghost had caused Gascoyne's silence and the dripping wrists of the American poet? I took my problem to the princess, who shook her wise beautiful head. 'Dear boy,' she said, 'you poets are temperamental people.' I loved the princess, but her answer disappointed me. Perhaps nobody who wasn't a poet could understand.

Rome, full of beautiful women, filled me with frustration. So aware of their bodies under their clothes, so aware that the men around were aware of their bodies, the young actresses primping their way down the Via Veneto were the incessant objects of my lust. I actually met some of them, on the occasions when I drank with Italian writers, but their presence paralysed me: scented, stroked, no hair out of place. A flutter of Italian came from their petalled lips, only ceasing when they threw back their heads to display round white throats and send deliberately projected laughter towards the café awning.

I had become a great deal more confident. Travel had done it for me, probably, and the princess: I was still quiet, but I could now take part in a conversation without strain. However, towards women my attitude remained the same: I was too terrified of making a fool of myself to ask a girl out. I, therefore, adopted a cool, disdainful attitude towards the young women I met, to conceal my desire and fear, and thereby confirmed everyone's opinion that I was homosexual.

After some weeks in Rome, I decided to try somewhere else. The idea of islands appealed to me: Sardinia and Sicily were my chosen destination. With considerable difficulty, I packed my case myself, and departed for Sardinia.

I landed in Sassari, in the north of the island, a tilted town that climbed the side of a hill. I had booked, through an agency, into the biggest hotel, and into it, unshaven and tired, I wandered one crisp clear day. An effusive manager welcomed me (I appeared to be the only guest), consigned my case to a porter, and informed me that the receptionist would collect my passport. The receptionist took some time to appear, but when she did she turned out to be a pretty young blonde. Her breasts, nearly as splendid as Aunt E's, swelled out her pink sweater, and as usual I concealed my little leap of desire with a cold and disdainful expression, which she answered in kind.

I went up to my room, had a bath, changed, and explored Sassari. Everywhere I went in the tilted streets I was followed by long trains of intent children. They had obviously never seen anyone my colour before, and were anxious to drink me in. After a day of this, I returned to the hotel anxious for a drink myself. I had just ordered one in the bar when I found the receptionist at my elbow. To my surprise, she smiled a very sweet smile, and then raised her arms to arrange her hair in a way that ensured a certain effusion of bosom under the pink sweater.

'I speak French,' she said in French. 'My name is Raffaela.'

'Oh yes?' I murmured.

'I come from Milano, and I am here to study hotel management. But Sassari is very boring. There is no culture here. In Milano we have all the arts. Here there are none. However, there is a cinema. There is a performance tonight. Would you like to come? I feel it is our duty to care for our visitors.'

She hadn't told me that the hotel manager was coming too.

Winter or not, the night was dry, hot, and dusty. The manager drove us to a plaster-walled hall, whose tin roof confronted the galaxies afloat above. A large and noisy crowd sat on wooden chairs inside. We sat down too, Raffaela in the middle. A Disney film, dubbed into Italian, started. As it started, I had the peculiar, detached, weightless feeling I had so often experienced before, of being separated from my body, and as though from a long way off I felt the weight of Raffaela's hand in my hand. This warm and solid object was something I did not know what to do with: I turned it about helplessly, in my fingers, and, still as though from a distance, noticed that Raffaela's other hand was entwined with one of the manager's hands. After the film Raffaela smiled a flushed happy smile and said, 'I hope you liked it.' I said I did.

Thereafter, throughout my fortnight in Sassari, I seated myself, every night, in the bar. The manager usually served, and a crowd of friendly Sardinians milled around, buying me drinks, and trying to explain dirty jokes to me in Italian. But at a certain time Raffaela floated in, blonde, pretty, bosomy, and there was a silence. The crowd rifted. She sat down beside me, and started demurely to sew. The crowd went to the bar, and appeared to chaff the manager, whose face at these moments became unhappy and sweaty.

Raffaela told me how miserable she was in Sassari, and how she had loved to play the violin. I told her I was a poet. 'Ah, when I saw your beautiful eyes,' she said tenderly, 'I knew you were like me.' Though unused to this sort of conversation, I retorted gallantly that her eyes were beautiful too. Sometimes she bent towards me, and her hair brushed my face. I tried not to look down her blouse. She was unhappy, I remembered, and I felt compelled to play the role of *preux chevalier.*

The night before I left, Raffaela whispered, 'You haven't shown me your poems.' I suggested that I bring them down to the bar. 'Oh, not here,' she said. 'There are too many people. I'll come to your room later, but we must be very quick. You see, I sleep quite close to the manager's room. He,' she explained, 'is my uncle, and he swore to my parents that he would look after me.'

I retired to bed in a state of nerves. Eventually, there was a knock at the door. Raffaela floated in. 'Oh,' she whispered, 'I'm so tired. May I lie down?' She lay down on my bed, and smiled a gentle, absorbed smile. 'It's very hot,' she said, and undid the top button of her blouse. I averted my eyes chivalrously, produced some poems, and began, laboriously, to translate them into French.

'Oh, how beautiful they are,' Raffaela murmured. 'How beautiful.' She rubbed her nyloned feet slowly together, with a noise like that of Eve's serpent. 'I haven't much time,' she added, rather briskly. I wavered above her. I knew precisely what I wanted to do, but it seemed to me it would be awful to betray the trust of someone who had actually ventured to come to my bedroom, starved of culture, to listen to my poems. 'There are,' I said, 'a lot more,' and started once more on my translations.

I kept my eyes carefully averted from Raffaela, so that she could rest assured of my trustworthiness, and after a while was surprised to hear her sigh deeply and rise. 'I must go,' she said rather coldly, 'it's late.' I said, 'There are still quite a lot.' She said it didn't matter, and departed.

All next day, on the bus to Cagliari, the capital of the south, I wondered.

I was in Mycenae. I had arrived hot and dusty on the local bus from Corinth, my stomach in disorder after being loaded with bread, cheese, and retzina by the other passengers. I booked into the Belle Helene at the foot of the valley. Agamemnon, the proprietor, beckoned me into his office after lunch. 'Antichi,' he said, putting his fingers to his lips, 'very old, very valuable,' and produced a few bits of broken pottery. 'I sell,' said Agamemnon hopefully. I shook my head. He frowned. 'You American?' he inquired in a strong Bronx accent. I denied this. He beamed. 'Aha. You no American, I no sell. Drink wine now,' and he stood several drinks. He was a square-set, pleasantly shabby man with a grey military moustache. Outside his valley shook out its humped dramatic hills in the cold sunshine.

I had rummaged round Sardinia and Sicily for a few weeks, and then returned to Rome, where the princess showed me the proofs of my poems, the first I had ever corrected. I told her I was leaving for Athens. 'Well, dear boy,' she murmured, 'I'll send you some money there.' I protested that I had already been paid. She raised her beautiful eyebrows. 'But you're *bound* to need money in Athens. I'll send it to the American Express.' I sailed next day from Brindisi, and presently, across the short sea, a white headland rose into the dawn, bathed in the strange iridescent sunshine which is a property of Greece. As the ship chugged down past the broad white face of the headland, I leant on the rails and, looking up, imagined that the ridges and fissures in the rock detached themselves into the flesh of statuary, so that gods and dead Greeks floated in the substance of the cliff. This illusion of the past and present intermixed persisted in me wherever I went in Greece.

Except Athens. On later visits I knew in which cafés I should find the poets, Odysseus Elytis, Nikos Gatsos, or Nanos Valaoritis, and sought them out always. In this first visit I didn't, and patrolled the white city alone. I was disappointed because Athens was like any other city. But once, in Constitution Square, I was astonished to see hundreds of leaflets, like gulls, fly from a window and float upon the wind, while a hoarse voice thundered like the voice of Zeus, and the people turned wild dark faces upward to the falling and fluttering scraps of white. It was only part of an election campaign, but for one sculptural moment it was like a frieze out of history.

From Athens I visited all the usual places, but because the gold masks, lions, and beehive tombs of Mycenae fascinated me, I left it to the last. Now, under the patriarchal eye of Agamemnon, I started to walk the shaly road up the valley. The afternoon sun burned and stood still overhead. There was nobody about and no sound apart from the scrape and swish of my steps. I passed a couple of beehive tombs slotted into the hillside: it looked dark and cool inside, but I did not enter. I climbed the fortress hill to the Lion Gate. The massed, hewn stone, in the hot silence, hung like a promise or threat. Beyond, the burial pits, with grass and spring flowers shrouding them, absorbed me, and I passed, as I had passed at Kanheri, into a concentrated fixity, studying an ant, a grass-blade, the porous skin on my hand. Nothing moved except the sun: the only sound was the boom of the wind as it slapped at hollows in the rock. For a century I stood on the hill, with time below me.

Afterwards I remember descending endless slippery steps into the belly of the fortress, and emerging at last at an embrasure that stared from darkness down a sunlit thicketed hillside to the valley. When I came up once more, the sun was dying: the wind had turned cold, and hooted like an owl: the fortress hooded itself in shadow. Prescience of blood filled me with a static sort of fear, and I scrambled down the hillside and walked fast all the way back to the hotel.

This first visit to Mycenae later influenced much of my work, poems in which images of kings, hills, and burial recur. I did not know this then, but was very elated, and consumed a quantity of alcohol before, during, and after dinner. Then I decided to walk to the hill tombs. Agamemnon, clearly acclimatized to the oddities of his visitors, furnished me with a torch and a bottle of ouzo. It was very dark outside, the wind had picked up density and volume, and made a rustling, crashing, and roaring noise all round me as I leant into it. I fought it all the way up the road to the nearest tomb. The entrance was closed, but I scrambled up on the hill above, lay down, sipped my ouzo, and looked at a vast yellow moon dragging clouds across the sky. After a while, above the roaring of the wind, I imagined that I heard a deep, vibrant humming, as though the former occupant of the tomb below me was singing in his sleep. I listened, entranced, for some time before I stumbled back to the Belle Helene. All night the walls of the hotel creaked and swayed in the wind as though they were planks of a ship built perhaps by Ulysses.

On my first day in Iraklion, the capital of Crete, I was puzzling over the cauldrons in a taverna kitchen, trying to work out what to eat, when a stocky man with a moustache approached me, and said, 'Allow me to suggest another place. This place is very bad.' As usual, I allowed myself to be led, and followed him out, pursued by the imprecations of the proprietor. 'I am Carrousis,' said my new friend, once outside, 'here is my card.' His card, a very grubby one, said he was a guide. I eyed him warily, but he made no approaches. He led me to another taverna in silence. Then he said, 'Permit me to order. I can recommend the *kirios* to try the cheese pie.' He ordered, and vanished. Later, mellowed by an excellent lunch, I ambled out into Venizelos Square, and suddenly observed Carrousis at my elbow. 'I hope,' he said, 'that the *kirios* enjoyed his lunch. Permit me to buy him a drink.' Half-an-hour later, full of raki and goodwill, I employed him to charter a car and show me round the island.

Carrousis had worked under Pendlebury, the archaeologist who was killed in Crete during the war, and he knew his profession. He was, I think, the only good guide I have ever met. He had no patter: he only explained what I asked him to explain, and he explained laconically and without fuss. He took me all over the island: he even, though plump and elderly, scrambled with me up the slopes of Mount Ida to the rocky Khameres cave, one of the holy places of the Minoans. At first, however, he was a little aloof: he had the withdrawn pensive appearance of a seal, with his whiskers and mournful eyes. He was, in fact, a proud man, and had perhaps suffered too many rebuffs from tourists to attempt friendship with one. When we lunched in some village taverna, therefore, he sat apart with the driver, leaving me alone with the excellent lunch he had ordered.

He always addressed me in the third person, as 'the *kirios*'. It got on my nerves.

Eventually, one day, as we were prospecting the ruins of Gortyna, a shepherd rose out of a wilderness of thistles and inquired where I came from. He spoke a kind of Italian, and informed me that he had been a guerrilla, with Pendlebury, during the war. Once reassured that I was not German, he elaborated on this.

'Italiani bad soldier. Fire rifle, Italiani run, Italiani kaput. Tedeschi good soldier, Tedeschi brave, no run. But Italiani very good man, like children, kind. Tedeschi bad man, shoot children. Bad soldier, good man. Good soldier, bad man.'

This piece of philosophy impressed me. Apparently it also impressed Carrousis. As we ate a picnic lunch in the shade, he unbent. He talked about the occupation of Crete, and his friendship with Pendlebury. That night, in another village taverna, the driver and he both sat at my table. We started to buy each other drinks, and to converse on subjects other than archaeology. Carrousis's wife had died in the war, leaving him with several children to rear. He had developed arthritis in his hands, which prevented him from doing archaeological work. So he had become a guide. But he was perpetually short of money, because tourists preferred guides with a patter, and perhaps a line in local humour.

He started to adopt a very fatherly attitude towards me. He introduced me to his unmarried daughter, a considerable act of friendship on the part of a Greek, and particularly a Cretan. He gave me advice on life, most of which was sensible, but all of which I have forgotten. We had a marvellous time. In those blue brilliant days, climbing against the senile white-haired mountains, with the glittering sea spread out beyond the vineyards and groves of olives: or driving through the hot plains, occasionally stopping at a poor, dusty village with beautifully carved lintels above the doors, to drink coffee with a brigandlike headman, we became friends. There was no part of Crete he did not show me, and explain to me. We called each other by our first names.

But at last, the day before I left, he brought me his bill. I was appalled. It was three times the price he had quoted at the start. It meant that I would have just enough left to pay the hotel, and would have to return to London at once. Friendship and treachery, someone had told me, were closely allied in some Greeks, but I could not believe it of Carrousis. Because we were supposed to be friends, I didn't want to haggle with him. I paid him, but I was full of hurt and fury. When he invited me to have a farewell drink with him at his house, I coldly declined. He was obviously hurt too, but I didn't care, in fact I was pleased. He went off quietly and proudly. His last words were, 'I hope the *kirios* has a pleasant voyage.'

Next day, smouldering still, I went down to the harbour. Carrousis was on the quay. He came up rather awkwardly and said, 'I have arranged for the *kirios* to have a single cabin, and I have ordered his meals from the steward.'

'What do you charge for that?' I inquired, and was instantly ashamed of myself.

Carrousis flushed deeply. He said, 'I'm sorry that my charges were more than you expected. Here is half the money back.'

He pushed it into my hand. I was pleased and repentant all at once. 'Don't be silly, Theodosius,' I said. 'I had a wonderful time, and it was worth much more.'

He smiled, but continued to press the money on me. I continued to refuse it. Eventually he laughed and said he would buy me a drink instead. So we had one, quickly because the boat was due to leave, and he waved goodbye as it surged away from the Cretan coast. We had parted friends, but not quite the same friends as before. For the first time I thought about money as something in itself, an entity which affected relationships between people, and decided that money was a terrible thing.

The princess saved me. When I returned to Athens £100 was waiting at the American Express. More scrupulous then than now, I wondered if I should accept it, then decided I could pay it back in kind, with the poems I had written in Greece. I bought Frank Harris's autobiography in the five-volume Olympia Press edition, and took the Orient Express to Belgrade.

Just before the Yugoslav frontier, sudden doubts overcame me. I knew that Harris's book was banned in England. I wondered if it was also banned in Yugoslavia. There was no logical reason why it should be, but I wondered. I was not yet eighteen, so it seemed to me highly likely that if it was banned, I should spend some considerable time inside a Communist prison. I seized a moment when the compartment was empty to stuff the five volumes into the ventilator. The result of this was that for the next five hours the temperature in the compartment rose steadily, till it resembled an oven. Streaming with sweat, I climbed out of the Orient Express into a wilderness of Belgrade snow. Thickly it carpeted the ground, and thickly it fell from the sky, which was pitch dark, since it was two in the morning.

I shivered my way down the platform till I found a decrepit and toothless porter, who spoke a mixture of German and English. I demanded a hotel. There were no taxis. He heaved my case and typewriter to his shoulders, and plodded ahead of me through the arctic weather. We traversed numerous deserted, snow-covered streets, till we came to the Moskva. It was full. The porter, a phlegmatic man, led me to two more hotels. Both were full. He then conducted me to the tourist office. Despite the hour, it was open. As we entered, like two travelling snowmen, an elderly official from behind the information desk bounded forward, kissed me loudly on both cheeks, and exclaimed in English. 'Ah! My African brother!' For some reason I was infuriated, but my supposed nationality seemed to work wonders. Within minutes he had found me a room in somebody's house. I paid my rent to the official. Then the porter, who was nauseatingly cheerful, and I set off on another terrible trek through wind and snow. After about half an hour, I began to feel like an icicle. Doubts assailed me as whether I would ever thaw out. Suddenly the porter dumped my luggage in the snow. 'Is it here?' I chattered, relieved. *'Ja, ja,'* said the porter. He took me by the arm and led me for some distance past faceless houses, till we arrived at the foot of a large statue entirely covered in snow. The porter pointed at this. 'Tito,' he said. *'Ist gut.'* I restrained an impulse to hit him. 'How far are we,' I asked carefully, 'from *das Haus*?' *'Ja, ja,'* he said. We plodded back to my luggage and the journey continued.

We reached the house at last. A cheerful Serbian maid opened the door, and whisked us into a warm kitchen, where an enormous wood stove crackled and spat. I paid the porter, and, dripping with melted snow, followed the maid to a large and handsome bedroom. Into the snowdrift of an immense bed I sank, wet, cold, and miserable, and slept heavily.

When I awoke next morning I felt very ill, but felt also that I must bestir myself. So I rose and dressed. I noted, while I was doing so, that this was obviously a woman's room. There was a dressing table littered with cosmetics, and on the bedside table stood the photograph of a very beautiful, dark-haired young woman with a child.

The originals of these photographs were seated in the kitchen. The woman was even more beautiful than in the photograph. She had very vivid violet eyes which contrasted with her raven hair, and a pearl-pale Slavonic face. Her daughter, who was about six, looked very much like her. Also in the kitchen was the maid, and to my dismay, the porter. He looked more decrepit and toothless than ever in the day.

'How do you do,' said the beautiful brunette, in French. 'This is my house. You are very welcome. Please have some coffee.' I drank some coffee, while the porter nodded and winked conspiratorially at me. Presently I inquired what he wanted. 'He says,' translated the lady, 'that he will show you round Belgrade.' Though I could not imagine a more undesirable guide, it struck me that, since I didn't know where I was, and spoke no Serbian, he might be useful. So we departed together.

I had no idea where we were bound for, but the porter did. Halfway down the snowy street, he stopped, pointed to a bar, made repulsive drinking noises, and said, 'Schnapps.' I replied, *'Nein.' 'Ja, ja,'* he said. *'Ist gut.'* Inside the bar he smacked down three rapid tumblerfuls of slivovitz, for which I paid. We then continued. But the porter's broken boots only seemed capable of leading him to bars. Utterly helpless, since I would have been lost without him, I followed him through about six. Meanwhile I began to shiver, not only because of the cold. I could feel my cheeks burning with fever, and an iron vice seemed to have fastened round my chest. Frank Harris had bequeathed me a very bad chill. Finally I said to the porter, *'Das Haus.' 'Nein,'* he replied defiantly, 'schnapps.' I didn't even know the address of the house, and was starting to feel as though I would collapse. In the next bar I waved a fistful of dinars in the porter's face. He put down his slivovitz and squinted at them. '*Raus,*' I said. *'Das Haus.* Then *sie haben* this.' He appeared to understand, and we crunched back through the snow. The house, to my surprise, was only five minutes' walk away. Once there, I did collapse, and was put efficiently to bed by my hostess and the maid.

They didn't report my illness to the tourist office, which they were supposed to do, so that I could be removed to hospital. Instead, they nursed me, fed me broth, herb tea, and medicine, and supplied endless hot bricks for my feet. My hostess went into town and found some English magazines. She would sit and talk to me in a soothing husky voice. Her name was Dragika, and she had been a widow for three years. Her husband, an engineer, had been killed in an accident, and since then she had let rooms to guests to supplement her income. The room I slept in was in fact her bedroom.

Dragika's brilliant violet eyes brightened and darkened like a cat's, under her long dark lashes. One day, when they were dark, she told me that she had been raped, when she was twelve, by a dozen German soldiers. I felt sorrow and pity: her gentleness when she described the incident touched me terrifyingly. She was now about twenty-five. I fell, naturally, madly in love with her.

At the same time, I didn't see what I could do about it. I was a stranger in transit, and very young (angrily, I realized this), and our lives, really, were utterly disparate. When, convalescent, I sat by the stove in the kitchen playing with Dragika's daughter, Nevenka. The maid fetching me endless cups of coffee, my eyes followed Dragika about painfully, imprinting her upon my memory before it was too late. Finally, I was well. Dragika took me round the city. She was a much better guide than the porter, and also I was delighted to be with her. But a great guilt preyed on my mind. Returning home the first night after I was well, I said, 'I know that I'm sleeping in your bed, and you sleep with Nevenka. Why don't you sleep in your own bed? I'll sleep in the kitchen.' Her brows lifted above her marvellous violet eyes, and her husky affectionate laugh answered me. *'Bien,'* she said. 'I'll sleep in my own bed. But you sleep there too.'

So I did. Everything was suddenly very simple.

9

> I sowed my wild oats
> Before I was twenty.
> Drunkards and turncoats
> I knew in plenty.
>
> —'Song' from *Poems* (1960)

It was spring in London. Sticky buds that smelt of semen unclenched on hedge and tree. All the young women looked so pretty that one thought of the pink buds on their breasts. Through the cruel and comely month, inhaling the weather, I went to see Mr Eliot. Some time or other we all encounter our idols, but I had had no idea that my time would come so soon. It had been arranged partly through Stephen, and partly through my having sent Mr Eliot my poems.

The afternoon sun slanted through his window, laying a malleable bar across the office desk. He was physically much larger than I had expected, not only tall but heavy, in a way that accentuated the gravity of his manner. His attentive aquiline head seemed bowed a little always, but his eyes were very kind. He said he had liked some of the poems very much: 'they show great promise.' But, he said, if the best of them were selected, there would be too few for a book. 'I believe,' he said, 'nowadays, that a first volume should be…substantial.' When I had written more, perhaps I would send them back. Fervently, I promised I would.

An inward dance of elation possessed me. Here was the man, he had suffered and been there, he had followed out the course of his poetry to the finish, and he liked some of my work. My feeling towards him was peculiar. His poetry and criticism were part of my mind and sensibility: like a son, I had inherited areas of myself from him. But physically he was a total stranger, and I could not really connect the hand that lay on the desk with the hand that had written in my mind.

He inquired very kindly about my plans. I told him about Oxford, and about my intention to remain in England. 'Have you thought,' he asked, 'what profession you will take up after university?' I said I hadn't. He looked at me keenly and said, 'Perhaps the academic field would not suit you. But it's very hard for a poet to live by his pen. Journalism demands a special talent.' After a while he said he must leave. We walked a little way together. His stooped immensity sheltered me.

After that I sometimes saw Mr Eliot at literary parties. He had remarried, and, like a boy in love, clasped the hand of his young wife always. I was very glad that he was happy.

I still frequented Soho. One afternoon, drinking with Oliver in Jenny's, he suggested we call on David Archer. I didn't know who David Archer was. 'He's just started a new bookshop,' Oliver said. We strolled round the corner into Greek Street and entered a handsome new bookshop opposite the Palace Theatre. Its only occupant was a tall elderly man who held himself so rigidly it seemed as though he were afraid he would explode. This was David Archer. In the 1930s he had run a now legendary bookshop in Holborn, from which, under the imprint of the Parton Press, he had published the first volumes of Dylan Thomas, George Barker, and David Gascoyne. Later he had had a bookshop in Glasgow, and from there, under the same imprint, produced W.S. Graham's first book.

The Greek Street shop was the first one he had had since 1942. The top room was a long rectangle, the front half of which was the saleroom for new books. In the back half was a small but excellent lending library, consisting mostly of rare books, and a coffee bar. Archer planned to start a gallery in the basement, also part of the shop. He showed us round with a prim nervous smile, and frequently apologized for the fact that he was not yet doing a roaring trade.

Presently Oliver informed him that I wrote verse. 'Yes, I thought you did, somehow,' Archer said, and laughed heartily. He began to ask me if I had met any poets. He was very solicitous about this. 'You ought to meet some, really,' he said. 'Fun for you, what?' He fumbled on his desk. 'Do you know, I can't find my address book? I think I'm going out of my tiny mind. Ah, here we are. Now George, you see, George Barker that is, is in London. You ought to meet George, really, what? I'll phone him then, shall I?' He phoned, and said, pleased, 'He'll meet us in the pub across the way.'

Later we crossed the road to The Coach and Horses, and there found George Barker, cowled like a monk in a duffel coat. He fixed me with hypnotic blue eyes, and said, 'So you write verse, too, baby. We are honoured. There are few Hindu princes amongst us versifiers.' Archer, an immense number of magazines clenched rigidly under his arm, floated around, buying drinks. He did not speak, but looked very pleased, like a scoutmaster who sees that his troop is happy. After a while an enormous man, with a lion's head maned in white, burst in through the door, and flung his arms round George Barker. He was introduced to me as the poet David Wright. I talked to him for a while, but after I had finished a short disquisition on my doings in the last year, was rather offended when he turned to Barker and demanded what I had said. 'No offence, honey dove,' said Barker, who had been watching our conversation with relish, 'no offence. Our South African friend is as deaf as the womb.' He then turned to Wright and, enunciating carefully, inquired, 'Ain't you, baby?' Wright, who had watched his lips with rapt attention, nodded his

Yeatsian head in a satisfied way. I found at this first encounter, however, that he could not lip-read me, I mumbled so, and most of our conversation was carried on through notes on the back of envelopes.

Next day I sent my poems to both Barker and Wright. They both wrote back to say they liked them. Thereafter we often met for a drink in The Coach and Horses, and I began to frequent Archer's bookshop. In its early days, the shop assistants, when Archer was out, included Barker, Robert Colquhoun, Tristram Hull, who edited the literary magazine *Nimbus,* and myself. But Ralph Abercrombie, the son of the poet Lascelles Abercrombie, took over as manager, and things became more normal. Abercrombie, a kind, dryly witty man, watched Archer as a trainer might watch an unreliable animal. One day we were drinking in The Coach and Horses when a ragged old man, with a distinctly unstable look in his eye, wandered in. He stumbled up to us and produced a very dirty copy of the Bible. 'Half a crown,' he said. 'Please, Ralph.' Ralph gave him half a crown and he handed over the Bible and departed unsteadily. I inquired who he was. 'That,' said Ralph, rather thoughtfully, 'was the manager of David's last bookshop.'

It was all strange and funny, but full of excitement for me. It was cut short in the summer. My father wrote to say that my mother was now out of hospital, and it might be a good idea for me to fly back to India for my eighteenth birthday, and spend some time with my mother before I went up to Oxford. India had become very remote to me. I didn't really want to return, for however short a time, but I did.

I landed in Bombay full of confidence. This confidence had been instilled in me, over the year I had been away, by Spender, Forster, the princess, Dragika, Eliot: by new places, faces, voices: I was adult, I thought complacently, at last. The airport, under its cowl of hills, shimmered with heat: as I descended the ramp, flies danced in my face. My parents were waiting: my father as calm and solid as ever, my mother slight, pale, possessive. They had more grey in their hair than I remembered. So had Kutthalingam, who wept with joy when he saw me. '*My* young master has come back...' I wanted to respond, to be happy, but I felt exiled from this life to which I had returned. I had put tentative roots down in London, and their tug made me homesick, though I had come home.

The flat and the servants were exactly the same. I had resolved to surround my mother with patience and love, to undo with care all the horrors I felt my impatience and unlove of the past had knotted round her. The difficulty was my own temperament. In the last year I had grown into a habit of not staying at home, except to work. So I was restless in the flat. I needed to visit Nissim Ezekiel, or go out to drinks with my father, or just walk. But my mother seemed to have lost all desire for any contact with anyone except me. She would sit plaiting a rosary in her fingers for hours on end, gossiping with me about the church she attended, her relatives, the weather, and my childhood. She appeared not to share any of my interests, nor I any of hers. The trouble, I suppose, was that apart from the terrible yoke of blood that held us together, we were total strangers: we had seen little of each other in the last ten years. For all my guilt, my shamefaced love, and my desire not to hurt her further, I needed to see other people. Whenever I announced that I was going out, however, my mother reacted violently. She could not bear me to be away from her, and the result was that we quarrelled: squabbling, petty quarrels which always ended with resentment on one side or the other. I was sullen if I eventually stayed in: my mother was angry when I didn't. She took my desire to meet other people as a further rejection of her. It could all have been solved quite simply, I imagine, if I had been willing to humour her: but I saw in her possessiveness an attempt to withdraw me into herself, to deprive me of the identity I had found. So we bickered unhappily and insolubly, and after each incident I became more guilty, and more furious at my mother for making me guilty.

One gesture, I felt, one final compelling gesture of love, would erase the past years, but I had no opportunity to make it, nor really did I know what it was. So, for all the weeks of my visit, my mother and I confronted each other like unhappy dancers ignorant of what the next step should be.

When I was able to get away, Kutthalingam drove me about as he had done ever since my childhood. He drove me twice to Kanheri, and once more I sat on the crest of the hill and looked out over the arid valley beneath. Only a few months before I had stood on the hill of Mycenae, but with different sensations: here I felt no awe or terror, but a kind of vacancy, a hollowness waiting to be inhabited. I thought perhaps that was it: in Europe I had positive emotions, in India I sank into the dream in which the whole country was sunk. The emotions I had now I could not explain to Kutthalingam, as I had done the emotions of my childhood. He waited patiently in the car at the foot of the hill, till I came down like Moses, and accepted my absorption and silence now as he had accepted my confidences as a child. When I was ready to speak, he spoke to me. One day, he suddenly and almost proudly showed me his hands. They were rough and hard with work, but were also twisted, like black twigs.

'Arteerytees,' Kutthalingam said, still with a kind of pride. 'Doctor saying I must retire. Master giving me house and pension, but I telling him I no take it yet. Before I retire, I driving my young master one last time.' It must have been very painful for him to drive with his hands as they were. I was horrified, but said how glad I was that he had stayed.

Kutthalingam eyed me, from time to time, in a curious, doting way. One day, as we were driving along, he unexpectedly inquired, 'Young master going with womans yet?' I said yes. 'Ah,' he said. 'Young master grown up now. Only too many womans not good.

Young master finding one good girl and having children, then I be happy. Then I coming back to drive your son, like I driving you when you little-little boy.' He understood this sort of thing, but could not understand why, occasionally, I drank to excess. He gave me many dark warnings about the deleterious effects of alcohol on my health. He seemed almost hurt whenever, when I came out of a party, he smelt whisky on my breath.

One night, after a particularly lively party with some film people, I staggered down to the car, and passed out. When, painfully, I awoke, I discovered I was still in the car, which was parked in the garage at home. Kutthalingam, looking very anxious, was bending over me. 'I was thinking,' he said without reproach, 'if young master going home like this, memsahib very upset. So I bringing you here.' He fetched me a cup of tea from his quarters behind the garage. I had never in my life been in Kutthalingam's quarters, so, sipping my tea, I wandered in. It was a bare room, furnished only with basic necessities, but on one wall hung brightly coloured lithographs of the Hindu gods. Amongst these I discovered with a sense of shock, three small Kodak prints of my mother, my father, and myself.

I looked at him, a plump small man with arthritic hands, one of my oldest friends, standing there, pleased to be with me. He was as docile, as accepting, as the country of both our births. He expected nothing from me, and gave all he had. I felt utterly unworthy of him. But there was nothing I could say or do that he would understand, beyond the unsatisfactory compromise of a smile and a touch of the hand.

Before I left, I was delighted to find that Verrier Elwin, on one of his occasional swivels back from the jungle, was briefly in Bombay. I went to see him at the house where he was staying. He was exactly the same as ever, but like everyone else a little older. We talked about his work in Assam, and about an exhibition of paintings by tribesmen which he was organizing. 'I don't think I've ever asked you,' he said in his gentle way, 'do you like painting?' I said yes, Samuel Palmer, Cotman, and Crome. He laughed his little husky laugh, exhaling it through the flesh of one of the cigars which were his only luxury. 'What a very English trio,' he said.

Suddenly what had haunted me on this trip became explicit. My mother and my father had nothing to do with India itself: they were simply themselves, as I was myself, and our relationship had to be worked out independent of where we were. But the colours and smells of India, the emotions I had at Kanheri, the painful sort of affection I had for Kutthalingam all pulled me one way, and the new life I led abroad, with friends and work and a milieu I understood, more than I did India, pulled me the other. I told Verrier this, hoping he might explain: he was after all, himself an expatriate, only he had come the other way. He said, 'Let's go for a walk,' and we strolled down the seafront. It was sunset, the tide was sucking back over the rocks, the garish sky quivered as it left its heat. The ember of Verrier's cigar glowed irregularly in the gathering dusk. He said, 'You're in a peculiar historical position, you know. All your family speak English, and, really, you yourself are a very English person. Your reactions aren't Indian, are they? I can't explain that, but there it is. You seem quite naturally to live in a world of English poetry and English painting, and you are an English poet.'

He looped the firefly of his cigar over the seawall. The lights were on in all the houses, so that the Queen's Necklace, as it is locally called, glittered round the curve of the bay. White-clad people floated past us, murmuring in the liquid language that had never been mine. 'I love India,' Verrier said. 'I love all this. History does peculiar things to people. I feel far more for India than I ever did for England. India's my country. I felt I belonged here when I first came, and I do. And, you see, you're the exact opposite.'

'But there is a choice.'

'I don't think it's entirely a conscious choice. It happens without your knowing, almost. Suddenly, you are in a place which is your home.' We walked in silence for a while. He said, 'I wouldn't presume to advise you. But if I were you, I would stay in England. I have always had the feeling about you that you would stay there. There will be a lot of heartache, of course. Often, even now, I have vague moments when I long, say, for Oxford in the summer term, or London in early spring. You'll have those moments too, the other way. But I'm not sorry that I've settled in India, I'm glad. I hope you will be. While you write well, nothing will hurt you really.'

I have always remembered these words, partly because they were more or less the last I ever heard from Verrier. I never saw him after our walk by the sea. Now, like so many of the people who befriended me as a boy, he is dead.

On the day I left, my mother declined to come to the airport. She gave me a quavery smile as I said goodbye. 'I put a sweater in your briefcase,' she said. 'Be sure and put it on before you reach London. Otherwise you'll catch a chill. You know you've a weak chest.' She clutched my hands. 'There were lots of things I wanted to tell you, but there isn't time now. I hope you had a nice time at home, son.' Briefly I held her bird's body in my arms.

Kutthalingam said, as I left. 'Next time my young master coming, he bringing one fine son. Then I coming to drive him, and I dying happy.' I hugged him and went with my father into the airport. My father was rather subdued: of him, the only fixed point I had ever had in my life, I had not seen very much. I looked at him with the old deep familiar love, noting the grey in his hair with a kind of helplessness: a consciousness of time passing, rapidly, severing, scything, possessed me: nobody could fight time, love could not fight time. 'I'll try and come to London soon,' my father said, and then, as always at our partings, 'Try and be a good boy.'

The flight was uneventful, save that we had a breakdown at Dhahran, in the burning desert by the Persian Gulf. We sat thirstily for four hours in an airbase where the only liquid was warm Coca-Cola. Someone left a bottle of it in the sun, and was rewarded by a unique spectacle: it boiled. But it seemed only a little while after that we landed, in pouring rain and a cold wind, at the London airport.

Archer's shop had reached its brief period of high summer. It was now always full, but unfortunately not of customers. Every young writer in town used it as a club, drank free coffee there and borrowed the books. Nobody was able to enter the lavatory for some weeks because Bernard Kops, then penniless and newly married, had locked himself up in it to write a play. This play, *The Hamlet of Stepney Green,* was later a considerable success. From time to time Kops emerged from the lavatory and drank some coffee, his feverish blue eyes alight with excitement. In those days he was flushed and talkative. But then everybody was.

Another young writer who frequented the shop was Michael Hastings. He was about the same age as myself, a thin, darkly handsome young man with a bored and rather dramatic manner. 'When I'm not working,' he said, 'all I can do is scratch my belly,' and he would seat himself in Archer's swivel chair, put his feet on the desk, unbutton his shirt, and for hours on end show us what he meant. Michael had just written a newspaper article condemning the older generation, by which he meant anybody over twenty, and demanding that a teenage government be elected. He often scrutinized me closely, as though he saw in me a prospective secretary of state, but eventually seemed to decide I was not ministerial matter. Even younger than Michael and I was the poet Robert Nye, an apple-cheeked boy who stood and stared at everyone as though they were genii: I found him very sympathetic, it was only a few months since I had been the same.

Other, older poets frequented the shop too: gentle Dannie Abse, a doctor whose practice was in Soho, dropped in on his way to work: Christopher Logue arrived from Paris, looking, with hat, cloak, and stick, as though he had escaped from a German film of the 1920s. Because of this constant clutter of writers, the shop took on the air of a kibbutz: everyone who was there volunteered for work, and, under Ralph Abercrombie's austere direction, shifted shelves, counted stock, or served. But there were few people to be served: normal customers, looking in and finding the place filled with eccentric young men who all knew each other and all talked loudly to each other, drank coffee, and dropped ash everywhere, would depart hastily. Those who stayed found it difficult to buy anything. Archer had an aristocratic prejudice against taking money from them, and he either recommended them to another bookshop down the road ('Silly me, I've got nothing readable here, really. The other shop's *much* better') or gave them books free. Ralph Abercrombie stopped this when he was there, but since he wasn't always there, the turnover was mostly low.

One day when I was having a drink with George Barker in The Coach and Horses, Archer came across the road. He stood looking at us twitchily for a while, then, in the embarrassed way of someone requesting a favour, inquired, 'Would you mind very much if I published your poems? As a book, I mean.' I stared at him unbelieving, and said I wouldn't mind at all. I had had ideas of sending a new collection back to Eliot, but to be published by the Parton Press, with its unique record, seemed to me even more of an honour, and I was very fond of Archer.

'An excellent idea, David,' George said. 'While you're about it, why not republish my "True Confession" as well?' This was a long poem that had been printed in a small edition in 1948 but which George's publishers had refused to include in his *Collected Poems* on the grounds that it was blasphemous. Archer seemed delighted at the idea. We sat down and talked about it. 'Honey dove,' George told me, 'your poems is good poems, we all know that, but if they isn't beautifully produced they isn't going to come over properly. You choose the paper and the type, and mind that our publisher here allows you wide page margins. Thass the way to print pums.' He recommended various typefaces to me. Ralph Abercrombie later showed me a book about type, and I eventually selected a twelve-point Plantin as having the feel I wanted. This was the first important lesson I learnt about the production of books of verse.

Now, intoxicated with triumph, with my first book under way, I wandered through Soho as through Elysian fields. Archer, having accepted me into his private fold of poets, followed me with a paternal eye. From time to time he would rush up to me, in the shop or in the pub, press a matchbox into my hand, and rush off. I was trying to give up smoking, and threw the matchboxes away, puzzled: till one day someone asked me for a light and I opened the box with which I had just been presented, and found a five pound note wadded up inside. I realized I must have thrown away nearly £100. I told Ralph Abercrombie about this. He nodded his intelligent head. 'That was the way David's last bookshop went bust,' he told me.

Now, from more than ten years away, I look back with a kind of despair on the boy I was. The moment when Archer decided to publish me was the moment I should have drawn my horns in, gone quietly away, and worked. Nevill Coghill had in fact arranged for me to stay with people in the country for the two months before the Oxford term started. However, weakness of will betrayed me. I enjoyed Soho too much: the company of other poets, the acceptance of eccentric behaviour, and the alcohol. And I was shy still of new people, people outside the charmed circle I had entered. I had been assimilated into a society which was itself not assimilated into normal English life, and I was afraid of the challenge which normal life presented. But the person I was then would have disliked the person I have become, and not understood him: and perhaps the person I have become cannot understand the person I was. It is the mission of the son to destroy the father, and now I have become the father of my boyhood self. Anyway, I stayed in Soho. In the morning I dropped into the bookshop, and talked to Archer, or Ralph Abercrombie, or whoever else was there. I generally lunched across the road with Ralph, and then went drinking. I had now graduated from Jenny's basement to an upstairs club where the *haute Boheme* was to be found. The club was run by a large affable woman who possessed a pleasant cynicism about people, but also two poodles. It was frequented, amongst others, by numerous painters. One of these was Francis Bacon. Tough and stocky in jeans and sweater, he surveyed everyone with cool pale eyes which sometimes had a curiously anxious look. The eyes always seemed watchful, though the strong round face often broke into laughter, or frowned with sudden concentration. Bacon had extremely good manners, and answered questions about painting with a humility and formality which were almost touching. He gave an impression of great strength and great aloofness: when most kind and friendly, he seemed also most remote. Sometimes, he made remarks about life in general, but made them as though asking a question: 'Nobody stays in love,' or 'Everyone is a drifter,' with an unspoken query at the end. He could be extremely vicious to people he did not like, but generally remained watchful and calm, except for sudden bursts of hilarity in which he would crowd the bar with bottles of champagne.

One day a society painter in Chelsea asked Bacon to come and look at some of his work. Bacon was in Soho that afternoon, and he suggested to myself and someone else that we should accompany him to Chelsea and go on to dinner. We arrived at the painter's impeccable house, and he welcomed Bacon effusively and us rather less effusively. In his studio, which was as graciously lived in as the rest of the house, a quantity of drink was laid out, with crisps, olives, and nuts in a tasteful colour scheme. The painter poured out the drinks, then asked if Bacon were ready to look at his work. He drew back a curtain to reveal a neat row of canvases hung on the wall. They were mostly landscapes. Bacon went and looked at each one carefully and at length. When he had finished, he turned, met the painter's expectant eyes, and burst into a cataclysm of high, wild, clear laughter. It was one of the purest acts of criticism I have ever seen. When Bacon had stopped laughing, he began to talk gaily and courteously about subjects unrelated to art, and eventually persuaded our shattered host to be happy.

This incident conveyed to me a strong sense of the difference between the practitioner of an art and the artist. I wrote a poem, 'Landscape Painter', about it. Much later I wrote another poem about Bacon in the Soho club. The club supplied me with considerable material, though I did not use it for some years. In it, through the presence of so many writers and painters, I felt an atmosphere of enormous intellectual excitement. This was partly my imagination, but it existed in the sense that one frequently heard witty or intelligent conversation there, and with the curtains drawn on the afternoon sun, sealing off the world, there was a conspiratorial air in the dark carpeted room, as though all the drinkers were revolutionaries, plotting against society. But as the afternoon waned and the night took over, a sullen quality came to people's faces: the roar of conversation became more hysterical and scattered: there were lonely men in corners, staring, and sad patterns squinted up from the carpet. In those days my capacity for alcohol was considerable: after a day on whisky, I was still not drunk: only glazed and detached, so that my eye could still photograph, in one corner of the bar, Lucien Freud, with the large fixed eyes and nervous hands of a refugee, talking intently to Bacon: in another the kind detached faces of Colin MacInnes and Archer: elsewhere a solitary starer, who seemed to look beyond the smoky room to a time and place perfect as the blue flower of the Mediterranean. This solitary starer I saw always in the mirror: it was myself.

It was here that I first met K.

I first saw her perched on a stool at the bar, surrounded by men, whose remarks she punctuated with a noisy, emphatic laugh. She was twenty-five. She had the same pale skin, long dark hair, and intensity of the eyes as Dragika, but her temperament was clearly different. On this first occasion, her escort was a tall handsome young man with a kind and serious face: he stood a little back from the group around her, sipping a beer. At one point, when he asked her to have a drink, she turned and said with a dramatic flicker of the eyes, 'Piss off, darling. Can't you see I'm busy?' In her high-pitched voice, which emphasized certain syllables as an actress does, the words brought back an atmosphere of the 1920s, with their bored young people in bars.

I met her through Archer. 'She's a one, really,' Archer said, with the delighted smile with which he always described the vagaries of other people. Then he began to talk about the production of my book, and I forgot about K.

A few days later, however, she swept into the bookshop. Archer had employed her to rim the coffee bar at the back. She discharged her duties with a sort of ferocious efficiency, and was constantly surrounded by young writers, with whom she carried on bantering flirtations. I observed her with awe from afar: she was quite unlike any other woman I had ever met. One evening, as the shop was shutting, she announced that she wanted to go to the cinema. There was nobody around except me, so I volunteered to take her. Curiously enough, it was the first time I had ever taken a girl to the cinema. It made me feel proud and male. Afterwards we had a drink together. Deprived of a large audience, she was quiet and rather unsure of herself, and I began ro feel a protective warmth towards her.

My book was held up for a while, because Archer wanted to bring George's out first. However, I had already chosen the paper and the type, and was starting to think of a cover. Archer introduced me to a small, talkative man named John Deakin, whom I think of now as one of the best photographers alive. He had started off as a painter, but once he started taking photographs obtained a considerable amount of fashion work. His eye was restless, however, and would not settle: he threw up his lucrative employment, and gipsied his way through the capitals of Europe, pointing his camera into cemeteries, flea markets, and alleys, or at, chipped walls covered with graffiti. He could not sell these photographs, but they were very beautiful, and when he showed them to me I was fascinated by one of a wall in Paris, into which children had chipped faces. It was a pale, delicate grey, the loops and squiggles of the children contrasting with the cracked, worn texture of the wall itself. I chose it for my cover.

Now Deakin and I often drank together. He was voluble and sometimes witty, but rather prone to accidents. On one occasion, leaving a restaurant, he attempted an exit in the grand manner. '*Au'voir, mes amis*,' he cried, and swept into a balletic pirouette which sprained his ankle, so that he had to be carried ignominiously out. Another time, with a hangover, he burst into a pub and demanded a glass of white wine. The barman mistakenly poured it from a bottle which contained a colourless furniture varnish. Deakin drank it in one gulp, and this time had to be carried to hospital. This constant rain of small accidents which fell always about him served to make him in some way rather lovable.

However, there was an ominous quality about it, too. Everyone connected with the shop seemed to become increasingly accident-prone. Archer mounted an exhibition of mobiles in the gallery. The largest one, which hung from the ceiling, was a kind of iron windmill. The night before the opening, David Wright, Ralph Abercrombie, and I went down to inspect it. 'Does it move?' inquired Wright, and pulled at one of the flanges. Not only did the windmill move, it spun round fiercely, and caught Ralph a sharp crack on the head, knocking him unconscious. Shortly after this, at the opening of a Bacon exhibition, a brass bolt from an overhead window became detached and plummeted down. It landed, of all likely places, on Ralph's head, and knocked him out once more. Deakin and he, both swaddled in bandages and plaster, sat commiserating with each other in the shop, like twin omens of doom.

Things were falling apart, and the centre, Archer that is, could not hold. Slowly the group of poets that frequented the shop dissolved. Michael Hastings went to America, Bernard Kops's play became successful, the others retired to work. Archer himself seemed to become more and more nervous, and started to disappear from the premises for long periods. In his absence, Ralph obviously needed an assistant. Archer, moved no doubt by motives of charity, employed a young painter who had just left a mental home. The painter, all his first day, dusted the books with a feather duster. He did this intently, and without reference to anything that went on round him. On the second day, having no more books to dust, he started to dust Archer. Archer fled. The painter dusted Ralph next, then K., and finally me. One by one, we followed Archer into the pub across the road. From the windows we peered nervously at the shop, and observed the entry of customers and, immediately afterwards, their rapid exit, pursued by the painter with the duster. Nobody knew quite what to do. At length Ralph telephoned the hospital from which the painter had so recently been discharged. That evening a van called, and took him away. But it seemed to take away more than a lunatic artist: it seemed, somehow, to carry with it the shop's last hopes of success.

In this doomed atmosphere, my relationship with K. opened up. After our visit to the cinema, I acquired enough courage to invite her to lunch, and these lunches became daily affairs. Eventually we started to have dinner together as well. In this way we passed nearly the whole day in each other's company. Sometimes I wondered what she hoped for in life, while all this went on, but I put this thought out of my mind. The qualities in K. which at first had deeply disturbed me now seemed to me noble and beautiful. She told me that she had had an unhappy childhood, and I felt deep pity for her. When, exuberantly, she threw bread at strangers in restaurants, I was rather gratified, since it proved she was now happy. Her insecurity made it impossible for her to allow herself not to be the centre of attention in any room, and I accepted this as well.

I realized that I was in love with K. Though my behaviour must have made this fairly obvious, I took pains not to actually declare my feelings. I did not aspire to share the pedestal on which I had placed her. She began to tell me how much she would miss me when I went up to Oxford. I knew I would miss her, too, and wished I didn't have to go.

But October was on me, and a few evenings before the start of the Oxford term, I took K. to dinner as usual. Afterwards, walking down the street towards the club, she suddenly turned to me, and with a curious, speculative look in her eye, said, 'I've got the keys to someone's flat. They're away. We could go there if you liked.' I had no idea what she meant. She explained, 'You could make love to me.' I was horrified. I had not really felt any definite sexual desire for K: only a romantic love which had set her on a pedestal, far from drawn curtains and beds. But I was very touched: it seemed to me that K. was willing to sacrifice herself to me because she knew I loved her. This generous gesture of hers I resolved to answer with one of my own: 'I couldn't possibly,' I said. She looked simultaneously annoyed and amused: then she shrugged her shoulders and said, 'Well, let's go and have a drink.'

The doomed quality of the shop not only continued, but increased. The day before I was due to leave for Oxford, K. became very ill, and it was discovered that she was one of the handful of people in the British Isles who had typhoid. She had contracted this through eating a bad oyster at lunch with me. If I had believed in portents, this would have made me think very hard. As it was, I half believed in them, and I felt a kind of apprehension: about K., about the shop, about my book. Archer was very worried:

the health authorities had called, and told him that the premises might have to be closed for the quarantine period. Through my worry about K., I found time to worry about him: he turned a pile of bills over ruefully, and said, 'Dear, dear. Dotty me, really, I shan't be able to pay these.'

I wondered silently about the book. With the intuitive quality he had, he said at once, 'The book will be all right, of course. I've paid the printers quite a lot already, then, you see. That's the most important thing, the book, and we'll see that it comes out.' He smiled his amazing smile. 'Don't worry. I'm sure it'll be a success.' I was reassured, but didn't want to leave him like this, surrounded by bills and problems. They were partly my fault, because he was publishing me: just as K., running a temperature in hospital, was my fault, because I had fed her the oyster which made her ill. Full of guilt and apprehension, I departed for Oxford.

10

… With a huge dry thumb
He shifts the bowl of ink
Towards me. 'Master, write.'
Now he is not here.
Slowly morning leaves me.
—'Craxton' from *Poems* (1955–1965)

The wind out of Hungary was like a thrown knife. Wrapped, a Sioux chieftain, in a blanket, I squatted on the tailboard of a lorry amongst my companions. We had nothing whatever in common except our presence here, but because of it a curious fraternity had developed between us: coming down the Neckar valley we had flooded ourselves with brandy and told each other our life stories. Now there was nothing left to say, and we were content not to say it: to smoke, share one of the bottles that was left, and look at the heavy, starless sky. The landscape around us was flat and porous, with occasional parked vehicles, each with its firefly clump of cigarettes. A couple of miles behind us was a village, and in front of us was the border, ragged outcrops of barbed wire through which, sometimes, the refugees came. Somewhere in the night was the October Oxford I had left, its pubs alive with people, the gasfires hissing in rooms where boys sat with books: but its walls that had penned me in had dissolved. Around me instead was the space that was Europe, laden with cathedrals, forests, and people, surrounded by seas which were in turn surrounded by the world. It was as though, wrapped in my blanket, I squatted at the heart of the world, my name and my body far away.

They had been too close to me in my few days at Oxford. The new wing of the college, where I was to live, was only half completed. Its stairway climbed through scaffolding, past cold washplaces that smelt of football socks. The windows of my top-floor rooms squinted down into an unkempt cemetery. Above the tombstones, small eyebrows of mist were raised in perpetual surprise at death.

The other freshmen in the new wing draped themselves in college scarves, adorned their mantelpieces with college shields, and applied themselves ardently to the pursuit of nurses from the local hospitals. The nurses were not difficult to entrap: the freshmen talked of their triumphs as we walked to the library through the cold city that smelt of stone, books, and water. 'Lovely crumpet,' they said, and rolled their eyes like ponies. 'Wait till you meet Madge.' Madge, Elizabeth, Jennifer, the names pined after me as frost decomposed on the library windows. Daily the trains clattered my sad letters up sixty endless miles to K. in hospital in London.

K. was far away, London was far away, and they were my reality: Oxford seemed unreal, and I felt this more deeply when the revolution in Hungary flared up. The newsposters waved fresh events at me each day, from the outside world sealed off by my new world of grey stone. Eventually I could bear it no longer. Relief lorries had started to leave for the frontier: I left with one of them. I consulted nobody, but packed a minimum of necessities, and went. In London I called on K. in hospital: she was over her typhoid, but had been ordered to stay in hospital. She was petulant and frustrated about this: sat up in bed, puffing fiercely at a Gauloise, and snapping at the friends who sat around her. To me, however, she was charming, and gratifyingly apprehensive about my safety on the frontier. 'Take care of yourself,' she said as I left, 'I should hate it if you were shot.' This made me feel as though I were on some sacred mission. I departed on it.

It had brought me here, to the edge of the wire beyond which lay the black impassable sea that was Hungary. Away in the darkness someone called birdlike, unseen. The French boy beside me cocked his head. 'Perhaps,' he said hopefully, 'something happens.' I suggested that we go and see. Absently clutching the bottle, Rainier wandered off towards the wire. I followed, stumbling in the frozen tussocks. We went a little way down the wire, and Rainier stopped and bristled, houndlike. '*Regarde,* a man,' he said. On the far side a swaddled dark shape detached itself from the darkness. 'A refugee.' 'Oh, no,' Rainier said, 'he is armed.' We stopped: the man came forward to the wire, his boots crackling the frost. I scraped a match into flame: he was a soldier, we saw his ghostly unshaven face in the faint glare of phosphorus. He addressed us hoarsely in a language neither of us knew. 'Take care,' Rainier muttered, 'we wish not to be shot, eh?' But the soldier pushed a thick hand between the wires, with two cigarettes fanned in the fingers. We accepted them: in the flame of my next match we saw his face once more. The light distorted his smile.

He squatted down on his side of the wire. So did we on ours. The three cigarettes glowed and waned, glowed and waned. Our mutual silence was impassable. Things we would have liked to ask or tell each other filled it: he was our enemy, we were his, but we had materialized to each other as human shapes, and the first instinct in all of us had been to communicate. I felt a more curious tenderness and pity for the humped smelly shape on the far side of the wire than for any refugee. I wanted to ask him about his family and his home: instead I passed him the brandy. We all had a drink. Afterwards he grunted and rose, shaking his heavy body: his thick hand came through the wire, and shook each of ours. It was hard and felt rather dirty. He made what I took to be a speech of thanks, turned, and crunched away through the frost into darkness. He became invisible. Where we sat it was terribly cold.

I returned to Oxford to find myself in trouble. Mr Christie, the principal, called me to his study. He was a very kind man; you could see it in his blue eyes, which were deeply worried about me, and hear it in the soft, academic inflections of his voice. 'You must never do that again,' he said. I promised I wouldn't: a rash promise.

The misty term folded me in once more. The university poets of the time called on me in my eyrie in the new wing. They were intense young men who all looked very much alike. Though they were followers of Leavis, and despisers of romanticism, one wore a cloak, another habitually drank Pernod, and a third smoked black Russian cigarettes. They gathered weekly in one another's rooms, where, surrounded by flasks of Spanish burgundy, they read their verse to each other, while sharp critical comments arrowed through the air. I attended one or two of these seminars, but didn't like them. Partly this was because everyone took it in turn to attack my work, in a strange peevish way that did not seem to me to do with criticism: partly it was because there was a smallness about it all, a doctrinaire regimentation of taste, which made such meetings pointless. These poets always spoke with particular distaste of two other university poets: Julian Mitchell and Peter Levi.

Julian Mitchell, however, wrote and asked me to have a drink. He lived in rooms at Wadham, bright rooms full of paintings, books, and invitations to parties. He was tall and fair-haired, with a fresh, ingenuous face, and an immense enthusiasm for the world which had filled itself with so many beautiful and exciting arts and people. This enthusiasm concealed a rather touching shyness and uncertainty about himself and his own work. But he was full of projects for magazines he wanted to start, films he wanted to produce, poems he wanted to write. In the fullness and excitement of his life he was the most alive person I had yet met at Oxford.

I did not feel Julian's real talent was for poetry, but I had no such doubts about Peter Levi, who was also there when I first called at Wadham for a drink. Peter was tall and very beautiful, with dark wings of hair stroked back from a pale and rather nervous face. He was a Jesuit novice: somehow his collar did not fit in with his jerky, rapid speech and movements, and the sudden enthusiasms he shared with Julian. He had the awkward grace of an antelope or a schoolboy. He would laugh a lot, then suddenly an extraordinarily frozen, remote expression would come to his face, as though he had just remembered original sin. The poems he wrote at this time had the same feel, both clumsy and graceful, as their creator: and a kind of transparency and clarity of eye, like that of an invalid.

Julian and Peter showed me what Oxford was about. We walked in the cold meadows, with Christ Church looming up behind us, mist adhering to it like wet linen: through echoing libraries and museums, with gowned dons rustling by: we sipped coffee in the Kemp, and beer in the Turf: and, incessantly, we talked. We talked about poetry, religion, sex, the usual subjects of the young: we talked all day, and into the night. We kept up a sort of guerrilla warfare with the Leavisite poets, who excluded us from their anthologies and magazines: 'When we have our magazine,' Julian said gaily, 'we'll keep them out of it.' This gaiety pervaded all our conversation: we would have sudden causeless bursts of hilarity: I was suddenly aware I was young.

More friends collected round us: Del Kolve, from my own college, an American Rhodes scholar; Patrick Garland, a poet and actor; and an American poet, Kenneth Pitchford. Pitchford was a stocky young fellow from the Middle West, who had studied creative writing under Theodore Roethke. Some of his poems were very fine, but he read them and spoke of them with a solemnity that made his friends feel rather mischievous. He was very suggestible: after his first stay in London, he returned to Oxford wearing a bowler and carrying an umbrella. After his first stay in Paris, less forgivably, he returned with a beard and a beret.

The beard was aesthetically very displeasing, and we all made unkind remarks about it. Very shortly, Pitchford lost it in a most uncanny way. He had developed a habit of walking in his college garden late at night, loudly reciting his own poems: and when thus occupied one midnight, disturbed an owl, which swooped from its nest and tore his beard out by the roots. He bore the scars for days afterwards, and was not comforted when Peter Levi reminded him that the owl was after all the guardian bird of poetry.

The gay and luminous surface of my friendships did not preclude a deep seriousness beneath. I was able to share my sadnesses and confusions with my friends in a way that I had never before done with people of my own age. This enabled me to forget my nostalgia for a Bohemian life in London: but it did not enable me to forget K.

During the Christmas vacations I took rooms in London. Almost every day I went to visit K. in hospital. She was by no means tranquil. She repelled the solicitude of her friends angrily. Her bitterness surprised me, but I felt sad for her, and certain she had been wronged by life, though I could not quite say how. I sent her constant flowers and books, and received a sharp letter from my bank.

Soho was much the same as ever, a mill of drinkers and talkers: it bored me a little now, and I did not frequent it as much as before, except to visit Archer. He sat in the lit and empty shop, surrounded by unsold books and unpaid bills, a tense look on his face. Ralph Abercrombie had left, and the coffee bar at the back was closed. The shop had failed, and to this Archer was resigned: but he had determined that my book must still be published, and in this fixity of purpose I saw once more his unique and remarkable personality. Daily, at his brisk stiff walk, the usual mass of newspapers and magazines wedged into his left armpit, he went down the road from the shop to talk to the printers. Publication was promised for the autumn. 'How I'll pay them,' Archer said ruefully, 'I don't know. But we'll manage somehow.' We occasionally lunched together, and he told me stories of his Parton Street shop, of how he had met, in turn, Dylan Thomas, George Barker, David Gascoyne, and Sydney Graham, and published them. 'Frankly, I never read a word they wrote. But I sensed then, you see, there was something about them… I sensed they were good.' I saw him as a dowser, waving a hazel wand not over water but over the brows of poets.

One day I inquired what Archer thought I should do about K. 'Er, well,' he said, turning slowly crimson, 'I don't really know, you know. It's difficult to say, isn't it? She is, er, a very lively girl, isn't she? You ought to bear that in mind, then, you see.' It transpired that he meant that K. had had a number of lovers. This saddened me, but I told myself that they had all obviously taken advantage of her trusting nature.

I saw her in hospital just before I left. I was the only visitor, and throughout the hour I was allowed, K. looked at me with brooding dark eyes alight in her pale beautiful face. She was unusually silent. As I rose to leave, she asked abruptly, 'Do you love me?' I answered, shakily, in the affirmative. 'I love you too,' she said. The oddity of such a remark at such a time did not strike me. I returned worried and elated to Oxford for the new term. That evening Julian dropped in for a drink, and I told him my problems. He was obviously deeply perplexed. 'I think you're very unwise,' he said. 'But certainly all you can do is wait till she's left hospital.'

A few days later Archer telephoned from London to say K. had left the hospital.

My second term at Oxford was buried in the deepest part of a dank winter. It was too cold to walk far, and at first I stayed in my room, trying to write, or to study for my prelims, due at the end of term. I could do neither, being obsessed with thoughts of K. I had no idea what I should do. I longed to be with her, but the complications in the way seemed insuperable. She was eight years older than I was, and I had very little money. When, as I was sometimes able to, I looked at my situation coldly and from a long way off, I saw myself as a rather foolish young man. But once K. had left hospital, I started to break my promise to my principal, and shot off to London for the day, without leave, once or twice a week, to see her and take her out to lunch. She seemed more beautiful than ever. At our lunches we held hands under the table, and an extraordinary intensity of feeling radiated between us, as though the separating air vibrated. Nothing else happened, however, for some time. When inevitably it did I was overcome with horror at myself, the monstrous seducer, and I fled to the shelter of Oxford like a child.

Term ended, and I debated with myself whether I shouldn't go abroad for the vacation. It would have been sensible, but I felt also that it was cowardly, and the pull of K. took me back to London, and our affair.

Soho swallowed me. K. had been a habitual denizen of the place since the age of seventeen, some eight years before. She knew the clubs and the restaurants, and moved through them like a queen, hailing her friends in the loud, deliberately affected voice which she seemed, like an actress, to assume for the public ear. With her, I surrendered whole days to alcohol, interspersed with occasional, expensive meals. I came to love the atmosphere of a pub at opening time: nobody there yet, the barmen discussing last night's incidents between yawns: the leathery taste of the first whisky, then suddenly a warmth of feeling that made one's mouth witty and alive. So one's mouth was ready for the acquaintances who came busily in, and one's ears ready for their wit, and one laughed and enjoyed oneself till, very late, it was time for lunch. Afterwards the upstairs club, where everyone was gay and happy, and made bawdy jokes: then bed.

This did not happen every day: even K. could not extricate herself that often from the demands of a normal life. But when she wasn't there I continued the routine by myself, because I was unhappy at her absence and because it was pleasurable. On days when she couldn't get away, she herself was unhappy: the next day she would tell me how unhappy. Everything she said I absorbed with pleasure, each remark she made a new shaft driven into her mind, opening it up to me.

One lunchtime I was with K. in a Soho pub when a previous lover of hers came in. He was very untidy, his eyes were haggard, and he went to the bar and bought a drink. K. and I sat on at our table, and K. began at once to talk rapidly in a loud insecure voice. The young man didn't look at us, but I looked intently at him. My unhappiness in the past few weeks, my worry which had been part of the unhappiness, seemed unreal before the bitter look in his eyes and mouth. Suddenly he swung from the bar, making a decision, and walked to our table. Before he could speak, K. said in a contemptuously friendly tone, 'Oh, piss off, darling.'

He stared at her with a bewildered and harassed look, as of someone whose debts have suddenly become too much for him to repay. Then he hit her, with an open palm, in the face. I was in the act of rising to intervene when he turned and hit me too. I sat down heavily. He had cut his hand on the glasses that littered the table, and bright thick blood dripped down into the bright thick splinters. I stared at this iridescence of glass and blood in a kind of trance, till the landlord of the pub came up and demanded that we all leave. Outside, in the street, I said to the young man, 'We'd better go somewhere and talk.' He stood with the thick blood falling from his hand into the pavement, looking dusty and hopeless, and said, 'Yes.' We went to another pub. The blood continued to leak vividly from his hand. I observed myself from a long way off as I left the pub, went to a chemist's, and bought antiseptic, lint, and plaster. I returned to the pub, and bandaged the hand of K.'s former lover, with a pallid and detached feeling that I was trying to repair a wound deeper than any that splinters could inflict.

The summer term had started. I came back to Oxford from Paris. I had gone there after a long talk with myself and with K. It was what I should have done before, I knew, and the knowledge made me more angry with myself, and guilty. This knowledge, however, did not damp my feeling for K., and when she wrote to me in Paris I replied. I did not see her when I came back to London, however, and when I reached Oxford once more, I was determined to change my life.

I had passed the prelims, which meant that I was sure of three clear years at Oxford. These years I meant to fill with work: but my own work, not the university's. I was not particularly interested in the study of English Literature, as my tutor, Reggie Alton, quickly discovered. The essays I did for him were full of involved metaphors and images, but utterly devoid of content: after I started one with the statement that Byron had been born with a silver spoon in his mouth, Pope with a wooden spoon, and went on to discuss the tactile differences between silver and wood, without further reference to the poets, Reggie surrendered. At all our subsequent tutorials, he flopped back in his armchair, puffing a cigarette, and looked wordlessly out of the window as I read my essays. From time to time he would eye me with a dry, amused, helpless air. We got on very well, however: he understood me.

Paradoxically, I was anxious to study Old English: I thought it might help me, as it had done Auden: but I found myself totally unable to learn it. This disappointed me, and disappointed my language tutor even more. However, my idea was to use the university, not let the university use me. My three years, free of responsibilities beyond the main responsibility to my poetry, were an ideal period, I thought, to polish and harden my tools, and extend my powers.

I discovered the joys of Oxford in summer. The golden stone fortresses where we lived were sunk in baths of light, through which sonorous bells sang: the quadrangles were of green velvet, with bright stiff flowers in rows by the walls. The river was stroked by punts and canoes, in which nubile young women lay in a petalled froth of skirts, like large dolls. Through all this my friends and I moved with a kind of urgency, as though we all knew it would not last.

Julian's magazine had started. It was supposed to be for Oxford and Cambridge, and was called *Gemini*: a glossy, handsome publication, financed by Willie Donaldson, as much an impresario when a Cambridge undergraduate, as he was later to be in London. The first issue contained poems by Sylvia Plath, Ken Pitchford, Peter, and myself, and went down very well: kind words were said about it in the London papers. Julian became very editorial and efficient: he rushed about the bookshops checking on distribution: he threw sherry parties. Then he handed the magazine over to me, and, in the same brisk, determined way, locked himself up for the last half of term to study for his finals, still a year away.

I got the second issue together, with the help of a few Cambridge writers. One of them was Andrew Sinclair, a tall young man, with a pleasant talkative face. He was working on a novel, and this seemed by his friends to be regarded as an amiable joke of his. 'Nobody,' one of them told me, 'can understand a word of it, not even Andrew.' This novel, *The Breaking of Bumbo,* when it appeared, was very successful, the first of a long sequence of books. Yet nobody would have suspected Andrew, at the time, of being a prospective professional: he sprawled about, laughed a lot, and did his best to appear inefficient. I myself saw the necessity of a mask, if I was to be a writer, and Oxford provided me with one. I now talked all the time, and was surprised to find I was sometimes fairly witty. I spoke with exaggerated irony and fantasy of people and poetry: the mask of the dandy behind the mask of the clown. From behind both masks I sometimes listened to my mouth talking with astonishment: a year or two before I would not have believed it capable of this shower of aphorisms and anecdotes. I had changed, I thought: but how? And was it for the better?

For better or worse, my mask, and my work, protected me from the thought of K. She still wrote to me, and I still replied, and was guilty because I did. I tried to put her out of my mind, but whenever I was not working or talking she haunted it. When Julian congratulated me on a lucky escape, I did not reply.

One afternoon Peter Levi organized a party. We punted upriver: sunshine fell through the trees on the leaf-coloured water. Peter took his collar off and rolled up his sleeves, revealing thin boyish arms: he dipped and swung the pole expertly, and drove us swiftly through the meadows. In one of them we lay under the trees, ate cold chicken and strawberries, drank chilled hock, and read out a play Peter had written. The afternoon was exquisite but somehow doomed: I felt we would not have many like this.

We punted back at twilight. When I came into college I found a message waiting for me. I was to phone a friend in London at once. Wondering, I did so. In a dead voice, he told me that K. had taken an overdose of sleeping tablets, and had been sent to hospital. 'You'd better come up,' said the dead voice on the telephone, 'as soon as you can.'

In the days that followed, trains spun me back and forth between Oxford and London. K. was discharged from hospital, and moved into a newly acquired flat. She came up to Oxford for a few days. It was splendid weather: I punted her on the river, and we lunched at the best hotels, and drank in my rooms or those of other people. I was anxious to show her off, and introduced her to all my friends. Her deliberately loud, carrying laughter, her constant flow of badinage, and her beauty seemed to fascinate them: none of them had ever met anyone like her before: they succumbed, they thought she was marvellous. K. blossomed in this atmosphere of adulation, and so did I, with her. We planned to marry when we were able. I was wonderfully happy, with a feeling that all problems had been solved.

But this idyllic quality, had I only known it at the time, applies by its very nature only to the start of any affair. The time comes when the beloved person ceases to be a symbol, and becomes a reality. Nobody is perfect in reality: this is the fallacy behind all romantic love. K. was not perfect, and neither was I. I soon found that she was very touchy: she looked for hidden implications in what I said: sometimes a casual remark from me would draw a sudden spurt of reaction from her. In many ways I was reasonably mature, but in one way I was not: I had never had to do with another person on so intimate a level, and I couldn't reassure K. as she needed to be reassured. In fact, when she saw some veiled insult in one of my remarks, when she said angrily that I really wanted to be rid of her, I tended to become abstracted, to withdraw into myself, wondering solemnly if what she said was true. It seems a little comic, looked at from far away, but wasn't at the time for I would be confronted then, suddenly, by a hostile person, not the person I knew, a person whose emotions were bared with a nakedness that appalled me. Her anger made her voice shrill, and mine uncertain. All this brought terrible images to my mind: this naked hostile emotion, to me, was associated only with my mother. The realization of these images shocked me, so that as when a child I withdrew still farther into myself, increasing her despairing, somehow sad violence of behaviour. At this early point in our relationship these quarrels were soon made up. 'It was my fault,' I would say, and K. would say, 'No, mine, I had an unhappy childhood.' These phrases were to toll like funeral bells throughout our relationship.

In the clamours and frenzies of this last half of the summer term, my concern for my work became extreme. It seemed that I never had any time in which to write. The dedication verse required had been split by circumstances. Words were suddenly brittle, and fell apart at my touch. In this difficulty of spirit my friends could not really help me: they had their own problems as writers: as yet, they were all still unsure. Julian had tired of studying for his finals, and reappeared bouncily upon the scene at the end of term. He told me he had decided to write fiction, and showed me several short stories which I thought brilliant. But he himself was hesitant about them. 'I haven't done what I wanted to do,' he said. Then, gaily, 'I will next time.' Peter wrote poetry all the while, but showed it to me indecisively. 'I don't really like it myself. But next time…' Their certainty of a next time shamed me: I myself felt a nerveless quality in my hand, and a space in my head which was no longer populated.

But I had one pillar to lean on, and strangely, it was my boyhood hero, Auden. He came to Oxford that summer as professor of poetry, and lodged in rooms in the Christ Church annexe in Brewer Street. Here I visited him on the first day of term, when I was still working well. I knew a numbers of poets by now, but the old awe still stayed with me: I came into the room as into church. It was a strangely bare room, and the curtains were drawn on the sunshine, so it was sepulchral as well. A heap of books on a table, a drink tray, and on the desk a litter of manuscripts, were the only tokens of life, apart from Auden himself, who surged up from a chair, grunting. He was a large, heavy man; his ridged, tousled head had not only, like most people's, a history, but a geography: there were mountains, rivers, and valleys in his face, which seemed made of whitish clay. However, it was a kindly landscape, something in the wry turn of the mouth and downward look of the eyes was benevolent. His gruff Oxford voice was rather incongruously spattered with flat American vowels: this gave it a somewhat hypnotic effect. There was a surprising delicacy about his hands.

On this first encounter, he delighted me by saying he liked

my poems. I showed him some new ones, which he fanned out on his knee, dropping ash over them as he peered at the words. His criticism, when it came, was the best I had ever had. He did not seem to believe, as most critics do, that a poem should or shouldn't be written in a certain way: he took it as it was, as a shaped object, and told one where it was misshapen. That he did this was to me in itself a compliment.

After this we met fairly frequently. He told me to call whenever I felt like it, but I did not like to do this more than once a week. However, I bumped into him now and then at the pub behind the New Theatre: and at three o'clock every afternoon, he set off from his rooms, red slippers flapping, and sometimes a demure white twist of shirt-tail fluttering under his coat, for a teashop in St Giles, where he said the only good coffee in Oxford was obtainable. Here, he made it known, he was available to any undergraduate who wished to show him verse. Every afternoon, in consequence, the place was packed by Somerville poetesses clutching folders full of sonnets about unrequited love in delicate, sticky fingers. They stared at Auden from afar, but seldom dared to approach him. When they did, he was unfailingly courteous.

He made none of the remarks most poets make about The Poet: he simply flumped down in his armchair in Brewer Street or his seat in the tearoom and was a poet: he filled crossword puzzles in with rapid fingers, the snowfall of papers on his desk deepened daily: he was always at work with words. He was sharp about their misuse. I showed him a poem once with a line about women swaying their long hair, like trees. 'That won't do,' he said crossly. 'It won't do at all. You can have trees swaying their long hair, or women swaying their long hair, but one swaying its long hair like the other won't do. No.' And he pencilled the image out. Another time, pointing to a line, he said, 'This is very good. It's your best line for a long time.' The line was, 'They fled in greatcoats to the night,' very much, I thought ruefully, like a line from an early Auden poem.

When I dried up, midway through the term, the very idea of Auden comforted me. I had the sense that he must have been through all this, and now stood solid on the far side. I went to him for advice. As usual, in the dark, bare room with its litter of papers, he offered me a gin-and-French, and asked me what the matter was. I told him, while he grunted, lowered his head, and rubbed a finger down the velvet arm of the chair. Finally, he said, 'It's not more than a few days since you haven't written any verse. Some people,' with his deep heaving chuckle, 'some people don't write for several years.' Put like this, my predicament seemed ridiculous. However, I plunged on to say I felt I would never write again. 'You'll get over it,' Auden grunted. I was silent. Then he looked up very kindly, like a veteran doctor prescribing for a hypochondriac, and said, 'Try translating a few poems. That might help.' Next day he called on me with an armful of folders. He had been asked, he said, to choose the best of some twenty volumes of verse submitted for a prize. He hadn't the time to read them. Would I do so, place them in order of merit, and write a short report on each?

In a youthful violence of emotion, I seemed to myself at this time finished as a poet, dead wood in which nobody could trust. To me, therefore, Auden's willingness to rely on my taste seemed a declaration of faith in me. It probably wasn't, but it comforted me at a trying time.

At the end of term I went to see him, and told him I had still written nothing. He gave me a kind but rather weary stare, and said, 'Perhaps you ought to be in love.'

'But I am.'

'Then it's the wrong person,' said Auden shortly.

The summer vacation started with a dark omen. Peter Levi, flourishing his famous stick as he came over Boar's Hill, was hit by a car, and dragged for some distance. He was sent to hospital with concussion: though his injuries weren't serious, they shadowed the end of term. Under this shadow, tilted into midsummer, I returned to London to live with K.

The pattern of my London life remained the same. Daily K. and I went into Soho. We always drank, and lunched, in the same places. Daily we saw the same people. Many of them were chronically without money, and much of their conversation was devoted to a discussion of whom they could next borrow from, or who could be persuaded to invite them to lunch. The gay and cynical manner in which such remarks were made struck me, at the time, as Bohemian and highly romantic: though even then I was aware of a kind of uneasiness that underlay it all. I had been taught that punctuality and courtesy were virtues: in Soho I unlearnt this: there it was thought smart to be neither courteous nor punctual.

In domestic life, too, my habits altered. I had always had a great feeling for ritual in my life. Each day was ordered, and its centre was my work. In the mornings I had been used to lay out my implements on my desk: pen, pencil, typewriter, paper: each in a fixed relation to each other, a fixed distance between them. Now, since I seemed unable to write, the other rituals fell away. My days became shapeless, unplanned, leading nowhere except to chance encounters and late parties.

My relationship with K. entered a new phase. I had always been rather silent: I liked to be alone as much as possible. I felt that in our life together, K. should accept this in me. She didn't. She needed to be reassured that she was loved by constant conversation and constant company. At first I was touched by this, and attempted to accommodate myself to her needs. But then romantic love suffered another knock. I found out how selfish I was. I was very aware of myself: the sound of my own voice, unwillingly emitted, became paralysingly familiar to me. As though another person, I found my inflections, my intonations, my very phrases, more and more predictable, more and more of a bore: thus, standing away from myself, I could see how forced and false many of my remarks to K. sounded, when, in a silent mood, I was compelled by her to talk. She was sensitive to it too: and her need for reassurance forced her into more furies. Perhaps these were meant to provoke some genuine reaction from me. They did; they drove me further into myself, and this made K. worse. However, I stayed in love with her. Partly this was physical, and partly it was that I had initially plunged myself so wholly into our affair. Worry prevented me from work: most days I washed it all away in whisky, and suffered from a perennial crapula.

During these expensive and painful ablutions, I noticed something that disquieted me. K. was insecure about many things, but not about her physical attraction. When she swept into a party, the heads of the men turned: they stared. Soon, in the centre of the room, K. stood with her drink, throwing back her long hair, laughing a throaty laugh, entirely surrounded by admirers. This made me furious; ironically, it also brought me closer to her, in that I didn't want to lose her.

Meanwhile, my account at the bank was rapidly emptying itself. The Soho days were expensive, and on top of it all were my Oxford bills. I started a rapid landslide into debt. When I considered that all this was my father's money, I felt confused and perplexed, but I tried not to consider it, and generally I succeeded.

There were the good times too: moments when everyone in the bar with us was suddenly funny and sweet: moments when we visited friends in the country, and K., in sweater and slacks, tramping down muddy lanes, loudly sang comic songs, and was unaffected and childlike. These moments were still frequent in our relationship, and at each of them a great sweetness flowed into me, and made me happy.

Archer's bookshop had finally closed. He had let the main floor to an agency, and retreated into the basement, which was now piled high with books and bills. At the end of September, shortly before the Oxford term was due to start, the clutter in the basement was added to by the arrival of numerous crates which contained copies of my book. It was the first time I had seen it. I turned a copy to and fro in my hands, opened it, looked at the poems which I knew like children. They seemed to belong to another part of my life. But the book looked handsome, and the poems stood well on the page, and turning it over in my hands I felt once more the flutter of power, the knowledge that I was a poet.

Archer flapped round over the books, with the air of a hen who has at long last produced an egg. He was even more proud of them than I was. He took an armful out with him, and distributed them, free, through the Soho pubs. At this time it seemed likely that this would be the only way anyone would ever read them, for there was no distribution organized. I was determined, however, that the book should be known. Archer and I, scrabbling on our knees in the basement in a thicket of brown paper and sellotape, sent off review copies: then, grimly, and with a briefcase full of copies, I tramped round London trying to persuade bookshops to accept them. This was a much harder task than I had imagined; several bookshops refused to stock them at all, even on sale or return; their shelves were already crowded, they said, and anyway poetry didn't sell.

When I had placed as many books as possible, I waited for the reviews. I opened the weeklies and the Sunday papers with trembling hands: but for days nothing appeared. Then, the week before I was due to return to Oxford, Edwin Muir reviewed the book in the *New Statesman,* and gave it high praise. Other favourable reviews followed. The book, after all the difficulties and the setbacks, was a success. I went to lunch with Stephen, and he smiled hugely, as though he were as pleased as I. 'I told you so,' he said.

My second year at Oxford started as the first had done, with wreaths of mist on the trees, and the gasfire hissing busily in the common room. I had been allotted new quarters: handsome white-painted rooms in the second quadrangle, which were said to have been occupied by Lawrence of Arabia. Occasionally, therefore, American visitors called, and asked to look round. On one of the stone windowsills there was a deep hollow. I informed the Americans that this was a hollow worn by Lawrence's elbow as he leant on the sill, day after day, staring fixedly at the view outside. They did not seem to believe me, though the window looked directly over the men's public lavatory in Market Street.

The rooms apart, everything was the same: Julian bounded in, flushed with autumn, to show me some new short stories. 'I'm writing a novel,' he said. I felt a little bitter that I had no new poems to show him. But he congratulated me on the success of my book, full of pleasure for me, and I thought that at least there was something I had done. Later Peter called: he had recovered from his accident, but still looked pale and unwell: it suited him in a way: 'Come beagling,' he said. So early next day I went with him to the woods outside Oxford, and there we watched the fighting and yapping dogs and the gaitered county people who owned them stream away through the cobwebbed misty trees. Peter and I walked leisurely after. He pointed with his stick at late flowers, called on me to admire the effect of a yellow disc of sun apparently entangled in naked branches, and discussed the habits of the hare. In this way we came through fields and woods, or splashed across icy brooks which rang like little bells. Ahead of us travelled the faint yapping of the dogs, and we glimpsed them now and then on the horizon. In this quiet relationship with my friend, which took less and gave more than my relationship with K., I felt completely peaceful, completely confident. Eventually, from the brow of a small hill, we looked down into a sudden sea of mist, on which, racing and reflected, shone the small gold disc of the sun. 'That's the kind of view,' Peter said a little breathlessly, 'which you and I will still be reminding each other of in twenty years.' I had lived so much in the moment of late that I had almost forgotten that there was a future: but Peter's words reminded me that it lay there, like the mist, unprospected and possibly hopeful. And looking at his pale meditative face I thought, yes, that is one thing I've achieved, in twenty years we shall still be friends.

11

> The last betrayal.
> The weather, winter.
> I left my trial.
>
> —'Song about the Usual Subject' from
> *Poems* (1955–1965)

The new scholastic year brought new people to Oxford. Amongst them were two poets. John Fuller was young and dark, with thick curly hair and a remarkably sweet expression. He was not shy, exactly, but entirely silent: one could spend a day with him, and scarcely hear him speak. By contrast his verse was crisp and ironic, filled with images like those of a brilliant child. At first I only saw John by himself, or with occasional friends from his college: later he began to appear with a beautiful undergraduate, Prue, whom he eventually married. They were rather disquieting, together: they sat with entwined hands, looking dreamily at each other, in total silence, wherever they were, and whoever they were with. This absolute happiness they found in each other caused much amused comment from their friends: but I think most of us were envious. In his silent way, John did a lot of work: university work, and his own work, which included several films where Prue starred.

The other poet was Quentin Stevenson. He had already obtained his degree, but had come back to do research. Quentin had had a volume of verse published, and was highly thought of by Edith Sitwell; he occasionally disappeared to London to lunch with her at her club. Very tall, very handsome, with fair hair and ice-blue eyes, he stalked about with an aloof air, which disappeared when he met a friend: then his face suddenly broke into an enormous, affectionate smile, and in a high and elegant voice, with lofty waves of the hand, he would tell one all about his latest work. Some of his work was extremely fine: he had one of the best ears of any poet I have ever met, and when he declaimed his verse, it rang superbly.

Another arrival at the university was an Indian writer, Ved Mehta. Ved had been blind since he was three: he had been sent to a blind school in America, and from there gone up to Harvard. His autobiography had been published in America, and had had a great success. Ved was stocky and dapper, dressed always in suits of excellent cut. His closed eyes and slow, deliberate movements gave him a sleepy air which misled those who met him for the first time: he was in fact exceptionally acute, reacting and observing always, and had a rather waspish line in wit. He led a different life from that of any other university writer in that he had a secretary, and attended club dinners frequently, resplendent in evening dress.

He intensely disliked people who tried to help him. Anyone who took his arm to assist him across the street was likely to be roughly shaken off, and thereafter, Ved would muse aloud about the solicitous person: 'He may be all right in some ways,' he would murmur, 'but there's something about him I don't like.' This independence led him into fantastic feats. Outside his college was a precipitous drainpipe that snaked past the window of his rooms: when, after a party, the gate was locked, he would ascend the drainpipe like Sir Edmund Hillary, and swing himself from it through the window like Tarzan of the Apes. Nobody who was able to see this drainpipe was ever foolhardy enough to follow Ved, but he himself never slipped or fell.

My relationship with him was a little different from my relationship with my other friends. This was because he was also

Indian, and he was much more Indian than I was. Though he had spent his whole adult life in America, he thought of India as his country, while I already thought of England as mine. He spoke Hindi fluently, and he intended to return to India and live there: he had roots in its soil. I didn't. In our relationship was a shared secret, the secret of the country seven thousand miles away, which none of our other friends had ever seen. Ved often spoke to me of his childhood: less often, I spoke to him of mine.

K. now worked as a secretary in London, which meant she was only free at weekends. Every weekend, therefore, I raced down to London to see her. This led to a good deal of trouble. Undergraduates who lived in college were supposed to sleep there: it was obvious, on certain nights, that I didn't. I had a series of difficult interviews with Mr Christie, and finally the Fellows of the College met to decide whether or not they should send me down. Not only was I constantly absent without leave, but my work was very poor. That they did not send me down was due to Mr Christie: he reminded the meeting, I was told by someone who was there, that University College had had to raise a marble monument to Shelley, to atone for sending him down, and that Jesus, a poor college, would not be able to afford such atonement for me.

So, precariously, I stayed on at Oxford. The precarious quality of my stay was in a way the least of my worries. My whole life so far had been conditioned to the idea that there was always money about, lots of money, to pay bills and entertain oneself with. But now there wasn't: what with K. and bills in London and Oxford, and overdrafts which I couldn't understand, I had very little money to play with, and it became less every day.

Now, looking back, I realize that in this, as in most other respects, I was too young for K. She was accustomed to men who had money, or could make it. Apart from my poems, I had then no means of earning money whatever. She seemed to look on my inability to take her out to dinner, or to pay a bill for the house, as a further proof of my lack of love. So I became silent and evasive. Trying to avert scenes, I fabricated imaginary sums, due shortly to arrive and settle all the bills. When these did not arrive, the scenes did, and were naturally worse than ever. During every such scene, the image of my mother came between us. I felt trapped in my own childhood, and in my dreams K. and my mother often turned into each other.

By this time I think K. realized, as I did, the magnitude of the mistake we had made. Our life together was almost that of enemies: neither of us trusted the other, and our mutual tensions, briefly released in bed, flared once more at dawn. Then, often, I wanted to break out of the trap I had constructed, and return to the work that had abandoned me. But a terrible invisible knot of pride held us together.

K. had, I now realize, many admirable qualities: she was brave, honest, and loyal to her friends. She was sometimes very perceptive, though her ideas were not thought out but felt. I think now that probably we could have been friends: the fatal mistake was for us to become sexually involved. We were too different as individuals to live successfully together. But at that moment we were locked together too violently for release, like fighting hawks that fall, claws fastened in each other's flesh, in a long slow spin, with the ignored reality of the earth banking itself below.

In the Easter vacation, K. and I went to Paris. The Paris I liked to prowl was a city where nobody knew me, but this was not K.'s idea. She preferred to spend the morning at the Deux Magots, have lunch at Lipp's, and then spend the afternoon in the Flore. Here there were always numbers of English people whom she had met at one time or another. In a way it was as bourgeois a method of visiting Paris as to visit it with a coachload of people from your own provincial town, but K. did not see this, and it seemed to me a lovable and childish illusion of hers.

On our first morning, sitting in the Deux Magots with K., I suddenly saw two unkempt and unshaven young men bounding towards us, and recognized one of them as Allen Ginsberg, the American beat poet, whom I had met briefly in London a few weeks before. Ginsberg's face had not at that time assumed the considerable quantity of foliage which was later to enshroud it. It was a sad, intelligent face, with large eyes that stared through thick spectacles. His companion was Gregory Corso, the other leading beat poet, a stocky yet faunlike young man with a wild look and an incessant flow of conversation. They sat down with us, and Corso asked K., 'Would you like to ball with me, baby?' There was no surer way to K.'s heart. She declined with a small, secretive, pleased smile, and at once exerted herself to be charming. Ginsberg and Corso seemed oblivious to these efforts: Ginsberg fixed me with a sad stare and demanded to know my views on God, man, and poetry. When I was slow to answer, he told me his, in a rapid and hypnotized voice, at great length, then fell into a deep silence, head bent and hands locked between his knees. Corso meanwhile described his experience of communicating with God as he watched a corpse being fished out of the Seine. Eventually they left, and invited us to breakfast next day in their hotel in Rue Git-le-coquer.

We went. Ginsberg and Corso lived in an attic at the top of the hotel, which they shared with William Burroughs, the novelist, author of *The Naked Lunch.* The attic contained three pallet beds, and a quantity of beat literature, stored away in suitcases which contained nothing else. Ginsberg and Corso scattered this literature over one of the beds, and advised me to read it, while Burroughs, a tall, angular man with a grey face, rolled up his trousers and showed K. the network of needle marks that covered his legs. When a pigeon moaned at the window, he hastily rolled his trousers down, and said in a quiet flat voice, 'Birds, I hate birds.' 'Cheeping, beaking birds,' cried Corso, springing to the sill. 'Fly away, bird!' The bird departed lazily into the March sunshine.

There was no sign of breakfast, but eventually Corso produced a sack from under the bed, fished some marijuana out of it, and proceeded to roll us all cigarettes. He showed me the way to smoke mine (K., I noticed, seemed already to know how) and the room filled slowly with sweet acrid smoke. My cigarette had no effect on me whatever, but it seemed to inflame Ginsberg and Corso. They dragged us off to a rendezvous with the painter Larry Rivers. Rivers had a young American woman with him, and they leapt at her, suggesting that we all strip and make love on the pavement. 'Like William Blake and the angels, man,' cried Corso. The girl became very upset and burst into tears, and the poets were much concerned, petting her with repentant hands, and offering her poems and candy which Corso pulled from his pockets.

After that we spent a lot of time with Ginsberg and Corso. I came to like them both very much. Corso had immense charm, the charm of a wicked schoolboy, which he used very consciously. Both Ginsberg and he talked the beat dialect which was later commonly employed by adolescents everywhere, but was then totally new to me. Ginsberg himself was very serious, and given to long silences; though some of his statements seemed absurd, they were absurd in a consistent, rather beautiful way. He told me, for instance, that in his poem, 'Howl', he had invented a new kind of prosody, undreamt of before: and that he had had a vision of William Blake in his apartment in Harlem. I inquired what Blake had worn to the interview. 'Oh, like a toga, man,' Ginsberg said, 'the kind of clothes all the people wore in those days.' He also told me of his first encounter with Corso. 'Gregory was just out of prison,' said Ginsberg reverently, 'and one day I went into this bar in Greenwich Village and he was sitting at a table. He was beating it with his fist like, and shouting out that he was a great poet. So of course I knew at once that he was a great poet.'

And they were both poets: neither could have been anything else. Their methods were far from mine: they believed in verbal extravagance and visions; I didn't, but I respected their beliefs.

Also I admired some of their work. I invited them to visit Oxford in the summer, and to read there.

I had hoped that Paris, the new air, the new people, would help K. and myself to repair our own relationship. There were gentle, civilized evenings with the Greek poet Nanos Valaoritis and the American novelist Theodora Keogh: but there were also periods when both K. and I drank heavily, and in these periods bitterness broke out in us both. It was as though we were not only closely intimate, but also total strangers: we wounded each other with every action, and we knew how to wound each other most deeply. After one violent scene I sat on the bed of the hotel room, which seemed now like a cell in which we were locked together. It was curiously dreamlike: the image of the cell came out of one of my dreams. K., standing across the room, said bitterly, 'I suppose now you'll want to leave me.' 'Anyone who behaves as you do,' I said, 'deserves to be left.' She was silent, and when I looked up I saw with amazement and a sudden sort of tenderness that soundless tears were pouring down her face.

The summer term came. I returned to Oxford with some relief: the stresses of life with K. had worn me out. I now had nightmares of our life together, going on in endless circles forever, and in my waking moments could still find no way out of this nightmare to which guilt and responsibility had fastened me. As often before, I told Julian about my troubles: but he was no longer the gay companion of earlier days: his finals were at the end of term, he was methodically working for them, and simultaneously on his stories. He seemed to sense the direction and flow of his life in a way that I couldn't. It seemed to me that at the start of Oxford I had been older in spirit than most of my friends, but that I had stayed the same, while they advanced, and were now older than I was. 'Honestly,' Julian said testily, 'you'll have to make a decision some time.' 'I know,' I said humbly, like a rebuked child.

As summer put flowers back in the college quadrangles, Ginsberg and Corso announced their impending arrival. I went up to London to collect them, having previously arranged readings at my own college, at New College, and at a couple of other places. I was astonished to find them in the care of Archer. 'Oh well then, you see,' Archer explained, when they were out of the room, 'I was introduced to them at a party. Charming chaps, what? And really talented, I think, too… I can sense it…' and he waved a vague hand into the air.

They were exactly the same as in Paris: Allen Ginsberg mostly remote and dreamy, with bursts of volubility; Corso mostly voluble, with spells of silence. England, to him, was the home of his heroes, Chatterton, Blake, and Shelley, and Shelley's particular home to him was Oxford. He made me promise to show him Shelley's statue at University College, and perhaps then help him to find Shelley's rooms.

On the train going up, in a spirit of anticipation, the poets rolled marijuana cigarettes and proceeded to smoke them. The compartment filled with a distinctively odorous smoke. Fortunately we were the only occupants, but then, to my horror, the ticket collector arrived. Smoke billowed back at him as he opened the door, and he sniffed it with a faintly puzzled air on his large ruddy face. 'Funny smell,' he observed. 'American cigarettes,' I explained hastily. 'These gentlemen are from America.' The ticket collector observed, 'I've never smoked one of them American cigarettes.' 'Try one,' invited Gregory, and ignoring my frantic gestures of appeal, presented him with a fresh marijuana cigarette. 'Thanks very much,' said the ticket collector, and, dubiously sucking at this novel kind of nicotine, he moved on.

On our arrival at Oxford, a reception committee consisting of Peter Levi, Quentin Stevenson, and Del Kolve met us. The reading at my college was scheduled for that evening. Del informed me, to my horror, that Mr Christie wished to be present. It was too late to do much about it. I placed him on the platform, between Allen and Gregory, and left the rest to providence. At first providence did very well: Allen read 'Howl' in a fierce apocalyptic shout, then Gregory read some lyrical poems. Mr Christie bent his silver head and listened attentively, tall body stooped forward: though this was not his kind of poetry, he seemed struck by some of it. At last, however, Allen stood up to read his final poem. It was a poem about flying over Kansas, and ended with the poet looking down and thinking of 'all the people fucking down below'. As Ginsberg roared out this climactic line, Mr Christie's head jerked up, and a very strange expression came into his face. Allen misread the expression as one of approbation, 'Isn't that what you think of in an aeroplane, man?' he demanded of my principal. 'Don't you look down and think of all the people fucking down below?'

Our tripper's tour round Oxford was crowded with similar difficulties. I took Gregory to look at Shelley lying obscene in white marble at University College. He inquired if he was allowed to kiss the statue's foot. I said probably not. He then demanded where Shelley's rooms were. I had not the faintest idea, but indicated the nearest door. I hadn't dreamt that he would want to enter, but he did: he flung open the door and crawled over the carpet, kissing it reverently, inch by inch, while its occupant, who, prior to his arrival, had been making tea, stared at him in dumbfounded silence.

Later the visitors demanded to see Auden. Auden had specifically forbidden me to bring any beat poet anywhere near him, but they had found out where he lived from someone else, and since I could not prevent the visit, I went on it too. Auden, though surprised, was very tolerant. He either ignored Allen's remarks on prosody, or received them with noncommittal grunts. He then offered to show the beats round Christ Church Cathedral, and did so. At the end both Allen and Gregory turned to him with tears in their eyes. This, they said, was the high spot of their visit to Oxford: they would never forget how a great poet had shown them round a cathedral. They knelt and attempted to kiss the hem of Auden's garments: the turn-ups of his trousers, to be exact. Auden hastily stepped out of reach, gruffly said his goodbyes, and departed. Allen and Gregory got up and dusted their knees. 'That was a drag,' said Gregory. 'Man, we went right round this church with a guidebook yesterday.' This curious mixture of true innocence combined with a sharp eye for the main chance was very attractive. Somehow everybody took to the visitors. Sometimes the reaction was extreme. Peter Levi, in a forgetful moment, wrote a poem in which he described a walk on which Corso had walked on one side of him and Ginsberg on the other. It was as though, he said in the poem, he walked between Truth and Beauty. I could never work out which was which. Quentin, usually unexcitable, started to describe 'Howl' as one of the great poems of the century. We took the poets punting: they smoked marijuana as we eddied over green, scumbled water, in which trees trailed their arms. As we passed under Magdalen Bridge, amidst liquid shadows, the boom of a bell came to us through the yellow stone overhead. Gregory said in a childish, wistful way, 'I wish I'd been to school here.'

They stayed for several days. During their stay Edith Sitwell arrived in Oxford to read at the Town Hall. Quentin took Allen and Gregory and myself to the rehearsal. A large John Piper screen had been set up on the platform: to it, presently, came Dame Edith, in a long sibilant dress, on which dark, heavy necklaces faintly swung and clashed. She looked frail, but very queenly, and offered us her hand like a holy relic. Allen, however, was unimpressed: he told her that he was editing an anthology of verse illustrated with photographs of the poets in the nude, and asked her if she would like to contribute. Fortunately, Dame Edith took this very well, and declined in the most courteous way. She also rejected an offer of marijuana from Gregory because, she said, it made her feel ill. I thought she had the best manners of anyone I had ever met.

Later, however, when in her customary fashion, she had retired behind the Piper screen, and was moaning effectively behind it, things changed: the screen was not properly attached, it was swaying about, and she demanded to know why this was so. She demanded it once only, but the tone of her voice set people into manic activity. It was no use: eventually several bystanders, including Allen and Gregory, were commanded to hold the screen steady at each end. Dame Edith resumed: but barely a minute had passed when, unexpectedly, the screen tilted forward and fell with a resounding crash, hurling its supporters in all directions. The only ones undamaged were Allen and Gregory, who stood back with curious little smiles as Dame Edith rose on the now naked stage and demanded in outraged tones: 'What is the matter, pray?' Her voice brought all the bruised and dolorous bodies lying around her to their feet, and forgetful of their own sorrows, they rushed to reassure the great poetess. Later Quentin said thoughtfully to me, 'Someone *pushed* that screen, you know.'

Things became more frantic towards the end of the poets' visit. Even then, in 1958, they had numerous English supporters and imitators, and these flocked to Oxford when they heard that their heroes were there. The New College reading was a disaster, largely because it was invaded by numbers of them. The hosts, the college poetry society, were understandably exasperated by this. One hairy young man with large, bare, smelly feet ambled in and stretched himself out on a sofa. There he rolled a marijuana cigarette. The ceiling of the room was very low, and to the astonishment of everyone else present, the young man placed a match between his knobbly toes, struck it on the ceiling with a careless sweep of the foot, and lit his cigarette.

Quite apart from the uninvited hordes, the reading itself was not a success; I had forgotten to advise Allen and Gregory that New College was a stronghold of the CND. When Gregory began to read a poem about the aesthetic pleasures of a nuclear explosion, his hosts were outraged. There was a great deal of heckling, and finally the New College poetry society, led by Stephen Hugh-Jones, the editor of *Isis,* took off their shoes and threw them at the poets. Allen and Gregory packed up their poems and left. They were tightlipped and silent, with hurt eyes, like children who have been chastised for the first time. Peter Levi and I, indulgent nannies, nursed them out of their hurt, and the night, their last in Oxford, ended in riotous laughter. I never saw Ginsberg again, but Gregory and I met frequently over the years, in London, Athens, and Paris. Last time I saw him he was lying on a bed in a large empty room in the Plaka, saying bitterly, 'Allen's off on this holy kick, and I'm finished with the beat stuff. When I tell people I'm not a beat, I'm a poet, they don't believe me. They don't believe I've grown up.' He shook his head uncomprehendingly, and turned it away.

Towards the end of term I received a letter from Lord David Cecil. I did not know him well. I had met him occasionally, floating down the summer streets in a white suit and a straw boater from which ribbons fluttered. His remarks to me, delivered in a very rapid, lisping voice which I could hardly follow, were normally about the weather. I did not think that he was even aware I wrote verse. I was very surprised, therefore, when his letter informed me that he was one of the judges of the Hawthornden Prize, and that it had been awarded to my book.

Immediately clouds of reporters and television cameras floated up to me from London. A literary prize is not usually the occasion for such a concentration of publicity, but there were several reasons for this. Firstly, the Hawthornden had not been awarded since the war. Secondly, I was the youngest person ever to win it, and the first non-English writer. Thirdly, the most important, there was a shortage of news that month.

So I found my face and the details of my life blazoned over the newspapers, and appeared for the first time before television cameras, incoherently answering questions about poetry. My reaction to this was dual: my ego, stroked and fed, expanded, and made me forget that I had not in fact written anything for a considerable time; simultaneously, I knew in my bones that this was a dangerous thing to have happened. The atmosphere of youthful genius that was building up round me was not an atmosphere in which I could get back to my work. I had wanted my poems to be known, and the award of the prize assured that they were: but I had not wanted them to be so publicized, so praised by reporters who knew nothing about verse. Poetry was not a matter to be touched by this sort of publicity.

The actual presentation of the prize was midway through the summer vacation. K. and I lunched at the Ritz with the judges, and during lunch she was all smiles. Afterwards we went to the ceremony. Lord David, Veronica Wedgwood, and L.P. Hartley, three of the judges, sat on the platform with Mrs Pandit, the Indian high commissioner, and Lord David made a speech. He alluded to the honour done to us all by the presence of Mrs Pandit, and indicated Miss Wedgwood with a graceful flutter of the hand then he praised the work of Miss Wedgwood, and bowed courteously to Mrs Pandit. After a few references to the rapturous irony of my verse, he finished, and I trotted up to the platform, and received my cheque and medal.

Later, as we were all drinking tea, an unknown man approached me. He congratulated me on the prize, and then announced that he had news that would please me even more. 'I am in a position to say,' he told me, 'that Her Majesty the Queen has read your book of poems and that she was graciously pleased with it.'

That evening K. and I threw a party. It was a great success. Stephen said, grinning a little maliciously, 'You'll be winning the Queen's Medal next.' Someone passed out in the lavatory, and Julian had to climb over a roof and through a window to unlock the door. David Archer somehow managed to fall into a dustbin in the courtyard, where he remained for some time, as though performing in a Beckett play. Everyone was very happy and full of congratulations, and for the first time that day I felt I had done something worthwhile.

When the party was over, K. turned to me and said abruptly, 'You don't need me any more.' Then she rushed into the bathroom, leaving me tired and shaken amidst the debris of the revels. Eventually I followed her into the bathroom. She was sitting on the edge of the bath, chipping away at her wrists with a razor blade. She had already inflicted a few minor cuts on herself. When I appeared, she looked up and said, 'You made me do this.'

I took the blade away from her. She was not really hurt, but there was blood in the bath and on the floor. Its strenuous red affronted my tired eyes. I felt nothing but a deep blankness.

The summer vacation passed slowly. It had become virtually impossible for K. and myself to have a normal conversation. Only a mutual possessiveness kept us together. She now had a post as a copywriter, and was away all day, but I still couldn't write, and drank heavily instead, and was glad when term came round once more.

It was my last year. Many changes had taken place in the structure of my university life. Quentin had left: Peter had departed to teach at Stonyhurst. Julian had achieved the First he had worked for, but had come back to do a thesis. He had taken a flat off the Woodstock Road. I myself had to move out of college for the first time. I was fortunate to find rooms in Polstead Road, near Julian, in a large house kept by an old couple named Kirkby. My sitting room, vast and Victorian, looked out over an elaborate, pretty garden tended by Mr Kirkby. Enthroned in a massive chair, I breakfasted here, fed by Mrs Kirkby with immense quantities of chops, kippers, eggs, porridge, and tea. Never much of an eater in those days, but not wishing to hurt Mrs Kirkby, I tended to wrap the surplus chops and so forth in newspaper, and conceal these parcels in my desk. After a while strange odours filled the room. It was not long before Mrs Kirkby discovered the parcels in my desk. She did not mention them to me, but I once overheard her inquiring of Julian, who had come to call, whether I was entirely right in the head. This apart, we got on splendidly, and after K.'s house it was very restful, and I was happy there.

Julian was not my only neighbour. Gill Thomas, another friend, shared a flat a few roads away with an American girl called Helen. I visited them often. Gill, blonde and very handsome, in a high-coloured Junoesque way, was the nearest thing to a sister I had ever had. In her flat, neat and very feminine, I had a strong sense of what women were really like. The sense of order, the desire to make things look attractive, the ability to take care of inefficient men: these all appeared in Gill and Helen's flat, and the atmosphere was pervaded by that strange quality, half childish and half callous, which is peculiar to women. When they giggled over their boyfriends, I was entranced: I listened with a curious intensity, as though to sounds I had never heard before. It made me very aware of what was missing in my relationship with K.

In my vast sitting room, looking out over the autumn garden, I began slowly and tentatively to write poetry once more.

There was an illustrious newcomer to the university. Allen Tate, the American poet, had arrived for a year at All Souls. He was small and neat, with a trim moustache and the soft accents of Kentucky. I had read and admired his fierce and haunted poems as a boy, but he was quite unlike them: full of mildness and courtesy, interested in the work of young poets despite the abrasions of forty years of literary life. Within a few days we were friends. Julian and I threw a lunch party for him. Cooking was a new interest of mine, and with cream, brandy, wine, asparagus, and veal I created a redolent casserole. When it was served an expression of dismay crossed Tate's face. The casserole contained exactly the ingredients his doctor had forbidden him to eat, and while the other guests devoured it happily, our guest of honour picked at a soft-boiled egg.

Tate's criticism was of a kind that was new to me, and I learnt much from it. He demanded precise technical skills, and was bitterly scornful of incompetent work. At the same time, he demanded that the poem bit, that it had its own teeth to bite with, not false ones. I showed him one of my new poems, a very misty piece of work about lying with a girl, 'on clods the colour of wet bread'. Scraping his small moustache with his forefinger, Tate gave me a sly and sardonic smile. 'Clods the colour of wet bread,' he repeated. 'That was very inconsiderate of you. Couldn't you find some other place to take the poor girl, like a macadam road, for instance, or a bed even?' I saw what he meant.

So I longed to satisfy his clean scrupulous intellect, and worked hard on my poems. The more I worked, the more I felt my gift returning, from the hazed distances where it had floated. The more I felt it, the more I worked. Tate's remarks about some of his own work fascinated me: he dismissed poems of his which I had admired for years, with a shake of his domed intellectual head. I began to see all poems I wrote as stages on a journey: if I was pleased with something I had written, I deliberately put it aside and tried once more, reflecting that in forty years the piece I was now pleased with might disgust me. In the case of many of the poems I wrote then, it has taken a much shorter time than that.

Julian and I began to give weekly lunch parties in his flat. I generally cooked, and we invited from half a dozen to a dozen people every Sunday. There was plenty of excellent wine from the college cellars, and these luncheons became rather famous in Oxford. Tate frequently attended, though confining himself to boiled eggs, and occasionally we had other dons, but the guests were mostly young writers. Ved and Del, Patrick Garland, John Fuller, and Prue came fairly regularly, but there were others, such as Alasdair Clayre and John Caute, who were shortly to become Fellows of All Souls, the novelist David Pryce-Jones, and a Korean writer, Peter Lee. The conversation at our lunches was some of the best I have ever heard. We were young people who knew each other, and felt no need to impress anyone, and we spoke always as equals. This was the atmosphere which is classically supposed to pervade Oxford, and I felt a deep melancholy, because it was my last year, and I seemed to be about to lose what I had only just discovered.

Another cause of my unrest was that everyone else seemed to know precisely what would happen to them when they left Oxford. They all had employment in view, or theses to write. I knew that even if I passed my final examination, for which I had done no work whatever, it was impossible that I should get the First which would enable me to write a thesis. Anyway, I didn't want to write a thesis. Vaguely, I intended to live by my pen. But I was already aware of the problems that this involved: I was vividly conscious of the army of penniless writers in London, elbows worn from leaning on bars, constantly borrowing from each other in order to be able to live, and I didn't want to be the latest recruit. Moreover, there was the problem of K., which seemed insoluble unless I made a firm decision, and I was unable to make it.

One day Julian, who had acquired a small car, drove me into the Cotswolds for a drink. Afterwards he decided to drive to his parents' house near Cirencester to pick up some books he needed. The house was a large one, filled with the presence of a family, and surrounded by smooth lawns on one of which Julian's mother sat, with dachshunds laying wreaths of themselves on her feet. It was a long while since I had been in contact with family life: it seemed familiar but distant, but snuffing at it as warily as the dachshunds sniffed at me, I felt a deep nostalgia for it. I thought for the first time in weeks of my mother and father and remembered the exact smell and texture of an Indian day. Driving back with my friend through the green and familiar landscape of my adopted country, I felt suddenly, and to my own surprise, a stranger.

During the Christmas vacations K. seemed quieter than before. She was happy in her work as a copywriter, but her tranquillity somehow puzzled me: it was like the surface of a quicksand, untrustworthy, I didn't know why. Our life was much the same: it carried us into Soho, amidst the witty and the corrupt faces.

Archer had now completely abandoned the bookshop, and lived uneasily in a small flat off the Edgware Road, stacked with newspapers and empty bottles. Nightly, he stared at the television, welcoming all programmes with the same delight and surprise. His financial situation was worse than ever, and though he tried to find employment with various publishers, they were all suspicious of his unique and eccentric flair, and would not employ him. I was saddened by this, but at the time didn't see what I could do, and in a tranquil, almost angelic way he seemed, despite his monetary perturbations, somehow content.

One night I wandered into Soho without K. The upstairs club was full of the usual faces, intense or smiling, none really benevolent. Amongst them was a friend of K.'s, a witty, cynical man who was browsing over a young man from the provinces, who had recently arrived in Soho. The young man had a round, open face, with blue eyes that were always wide and awaiting: he wanted to be a writer. At this moment he was very drunk, and swayed to and fro, his wide eyes absolutely blank. 'He's got no money,' said the witty man, 'and nowhere to sleep. Take him away, will you? He's a bore.' I took the young man downstairs, and he sobered up in the winter air. 'I'd better go to a telephone,' he said. 'If you lend me four pence, I'll phone somebody. They might put me up, if you'll lend me the money to get there.' His suit was the cheap neat tweed suit any young provincial might wear, but soiled and a little frayed since its arrival in London. He pulled awkwardly at the frays in the cuff of his coat, and muttered something about decency.

When we arrived at a telephone box he lurched in, and, head down, telephoned. I was standing outside, waiting, when I suddenly saw him straighten, and crash the telephone receiver violently into the glass pane of the box. The pane and the receiver both broke, in an explosion and tinkle of sound, and the young man staggered out and stood swaying. 'They won't put me up,' he muttered, and as the first policeman loomed obscurely towards us through the mist, seized my sleeve, and, his young smelly mouth to my ear, muttered, 'What has happened? What has happened to me?' In the mirrors of his eyes I saw, small and remote, the image of myself.

The start of the next term set off a series of explosions. K., when I had returned to Oxford, constantly telephoned and wrote in extreme phrases. She threatened to commit suicide. I couldn't understand this sudden new melodrama; I made constant trips to London to see her, as a result of which I missed several tutorials, and the dons of my college met once more to decide whether or not to send me down.

Mr Christie, I knew, was on my side: Reggie Alton, for whom I had done so very little work, and John Hale, the history tutor, spoke for me: but there were a number of more conservative dons who demanded my expulsion. I was apprehensive, not so much because I wanted to take my degree as because Oxford had become the staff I leant on. I did not want to be exposed at once to London. On the morning of the meeting, I paced Tate's rooms in All Souls for two hours, while he gently rubbed his moustache with his fingers, smiled in his ironic way, and poured me dollops of whisky. Eventually John Hale telephoned. Once more, he said, I was safe.

The Easter vacation arrived a few days later. I returned to London. K.'s disturbed mood continued. There had always been interludes of peace between our storms, now there were none. Even in this terrible time, I could not make the simple decision to leave her; there were too many complications in my mind. But K. now had frequently to visit the provinces on her firm's business; each visit allowed me a day or two's rest, during which I thought and drank. One day, as I indulged myself thus, the telephone chirped. It was a friend who told me, in the kind way that friends have, that K. was madly in love with another man. I put down the telephone and waited to feel outrage and shock. Instead, quite suddenly, I was filled with an incredible, enormous sense of freedom. It was as though the bars of a prison were being prised out from around me, till only a few remained: yet also as though there was some act I must perform to break down the final bars and be fully free. I did not wait to see K., but went out to a literary pub, selected a pretty young woman, deliberately picked her up, and went to bed with her. It was the only time we ever met. Next day, as I dressed, she remarked, 'Do you know, it's funny, I'm actually in love with someone else. Are you?' 'No,' I said.

It was true. It was done. I had pulled down the final bars. That day I left K., and went back to Oxford.

12

Sorrow has stopped your eye.
Your dream is desolate.
It calls me every day
But I will not enter it.
You know I will not return…

—'Letter to my Mother' from *Poems* (1955–1965)

I lay on my back in a punt, inert, looking up through summer leaves at the sky. Red wheels luminous with yellow turned behind my half-closed eyelids. The sun's colour made my body heavy: to move a hand was like shifting a mountain. If I moved my hand I could open the textbook that lay open beside me: but I didn't want to. The final examination, a week away, did not seem greatly to matter. What mattered was to inhale into my flesh all the rivery air of the city which I had first hated, then loved, and was soon to leave. It had been like this all summer. What I had missed in Oxford, through the life that had led me, I was determined to replace. I had done no bookwork: but, in a deckchair in Mr Kirkby's garden, had breathed roses and written verse, or had fed avidly on the company of my friends. The unity that had so long held us together would shatter with the end of term: we would fragment and fly away, each into his own future. I did not yet know for certain what my own future would be.

I moved my hand, very slowly, and splashed it in the dappled water. It gloved my fingers coldly, and pressed a twig into my palm. From the bank above me a husky voice inquired. 'Awake?' The girl looked down at me with large serious brown eyes. Perhaps my future was with her: at least, I hoped it would be. I had met her at a party, when I had resolved my attitude to women: a predator, I would prowl the forests of flesh, and attach myself to nobody. But at the party the girl had spoken to me in her husky voice, and looked at me with her grave brown eyes, and next day I had sent her flowers and asked her to lunch. She had a gentle, very feminine nature: she listened to all I said, and she had very good manners. So now I had built a new prosperous future round her. I was full of love, I discovered, only I hadn't been able to give it latterly to K., and the discovery of the love in me pleased and surprised me. I didn't know what to do with all this love, except to pour it out at the feet of the girl.

I poled down the river to Cowley. The girl lay on the cushions trailing a hand in the water like Ophelia: seeds of a poem twitched inside my head. I began to paste the lines into my memory in time to the lift and fall of the pole in the heavy water. We left the punt at Cowley and ran over Magdalen Bridge, down the High to All Souls: Allen Tate was having a party. It was full of my friends; they were full of talk about the examinations coming up. This irritated me, but only for a minute. I looked with love at the known faces around me, and back at the girl who stood beside me, poised on her toes as though ready to fly. There was something grave and mournful in her face, and when we left the party and walked down the warm twilit High, I told her so. She looked at me in surprise, her brows raised. 'Did you really think that?' she asked. I said fervently that I did. 'Sometimes,' she said, 'I don't think you know what I'm like at all.'

Earlier in the term Julian and I had driven up to Lancashire to see Peter Levi. Stonyhurst, where he taught, was an immense school full of echoing endless corridors that seemed to lead nowhere; outside were ornamental lakes where ducks ruffled and scudded, and immense, broken vistas of tailored turf. In these massive, somehow lonely environs, Peter lived a colourful untidy life. The boys who came to his study to learn Greek were allowed to smoke, the only place in the school where they were, and he encouraged us to take two of them down to the pub at the end of the road, where they acquired their first tuition in drinking. Behind this gaiety and apparent disregard for authority, however, was a new gravity. In this lonely place, high up in the moors, he had acquired a kestrel loneliness that showed itself only in his face. In some ways he seemed more unhappy than he had been at Oxford, which he missed, but he was also more peaceful. I had the sense that he was thinking more deeply about his religion than ever before. I remembered suddenly that it had also been my religion; somehow, though I knew Peter so well, the fact of his being a priest influenced me. His peace and fixity of purpose were attributes of the poet as well as the priest. I hoped for them now in myself, and took power from Peter as we paced the moors above the school.

I tended in those days to see my friends not as they were but as I imagined they should be. Julian and Ved, for instance, I saw as totally confident, walking the paths they had chosen towards the destination they had chosen, aware of every step they took. I now see that this was not really true: they were subject to the same doubts and fears as myself, but they handled them better, and refused to be as frequently and deeply swayed by them as I. I saw this faintly at the time, in a conversation I had with Ved a short while before Schools. Our conversations, as a rule, were frivolous and ironic, and we teased each other constantly. However, on this occasion Ved told me that he planned to return to India shortly. 'Do you want to live there?' I asked him. His lips pursed a little, and he murmured, 'I don't know, that's the trouble. Somebody's offered me a job in New York. I don't know if I should accept it. There might be something I could do in India...'

I had never associated indecision with Ved, and watched in surprise as he shook his head and went on, 'But would people like us fit in at home? I don't know that either. Do you know, the other day an Indian boy came round for a drink, he'd come up here for his three years, then he was going home. He never contemplated anything else. It's different for me. And for you, but it's not so different for you, your choice is straightforward enough, there's nothing Indian about you, Dominie, you belong here if you belong anywhere...you'd never fit in at home.' The idea that Ved thought my life simpler than his intrigued me, but suddenly I understood what he meant. I had put down roots of work and friendship in England which would keep me here whatever I felt about returning to India. I would always have, I thought, moments when invisible roots pulled me towards the country of my birth, like the moment I had had in Julian's car in the Cotswolds; but Verrier Elwin had warned me years before that I would have such moments, so that I would not be unprepared. In a way this conversation made up my mind not to live in India: in the previous months I had wavered a little in my determination to become an expatriate. What I would do in England was another matter; but in England, I realized, I would stay.

Schools were much less alarming than I had thought they would be. I was able to answer the literature papers, from private reading rather than study, fairly easily: the language papers were my difficulty. But I had already decided that it didn't matter what sort of degree I obtained, so long as I passed: so I pecked away at the language questions in the hope of attaining the minimum correctness necessary to pass them. This did not take me very long: for the rest of the time I sat up in my ridiculous harness of grey suit, white bow tie and gown, and watched the other examinees with detached interest. Invigilators paced the aisles, with austere and vigilant eyes, and involved themselves in a variety of dramas. One shy and antique don, looking fierce for the purposes of his post, spotted a girl who had brought her handbag in with her, which she was not supposed to do. He swooped on her in a flail of his gown, like a giant bat, seized her handbag, and emptied it on her desk. Out of it fell a compact, a lipstick, tissues, money, and a Dutch cap. 'I'm awfully sorry,' said the invigilator, 'I'm most awfully sorry.' He stuffed everything back, with averted eyes, and rushed off to the other end of the room. The girl watched his rout with maidenly amusement.

These small pleasures apart, Schools were a strenuous business, even for me, who didn't really care about them. Every day the faces around me looked paler and more worn; my friends stoked themselves up on benzedrine and black coffee, and burnt the midnight oil, while I slept peacefully in my Victorian bedroom. I could understand why it was that a few undergraduates commit suicide as their finals approach.

On the last day Patrick Garland, who was also sitting for English Schools, and I came out of the squat hall in the High together. Patrick looked as fatigued as someone who has completed the last lap of a marathon, but there was a look of achievement in his eyes, which I, though also tired, was without. Gill Thomas was standing outside, with the traditional bottle of champagne, and she enfolded us with an air of pride, and swept us off to the Botanical Gardens. We sat by the river. It was a warm, hospitable evening, and welcomed us to the responsibilities of being adult. Gill, always provident, had brought some paper cups with her: we drank the champagne from them, it had the tart chill quality of an unripe apple. Patrick asked Gill various questions about the paper we had just answered, then, with an abrupt and dramatic movement (besides writing poetry, he was an actor, though he became a BBC producer in later life) he shredded the crumpled question paper and let the scraps flutter from his hand like doves to settle on the greenish ripples of the river that swept by on its way to London, where we were all eventually bound.

Term was not yet over, and the next few days were an orgy of farewells. Though my friends and I knew we would meet again, we knew also that we would never have quite the same absolute relationship, the world would take that away from us. I began to wonder what I would do. As a child, my father had always tended to solve my problems: he wrote and suggested that I revisit India, even if I didn't stay there. My mother longed to see me, and so did he. I told Ved about this, and he thought it an excellent idea. He, too, was sorry to have finished with Oxford: he was returning to India, a little apprehensive, and he would be glad, he said frankly, for his own sake, if I were there too. 'Besides,' he remarked, 'what will you do in London? You'll have to write little articles for the newspapers, and they won't pay you much. If you come back to India and write a book about it, you'll make enough money to start off as a writer. Writers need capital too.' I thought about the girl I had happily committed myself to, but, as I had felt when I left K. to go to the Hungarian frontier, I felt there would be something romantic about such an exile. I wrote to my father and asked him to buy me a return ticket.

With this settled, I felt more at ease. On the last day of term I made a round of duty calls, saying goodbye. The two I most wanted to make were on Auden and Tate. It had been a remarkable experience, in its way, to have them both in Oxford at the same time: they had taught me more about my craft than anyone else had ever done. This was not only by criticism, but by example: their physical presence, and the presence of those sharp and sedulous minds, had reassured me that poets did continue, and need not necessarily burn themselves out or die young. They had given me much of their time and patience, and I was grateful.

Auden had slipped away from Oxford early, and retreated to his fastness in Austria, but Tate was still there. He was awaiting the arrival of the American poet Isabella Gardner, whom he was soon to marry. He kept checking his watch in an absorbed way, and absently poured out whiskies for himself and me. 'There's half an hour still,' he informed me, 'before she catches her plane. I should think right now she's having a drink with some of our friends in New York... Stanley Kunitz and his wife, probably...' He fingered his moustache with a small rapt smile. This romantic concern in him touched me so that for some reason I felt near to tears. I told him about my plans, and he listened, with an eye on his watch. 'If you come to America,' he said, 'you must visit us in Minneapolis.' I said I would. 'What happens if I visit the South?' 'Well, then,' Tate murmured with his ironic smile, 'you'll have to wear a turban to show you're not a negro.' He eyed me slyly and added, 'You'd look good in a turban.' We laughed together, and he glanced back at his watch. 'She ought to be getting on that plane almost this very moment. I wonder if she'll have a comfortable trip.' I left him there, sipping whisky and anxiously eyeing his watch. Other people had other lives: the world after all, much though I resented it, did not revolve round me.

My luggage and I arrived in London the next day. This final trip stranded me on the platform at Paddington with a feeling of loss. I had not found anywhere to live. I dumped my cases at Archer's flat nearby and set off to find one for myself. A number of the flats advertised said 'No Coloured', which gave me a strange sensation: it had been years since I had thought of myself as being any particular colour. I had been taught not to, and the idea of a colour bar filled me with sudden rage and hatred. I tended always to be unaware of things until they affected me personally, and this seemed a personal affront. To reassert myself, I raised my price range, and soon found a very expensive flat in Chelsea. I stayed the night with Archer, and moved in next day.

The girl I was in love with had also arrived in London, and I spent most of my time with her. We went to the cinema, or to riverside pubs, and I lived is a sort of haze of romance. My feelings were those of one who has found an oasis after annoying days of grit in his throat and shoes. Our relationship was very peaceful: it was more, though I didn't realize it at the time, like the relationship of very good friends than the relationship of lovers. In fact we were not lovers, there was something very delicate and remote in my care for her, as though I lifted her out of her flesh, and floated her intangibly in the air beside me. This sentimental quality in my attachment adversely affected all the poems I wrote about it.

On the night before I left for India, I reassured her that I would be back very soon. But with a faint irritation I sensed that she did not need reassurance: she would miss me, she said, but she didn't say she would miss me much, or for long. The brown eyes that always seemed to me so sad looked gravely at me: 'Take care of yourself,' she said. 'Don't drink too much.' I promised I wouldn't. Simply because her feeling for me seemed to lack the intensity I had hoped for, mine became more intense. I took her delicate head in my hands, and looking into her eyes said in the pregnant tones of MacArthur leaving the Philippines, 'I shall be back.' When I landed at Bombay, I was suddenly aware that I was a foreigner. The gestures and intonations of the people around me were strange. The quality of the dust, the trees, and the air were different from what I was used to. Then past the Customs my father put his arms round me, and a moment later my mother, who had been standing back, a little shyly, was all over me. She looked much older than when I had last seen her: there was a lot of white in her hair, and both her face and body had grown smaller. When I put my arms round her, she seemed weightless, as though one were to try and embrace a bird. She talked constantly about how tall I was, how thin I looked, how she would feed me up, and about the various delicacies she had stocked up on to feed me with. A few years before the fact that Kutthalingam was not standing by the car would have shocked me: now, seeing a bearded young Muslim chauffeur there instead, I simply accepted his presence and Kutthalingam's absence.

In the days that followed, I sniffed warily around Bombay. My eyes were those of a tourist: the beggars, the palm trees, and the teeming white-clad crowds were reflected in them, but did not penetrate. It was all very strange. Yet, naggingly, behind it all, there were echoes and scents which awoke some memory in me. Like a dream, the city was a new experience, which I knew that I had had before.

Ezekiel came to see me. He, too, was older, he had filled out physically and his hair was touched with grey. 'There are no new poets,' he said mournfully. 'Things are the same as they were when you were here before.' He himself wrote on, publishing his verse in local magazines, or bringing out books of it for the printing of which he paid. No publisher in India would touch English verse: and the difficulties of being published in England were considerable, from seven thousand miles away. There seemed to me a great courage in Ezekiel, and a gift which no amount of discouragement would dry up. I felt guilty that I had not been tested in the same fires; to me, whom Ezekiel had helped when I was a boy, the success he himself sought for had come easily. Yet for all my memories of Ezekiel, and my friendship for him, I could not evoke through him the dead emotions of my past. Five years full of other friendships stood between us. The city of my birth was still beyond my reach.

In my parents' flat, I moved about a little awkwardly, touching things. It was extraordinary to me, after my English years, to lift the telephone without thinking about the bill, to order a drink which the bearer fetched on a tray, to sit at a properly laid table and have lunch served to me. I was the young master of the household, come back from across the black waters, and the servants vied with each other to see to my comfort. It was a little disconcerting, after a bath, to find the bearer helpfully holding up my trousers so that I could step into them. I had forgotten about all this, and I could not adjust to it, knowing that I would have to go back to my other, more real existence.

Then, a few days after my arrival, the bearer, fetching my morning tea, said shyly, in English, which he did not speak well, but which he was forced to employ because I had forgotten my

Hindustani, 'Sahib, old driver come to see you.' Outside my bedroom door stood a thin, black old man in a vest and sarong. His hair was white, but the pug face was unaltered, and I saw it was Kutthalingam. He folded his hands and bowed his head in the gesture of greeting. When he lifted his head his eyes were full of tears. He suddenly plunged forward impulsively and hugged me as he had always done, saying in an incredulous and happy voice, over and over, 'My young master has come back!' He showed me his hands, which were now completely crippled by arthritis. 'I no good for driving no more. Master give me house and pension, now I sitting at home, but I hear my young master coming Bombay, so I coming also.' He had travelled from the depths of the south, several hundred miles, to see me. Though he was unable to drive, he annoyed the new young chauffeur intensely by sitting beside him in the front seat whenever I went out, and telling him not to go so fast, did he want to kill his young master? Or reproving him for grinding the gears: 'My young master not wanting to hearing such noises.' On one occasion I went to visit someone in the suburbs, and we parked by a small patch of mud, which I had to cross to enter the house. Kutthalingam, when he saw this, became intensely excited. 'My young master no must dirty his shoes.' He ordered the new driver to remove his uniform jacket, and before I could prevent him, flung it down into the mud. 'Young master walking on that.' The jacket was already beyond salvation, so I obeyed him, while the new driver looked on with an expression quite different from Sir Walter Raleigh's.

But through Kutthalingam I achieved what I had been unable to achieve through anybody else, a recognition of the city of my childhood. As we drove around, he would point to one place or another, and tell anecdotes about what I had done or not done there when younger. Some were rather shocking to me now: 'Here I waiting five hours, young master going somewhere else, forgetting to tell me': but he seemed to remember them happily, and to treasure these memories.

I had long talks with him, I think he was the least complex man I have ever met. He seemed to have organized his entire life and thought round the idea of service to my family. His dedication was absolutely simple: I wished I could achieve so straightforward a dedication to my work and my life. I once told a Marxist friend about Kutthalingam, and he muttered something about despicable slaves, but Kutthalingam was neither despicable nor a slave: he was a very proud man, he chose the direction of his life, and within it he was full of love.

I asked him if he was happy in his retirement. 'Oh, yes,' he said, '*my* young master not worrying. I very happy, I getting pension from master, I got my own house, everything.' What did he do with his time? 'I sitting in my house, and the other old men coming to see me. And I telling them about *my* young master in Ingiland, and how we all happy, when he was little-little boy.'

I was called on to read and lecture at various places: the British Council, the USIS, and some of the colleges. I also, to my surprise, received an invitation to revisit my old school and talk to the boys. For curiosity's sake, I accepted this, and found the place exactly as I remembered it: a grey barracks with dusty fields round it, populated by priests and pupils. These priests, like Peter, were Jesuits, but I could find none of the respect in myself for their cloth that I did for Peter's. However, I was as polite as I knew how, and lectured to a bored audience of boys, sprinkled with members of the staff who applauded loudly at everything I said. Afterwards I was invited to tea with the priests and the staff. As I was trying to balance a pink cake on my saucer, one of the senior priests came up and said sternly, 'I must speak to you.' I indicated that I was ready to gratify his desire. He said in ominous tones, 'We have heard that you have been involved with a divorced woman in London.' He obviously meant K. I had heard of the bush telegraph, but this was ridiculous. I murmured that my involvement had ended some time back. 'It is still a sin, my son,' he told me lugubriously. 'I trust you did not contemplate marriage with this woman?' I said that as a matter of fact I had. He was very shocked, and told me so. 'Are you involved with any other woman now?' he inquired. I intimated politely that this was a matter that concerned only myself. 'Well,' he said, 'I trust she is a Catholic.' He perhaps read my reply in my eyes, for he added, 'We must find you a good Catholic girl.' My alarm at this remark increased when shortly afterwards one of the teachers, a pretty girl like those at whom, in our adolescence, Mickey, Satish, and I had cocked lecherous eyes, came up and asked me if I danced. I didn't, I told her. 'There is a dance,' she informed me, 'at our church hall tomorrow, and I have nobody to take me. I wondered...' Hastily, I informed her that I was extremely busy the next day. 'We would like it,' she said enticingly, 'if instead of dancing, you read us some of your poems.' I made some evasive remark and fled.

After this, however, I noticed amongst the Catholics I met a dual intention towards me. They wanted to reclaim me to the fold, and they wanted me to marry someone. There was something very Indian about all this. It annoyed me intensely. The Cardinal of Bombay, who asked me to come and see him, reminded me that he had baptized me, and also that my mother was a devout Catholic and much distressed by my lack of faith. He was a very nice man, with long fingers which he plaited ardently together as he spoke. 'I realize,' he said, 'that you want to write poetry, but you will find that the greatest art is produced by devout Catholics. Who, for instance, are the greatest pair of modern novelists? Who are the greatest pair of modern poets?' I knew whom he would cite for the novelists, but was puzzled about the poets. 'Chesterton and Belloc,' he told me. After that I couldn't really take anything else he said seriously.

Largely to flee from further Catholic attentions, I moved up to Delhi, where I encountered Ved. Together we went up into Nepal, stayed at the palace of a hereditary ruler there, rode into the mountains, and eventually left for Calcutta. From here Ved flew to New York: he had after all, decided to accept the job he had been offered there. I went on to interview Nehru and the Dalai Lama, and wound up in the frontier state of Sikkim, in wild remote country. Here I crossed the Tibetan border and narrowly escaped capture by a Chinese patrol. I described all these adventures in the book I subsequently wrote.*

I wrote most of this book on my return to Bombay from my travels. This meant that I was at home all day, which greatly pleased my mother. She had been rather distressed by my absence, and on my return cosseted me tremendously. Our attitudes towards each other had changed a little, at least mine had. Hers was as it had always been when well, full of tenderness and love. I, on the other hand, still felt guilt for her illness, and, feeling myself now adult, I determined to try and make amends. Unfortunately, I chose a method of patronizing kindness: I would listen to all my mother's conversation intently, and interpolate remarks which made me, inwardly, wince at their falsity. I was solicitous with shawls when it became cool, lights for her cigarettes, and so forth, but there seemed to be no real communication between us. This was because my mother was physically a stranger to me: I was too shy to make the gesture of love that was necessary. But I tried to carry out all her whims, except for two. I steadfastly refused to go to church with her, which upset her: and moreover, the presence of my father complicated matters. He was the closest friend I had ever had, and I wanted to make the most of my time with him. But he was at the office all day, and only free at night, when he usually went to parties. His presence in the flat excited my mother, so he tended to stay away till late. However, I had an open invitation to all these parties, and sometimes my father and I dined out afterwards. These were the only times when I was really able to see him and communicate with him.

---

* *Gone Away* (Heinemann, 1960).

My mother did not like me to leave her in the evenings. She drank in every moment of my presence, and even when I was at work, to sit in the same room, in silence, her eyes on me, seemed to make her happy. Obviously, she felt that no minute of my stay must be lost. Frequently, she begged me to stay in India, or at least to prolong my stay, but my mask of kindness slipped a little when this came up: my mind was full of the girl in London, as it had been throughout my trip, and of my return to her. In a curious way I also felt homesick for London itself: its squares and houses, my flat in Chelsea, plane trees, the atmosphere of a pub, restaurants, friends, a nation whose gestures, speech, and habits I understood more deeply and instinctively than I did the gestures, speech, and habits of my own people. I tried to explain to my mother what I felt, but my desire to be away from India, and consequently away from her, hurt her. She had been perfectly well when I arrived, gentle and talkative: but the longer I stayed, the more upset she became.

At length, one night, I told her I would be out to dinner, news she received in silence, and went to my room to dress. I was tying my tie when I heard a scream and a crash outside. I discovered my mother breaking crockery, and talking to herself in a thick unnatural voice. I said gently, 'Why do that? I won't go out if you really don't want me to.' Next moment, a sugar bowl flew past my ear, and broke on the wall. My mother emitted a terrible scream. All the horror of my childhood returned to me: mixed with it were raw memories of scenes with K.: there seemed to be a wilful loss of control involved in this sort of behaviour which enraged me. My attitude of sweet reason disappeared: I grabbed my mother's arm and shouted at her to stop. In that moment, vivid as a photograph, the scene from five years back, which had taken place in this very room, under very similar circumstances, flashed into my mind. I released her arm and stepped back. But my sudden fury had silenced her: she gave me a very odd look, then, without saying any more, turned and went to her room.

I went out to dinner. When I returned, my mind was full of images of the scene with my mother. I couldn't sleep. I put on my dressing gown and went into the sitting room to look for cigarettes. When I found them, I lit one and took it into the verandah. I remembered that it was here that Kumar had died. The boy who had held the dog in his arms through the monsoon night, hating his mother, haunted the place, but I was not that boy. Looking up at the black sky in which sharper stars than those of England, sharp stars that had presided over my childhood, shone, and listening to the mumble of the sea to my left, I was filled with all the old remorse, and now with an instinct of pure love for my mother, a love that seared and hurt me. I noticed that the lights were on in her room, and put my cigarette out and went to her door. It was open. Inside the room my mother, quiet and pale, with red eyes, was packing suitcases.

She looked up when I came in, and said with a wan smile, 'Why aren't you asleep, son? It's late.'

'What are you doing?' I demanded, nodding towards the cases.

'I'm packing,' she said simply. 'I'm going away.'

'Going away? What do you mean? Where?'

'I'm going back to Bangalore,' she said, 'I'll stay in a hotel there. It's nice, at this time of year.'

'But what on earth for?'

She said, 'You know, when you were a little boy, I meant everything to you. You thought of me as your beautiful Mummy, and you thought everything I did was good. I wanted you always to stay like that, then. But you've grown up now, and I've been...ill, all these years. You don't remember me as I was. Sometimes I don't know what I'm doing, like today, and that makes you unhappy. I thought I would go away till you'd gone back to England, and that would make sure it didn't happen again while you were here. And perhaps some day you'll remember me differently...perhaps you'll feel as you did when you were a little boy.'

She blinked at sudden new tears and said, 'I don't want to hurt you, son, I love you.'

And suddenly, like a stream that breaks down a dam that has stood for years, the simple and truthful words I had never before said broke from me. 'I love you too,' I said. 'You know that, don't you?' and like streams that meet for the first time, we wept in each other's arms. And gradually, from that weeping and that close embrace, a healing and a peace came into the room and into our arms which held each other. All the troubles of my past and present vanished, in the unaccustomed cradle of my mother's arms. Her eyes, too, were peaceful, and full of love, as though after all these years she understood, and knew I understood.

So she stayed, and, a few days later, I celebrated my twenty-first birthday, in the city where I was born.

I left India at peace with myself. Something very important to me had happened: I had explained myself to my mother, there was love between us, the closed window that had darkened my mind for years had been opened, and I was free in a way I had never been before. My concern now could be for the future, for the girl in London round whom I had built it. She had been my dream throughout my absence, now I was returning to her in reality, a reality which I populated with further dreams. Contracts were waiting for me in London, money would be arriving in considerable quantities, perhaps I could propose marriage; though in my mind, like some rare forest antelope, she was too fragile for any net.

As soon as I landed in London I telephoned her. It was a day of late autumn, with a bright frosty sun gleaming above the airport buildings and the stranded whales of aeroplanes. She was in, and I told her I would be there in an hour: then I took a taxi to my flat, which I had kept on, and from my luggage I took the brocades and silks I had collected carefully all over India, and carried them round to her house.

She was trim and spry, her brown eyes smiled. I told her about my trip, and then dropped the brocades in her lap and said, 'These are for you.' She rustled them in her fingers, her smile became a little absent, she said, 'Oh, they're beautiful. But, you know, I can't accept them.'

My smile became a little mechanical. 'Why not?'

'I tried to explain to you,' she said softly, 'but I don't think you understood. I'm not at all like the person you think I am, you know. And I did try to explain to you.'

'Explain what?' I asked angrily, and felt the apprehensive flutter of my heart.

'Well, explain, quite simply, that I'm in love with someone else. And I'm going to marry him very soon. That's why, you see, I can't take these.'

I collected the ridiculous heap of cloth, and put it under my arm. I emerged from the house into the bright fortunate autumn sunshine. From where I stood I could see the coloured ribbon of the swan-laden Thames twisting away towards the sea. Gulls fluttered over my head with sharp yelps of joy. Looking up at them, fierce ecstatic birds, fighting the wind, I suddenly found myself laughing, and with my hands in my pockets, I advanced towards my future.

Epilogue

Goodbye now, goodbye, to the early and sad hills,
Dazed with their houses, like a faint migraine.
Orchards bear memories in cloudy branches.
The entire world explodes in a child's brain.
It suffers accidents. Now I am yours.

—Stephen Spender

13

> … When insecurely he had slipped,
> Trailed by a steamy sponge of filth
> Into the floodlit theatre, I
> Took him inside my arms and felt
> How soon our children make us die.
>
> —'For my Son' (unpublished)

I awake early as usual to the slap of newspapers on the hall carpet, and tiptoe downstairs in my bare feet, our dog Thomas pattering ahead. Mechanically I open the front door, lift an icy bottle of milk off the step, put it under my arm. The post has arrived. I take it down to the kitchen: on the way I push the garden door open, and Thomas squeezes through the aperture and departs into distance like a rocket. Alone in the kitchen, I boil a kettle, make tea, and read the post: an invitation to a party, a letter from Peter: the quarterly rates, hell. I take a cup of tea upstairs to Judith. She curls like a dormouse in the warm bed, burying herself in a starry sleep. When I kiss her cheek she wakes, yawning and rosy. 'Hullo, there,' she says.

'I'm going to do some work, love. Isn't Francis up yet?'

'Not yet, thank God,' she says, laughing. 'Thank you for my tea.'

I tiptoe downstairs to this typewriter, so as not to wake my son.

My study window looks out on the garden, denuded by winter. In the far corner Thomas is busy scraping up the last surviving bulb. I rap on the pane: he looks up, smiles, and continues on his mission of destruction. I wind paper into the typewriter and start my finger pecking at the keys.

I am nearly thirty now, and am still not quite clear how I arrived at this house and this happiness. But the unassailable fact is that I am here, and that soon Thomas will snuffle in from the garden, scattering soil over the carpet. After that I shall hear a faint, prolonged, indignant wail from the nursery, and then soon Judith will come downstairs, crooning like a dove to our fat son, held in her arms.

In the summer of 1963 I was standing morosely at the bar of a public house in Fulham Road. I was an established writer and all that, but the five shillings in my pocket were my total worldly wealth, till the next cheque came in. I was used to it: the hard lesson of all writers who live by their work had been drummed into me often. I tapped my fingers on the chipped bar, and waited, for what I did not know.

In the years that had elapsed since I had flown back hopefully to London on a sunny autumn day, I had achieved quite a lot of success, and quite a lot of failure. I had published a book on India, and a second book of verse: had scripted documentary films for television: had been eight months at the Eichmann trial in Israel: had visited Russia: had floated to and away from numerous women: had made a lot of money, and had spent it all. I chinked the two half crowns in my pocket together, and eyed the other customers without favour. Affairs, I had decided, bored me, and I had read all the books. I was sick of discussing poetry in pubs. I was also too restless to write. At this moment in my life, I was prepared to fail.

The swing doors slanted apart, and a malleable yellow bar of sunlight wedged itself between them. Through it came a girl in a blue dress. She was blonde and very pretty, with a soft, kind mouth, and in her cheeks a radiant and childlike flush of health. Her hazel eyes met mine, and though I had never seen her before, it was as though we recognized each other, and had known each other for a long time.

She was with someone I vaguely knew, and they came over to me. I was not surprised: it was as if suddenly my future had in fact crystallized, as though all events henceforward were predictable, from the moment she put her small firm hand in mine and said, smiling like a sun, 'Hullo, I'm Judith.'

Two years later, we were in a small village in the French Alps. It nestled in the shoulder of a mountain infested with wild boar and, so we were told, chamois. Our house, which we shared with George Barker and his wife Elizabeth, was primitive, and perched above the village rubbish dump: but we intended to live here permanently. I was negotiating for a house with a farmer in the next village. The sun was hot, the wine was cheap, there was no literary talk, except in the café where everyone discussed the contents of the daily paper. My third book of verse had just appeared in London, and whenever my publisher sent me a bunch of reviews, and some of them were unfavourable, I told Judith what a good place France was to live in.

One day we went for a walk north of the village, where the dusty road dipped in to a hollow full of trees. They drenched the earth with coolness: a rapid stream lisped past like David Cecil, and Alpine flowers sprouted between the rocks. I lay in the stream, which was icy and reviving, and read. Thomas, a puppy then, made splashy forays to me from the bank, yipping solicitously, then fled back to dry land and shook himself over Judith. She split a long loaf in two, anointed the halves with butter and thrush pate, and reached me one half. I munched it and continued to read. Above me the trees rose in a leafy spiral towards the bald blue sky. Judith suddenly said, 'I've got some news for you.'

'Mmhm.'

'I'm going to have a baby.'

I leapt out of the stream, alarming Thomas, who fled incontinently uphill, and said, 'Are you sure?' Racing birds filled the sky. Judith looked at me demurely, and said, 'Yes.'

I had never thought of being a father: another dimension seemed suddenly to have entered my life, rooting and deepening it, as though by this fact I had myself turned into a tree, feet hooked into the firm alive earth, hands extended endlessly upward, a bridge between future and past. 'We shall have to go home,' I said. 'He can't be a French baby.'

'Why not?' inquired Judith, and started to laugh. 'We'll call him Francis,' she said. 'It's your father's name, and besides it means 'of France', and he was conceived in France.'

'Supposing it's a girl?' I inquired, and held her close, as though our bodies were halves of a cradle that rocked the unseen child.

'It'll be a boy,' Judith said.

We arrived back in London at the end of summer, and hunted for a house. Eventually we found a small Victorian house in Islington. We had just enough money for the deposit, and moved in with no other furniture than a bed and a cooker. Later we acquired a kitchen table, at which I sat and wrote while Judith painted the walls, laid the carpets, and bought the furniture. Suddenly, to my surprise, I found I was living in an actual home of my own. I could not believe it, nor in the child whom, laying my ear against Judith's stomach, I could hear kick and move, alive in the dark and secretive way of a fish or animal. The incredible nature of the act of reproduction came home to me, and told me more about my own craft than I had known: the poem I had created moved darkly in Judith's womb, and other poems moved in my head and hand.

One evening in March, we were sitting on the sofa talking, when Judith said, in a conversational way, 'I think I'm going to have the baby.' I leapt up, rushed to the nearest telephone, at the pub opposite, and called an ambulance. The landlord looked at me with sympathy. 'Are you going to the hospital?' he inquired. 'You'll need this then, mate,' and he handed me a bottle of whisky.

It took all night. I sat and held Judith's hand in a small cubicle, and took pulls at the bottle in my free hand, till as a pale and bleary day broke over London, the nurse said the baby was about to arrive. Hastily, I concealed the remnants of the bottle in Judith's case, and then followed her into the delivery room. In gown and mask, like a medieval executioner, I stood beside her and tightly held her hand while the midwife and the doctor exhorted her to further efforts. Her face contorted, and became unknown: I squeezed her hand harder: slowly her face returned to normal, suddenly an expression of immense relief and joy appeared on it: I turned and the doctor was holding a strange bloody bundle, and slapping it, and a thin but powerful wail filled the room. 'It's a boy,' I shouted, and then, irrelevantly, 'It's fourteen minutes to six.'

'Hullo, Francis,' was all Judith said.

When I came back to the hospital later that day, the matron intercepted me at the door of Judith's room. 'Excuse me,' she said, 'but we're worried about your wife.' I was terrified, but her next question seemed rather strange. 'Does she drink very heavily?' she inquired.

'She hardly drinks at all. Why?'

The matron looked at me with pity and said, 'Perhaps she's concealed it from you. That often happens. You see, we found an empty bottle of whisky in her case.'

I leant back on the wall and roared with laughter. The matron was very offended.

A week later we brought Francis home.

I look down at the heap of manuscript on my desk with a sense of finality. There are nearly thirty years folded away into this small stack of paper. If my son reads it, when he is older, I hope he will understand the person I was, and accept the person I am. I do not hope anything for him, except that he should stay alive and himself.

I have managed that, sometimes with difficulty: what I hoped for as a child has come true, and the vocation I have always held to stays with me. There are new poems somewhere in the rubble of my desk, and there will be others. If I have not written as earthquakingly as I hoped when I was a boy, I have written as well as I could. And the brilliant bit of luck, for which all poets pray, and which they all chase through a lifetime, may yet descend, so that I write one great poem.

They have come downstairs. I cross the room to kiss my son, whose skin has an odour of baby soap and milk. He has English apples for cheeks, but somewhere behind them is a tinge of gold and olive, the colour of the country from which I came.